TWILIGHT OF THE TYRANTS

Twilight
of the Tyrants

TAD SZULC

ILLUSTRATED WITH PHOTOGRAPHS

HENRY HOLT AND COMPANY

30143

To Marianne

Contents

1 THE DICTATORSHIPS 3
2 THE DICTATORS 23
3 GETÚLIO VARGAS OF BRAZIL 41
4 JUAN PERÓN OF ARGENTINA 99
5 MANUEL ODRÍA OF PERU 159
6 GUSTAVO ROJAS PINILLA OF COLOMBIA 204
7 MARCOS PÉREZ JIMÉNEZ OF VENEZUELA 249
BIBLIOGRAPHY 305
INDEX 307

TWILIGHT OF THE TYRANTS

THE DICTATORSHIPS

1

The long age of dictators in Latin America is finally in its twilight. Since 1955 six dictatorships have vanished from the scene, four of them on the South American mainland. In Argentina, Colombia, and Venezuela the regimes of Juan Domingo Perón, Gustavo Rojas Pinilla, and Marcos Pérez Jiménez went down in the blood and fire of revolt. In Peru the dictatorship of Manuel A. Odría bowed out quietly under the mounting pressure of enlightened public opinion. In Brazil, where experiments in democracy had been going on since the preceding decade, Getúlio Dornelles Vargas made his exit by self-inflicted death in 1954 because he could not handle himself in a society of free men. At the present time one classical dictatorship remains in South America: that of Paraguay, a small and backward nation with an incredible history of dictatorial adventures.

On the sunny islands of the Caribbean and in the tiny republics of Central America the winds of freedom are blowing again. The assassination of General Anastasio Somoza in September, 1956, ended twenty-three years of his lusty personal rule over Nicaragua, and his son, who succeeded him, has brought a measure of liberty to his country. In Cuba, Fidel Castro's revolution was crowned on New Year's Day of 1959 with the overthrow of the stubborn dictatorship of General Fulgencio Batista. Only the realm of Rafael Leonidas Trujillo Molina in the Dominican Republic stands out, seemingly impervious to the influences of changing times.

Despite the short perspective thus far on political developments since the demise of dictatorships in all these nations, indications are that democracy, so late in coming and still taking its first shaky and tentative steps forward, is here to stay in Latin America. The pattern of events in the late 1950's suggests unmistakably that the republics of the south, so recently emancipated from the regimes of force, have finally crossed the great divide of their political destinies and taken the road toward constitutional order and stability. Sporadic recurrences of short-lived dictatorial adventures, always a possibility on the agitated Latin-American scene, would not signify a departure from this fundamental historical trend.

In Argentina, a country wracked by deep economic ills and troubled by the agitation of Perón's diehard followers, a free election was held in February, 1958. Arturo Frondizi, a civilian intellectual, was inaugurated as president and, weathering plots and conspiracies and pressures from many quarters, embarked on a courageous program of austerity and reform designed to restore the country to its predictatorial prosperity.

In Peru the fairly inept democratic civilian government of President Manuel Prado y Ugarteche was overwhelmingly preferred to any restoration of dictatorial military rule, even one as relatively mild as that of General Odría.

In Colombia, where a decade of civil war and difficult economic problems had combined to render the outlook for democracy gloomy, Alberto Lleras Camargo, one of Latin America's most respected civilian statesmen, smoothly took office in August, 1958, as elected president. When General Rojas Pinilla, the deposed dictator, attempted to conspire for a return to power late in the same year, the nation watched with approval as he was detained and packed off to prison aboard a warship.

Rojas was subsequently brought back to Bogotá and tried by the Senate in exemplary, painstaking proceedings. On April 2, 1959, climaxing what is the only recorded instance in Latin America of a dictator's trial by Congress, he was convicted of violating the Constitution and degrading the presidency. In finding him guilty, the Senate deprived Rojas of political rights as well as all other rights, honors, and pensions.

In Venezuela, a nation with virtually no constitutional traditions and no experience in democratic practices, elections were held in December, 1958, less than eleven months after the antidictatorial revolution. Rómulo Betancourt, a civilian political leader, was chosen as president over an immensely popular admiral who had chaired the government junta of the revolutionary interregnum and defeated two military plots aimed at arresting the democratic process. He took office in February, 1959, naming a coalition cabinet made up of Venezuela's three principal political parties.

The novel common denominator in all cases was that the vast majority of the populations in these republics supported the revolutionary shift to representative government and, for the first time in Latin-American history, the military stood squarely behind these changes that resulted in the curtailment of their own traditional power. In Argentina, Colombia, and Venezuela revolutionary military regimes guaranteed free elections and turned the power over to elected civilian presidents. In Peru the generals and admirals, who formed the backbone of Odría's dictatorship, donned their gala uniforms to watch the swearing-in of a civilian chief executive. As far back as 1945 the Brazilian army, which had forced Getúlio Vargas from his dictatorial chair, sponsored the provisional government of the president of the Supreme Court and supervised the three presidential elections held between that year and 1955. In November, 1955, the army ousted two acting presidents of Brazil in its perhaps exaggerated zeal to guarantee the inauguration of the newly elected Dr. Juscelino Kubitschek.

The last war, and the liberal sentiment that swept the free world with the Allied victory, resulted in the downfall of several Latin-American dictatorships, notably Vargas' in Brazil, and the loosening of political controls in a number of other republics. In Argentina it set off the deep turmoil that has not yet fully quieted down. But, for the most part, this sentiment had not yet filtered into the national consciousness with force sufficient to dislodge the old habits of dictatorship so deeply ingrained in many Latin-American countries. The military, with rare exceptions, still saw themselves as the fountainhead of stability, order, and progress. The conservative classes, in most cases, sided with authoritarian rule, and the people, by and large, were indifferent to change of rulers.

2

The fundamental factor in bringing the dictatorial era toward an end in Latin America was the rapid growth of political consciousness on all class and educational levels in the last decade or so. It accompanied the powerful economic and social ferment of the postwar period. But, as much as anything else, the dictatorships' own excesses accelerated what might have been a slower natural political process.

The revulsion against the shamelessly blatant practices of colossal graft and corruption, police brutality, thoughtless repression of all freedoms, and public and private immorality (which characterized in particular the regimes of Perón, Pérez Jiménez, and Batista) united powerful forces in these nations against their leaders and the systems for which they stood.

These acts of dictatorial behavior—murders, imprisonments, and tortures of political enemies; muzzling of the free press and servile adulation of the rulers by official newspapers and radios; cavalier looting of the national wealth to build up the bank accounts of the dictatorships' officials and to pay for the kind of opulent and orgiastic living at which men like Perón and Pérez Jiménez excelled—were too much even for the immensely tolerant Latin Americans. As the new generations had become tired of their nations' reputations abroad as nothing but lands of bananas, operetta revolutions, bemedaled dictators, mustachioed policemen, and official thievery, a sense of shame was added to that of indignation at the farces being perpetrated by their autocratic rulers.

The rich and the poor, the educated and the ignorant, professional politicians and idealists, took part in the great antidictatorial revolutions of this decade. While in all instances high school and university students were in the forefront of the rebel movements, representatives of most of the other population groups were drawn into them sooner or later. In Colombia the resistance to Rojas Pinilla was plotted in Bogotá's exclusive Jockey Club, in the board rooms of big corporations, in the banks, and in the offices of stockbrokers. In Venezuela young air force pilots touched off the rebellion, then the cry of defiance to Pérez Jiménez and his secret police was picked up by students, women, intellectuals, and professionals. In the climactic days of the January, 1958, revolution, workers from the Caracas squatter hills and housing projects fought the dictator's police in bloody street affrays.

In all recent instances of revolt in South America, businessmen and industrialists joined forces with the rebels, even at the risk that the ouster of reactionary dictatorial regimes could, as it in several instances did, open the way for radical left-wing influences harmful to their interests. This was true in Colombia, Venezuela, and even in Cuba; in Argentina the business class had been oppressed all along by Perón's demagogic playing of labor against capital and management, but the advent of democracy put a leftist politician in power in the person of Frondizi.

The Roman Catholic Church, for centuries identified with reactionary policies and regimes in Latin America, reversed its stand and helped to lead the antidictatorial revolutions in Argentina, Colombia, and, to lesser extent, in Venezuela.

This nearly unanimous condemnation of dictatorships could not fail to penetrate the armed forces, particularly the officers' corps. Not only were the officers subject to all types of pressure through their families and civilian friends, but many of the young officers had been trained in the United States and had returned to their countries with changed ideas about what was right and what was wrong. Unable to stand against the overwhelming current of public opinion, these leaders of the armed forces turned against their dictatorial chiefs. Some did it quickly and spontaneously, others slowly and reluctantly and only when it became obvious that a defense of the regime was untenable. Those irremediably committed to the dictatorships had to exile themselves along with their fleeing chiefs; others were temporarily imprisoned, as was the case in the Argentine revolution of 1955.

3

Seen as a whole, the antidictatorial movements in Latin America, followed as they were by the establishment of free governments in Argentina, Peru, Colombia, and Venezuela, constituted one of the most positive developments of the postwar era in the world's struggle for democracy.

Ironically, the United States government, which in its position as the free world's leader should have been the first to encourage this change, remained singularly aloof from Latin-American freedom struggles. On many occasions it went to the astonishing extreme of befriending the dictators and thereby identified itself with the local forces of reaction and oppression while at the same time its information services blandly were preaching our dedication to the principles of liberty.

Through a quirk in Washington's political judgment, the concept of antitotalitarianism was not applied to Latin America's dictatorships of the right in the same way as it was being set against Communist domination in Europe and Asia. Operating on the mistaken belief that the professed anticommunism of Latin America's dictators was an asset in the cold war—or that it was a guarantee of stability—the United States government, often influenced by Pentagon thinking, rationalized its hemisphere policies in terms of expediency of the moment and thin legalisms.

Acting on State Department instructions or interpreting them loosely, American ambassadors in dictatorial capitals maintained cordial contacts with local tyrants, in many instances considerably more cordial than required for the simple conduct of correct diplomatic relations.

Although flirtations with dictators go back many years— Dr. Milton Eisenhower's visit to Perón was one of numerous

examples of such policies—the best known incident involved
the award of the Legion of Merit to Pérez Jiménez in 1954.
Repercussions of this act are still heard throughout the hemisphere. Oddly enough, hardly a protest was heard when the
same decoration, in the rank of commander, was pinned, a
year earlier, in June, 1953, on General Odría, the then dictator of Peru.

But the award to the Venezuelan dictator was not made on
thoughtless impulse. He was given the medal as the price for
agreeing not to bring his personal feud with Costa Rica's
President José Figueres before the Organization of American
States. The State Department was worried by possible repercussions in the hemisphere should the dispute come into the
open; and the knowledge that Pérez Jiménez, in his vanity,
would settle for the medal led to the secret policy decision
to make the award. The grant of the decoration was also expected to influence Pérez Jiménez to continue the agreements
under which the United States military missions operated in
Venezuela.

The short-range objective was accomplished with the
award but, in the long run, the scheme backfired. Neither
democratically-minded Venezuelans nor other Latin Americans could understand why the United States was honoring
a man who two years earlier had annulled a free election,
exiled and imprisoned the victorious candidates, and, with the
help of the most efficient and brutal police this side of the
Iron Curtain, established the toughest dictatorship in the
hemisphere.

The State Department never publicly explained the real
reasons behind the award, which is probably just as well from
everyone's viewpoint because the Latin Americans were not
likely to be convinced by them. Not even a policy explanation existed, however, for the Navy gratuitously to name
Pérez Jiménez "Honorary Submariner" on the occasion of

the visit of a U.S. submarine to La Guaira shortly before the dictator's overthrow. Nor was there a good reason for Fletcher Warren, former United States ambassador to Venezuela, to write from his post in Turkey a letter to Pedro Estrada, head of the secret police, wishing him success in the fighting in the January, 1958, revolution. The letter was found in the destroyed Seguridad Nacional building after the revolution and, if nothing else, it provided insight into what must have been the relationship between Messrs. Warren and Estrada. There was no known reason, either, for the decorating in 1956 of Paraguay's dictator General Alfredo Stroessner with a United States military medal by a visiting American general.

So careful was the government not to ruffle the feelings of dictators that when Colombia's Rojas Pinilla objected to the presence of American Ambassador Philip Bonsal, one of the most distinguished Foreign Service Officers, at a luncheon for an editor whom President Rojas disliked, the State Department transferred Mr. Bonsal without protest.

In many instances the ambassadors actively discouraged their political staffs from maintaining any relations with members of the opposition, which, among other things, harmed balanced reporting from the capitals where they were stationed. This was notably true in Argentina before Perón's fall and in Venezuela under Ambassador Warren and his successor, Dempster McIntosh. That relationships did exist between the opposition and the embassies in these countries, and that the opposition leaders who today occupy key government jobs could be somewhat influenced in favor of the United States was due entirely to the personal efforts of dedicated lower-level officers who risked their jobs in showing better judgment than their superiors.

As a result of United States policies toward the dictatorships the impression spread throughout Latin America that, through our refusal to have anything to do with liberal and democratic forces there, we were helping to preserve tyrannical regimes. So entrenched was this idea that responsible persons in Argentina readily accepted the absurd rumor spread in Buenos Aires in September, 1955, that the United States fleet stood ready offshore to protect Perón.

The policy of never condemning dictatorships—or doing so in such a roundabout way as to be totally ineffective—amounted, in a basic sense, to failure of United States leadership in Latin America. While democratic Latin-American governments have been greatly tolerant of the dictatorships of their neighbors, and while public opinion everywhere in the hemisphere would have resented any overt acts of intervention by the United States, Latin Americans, who are sometimes given to double standards, did expect a prodemocratic leadership from Washington.

Whatever the reasoning, the United States found itself faced with a wave of resentment in Latin America—a resentment the Communists skillfully exploited, as in the case of the riots that greeted the arrival of Vice-President Richard M. Nixon in Caracas less than five months after the anti-Pérez Jiménez revolution.

The changes of recent years in Latin America—when Washington insisted on displaying cordiality toward the dictators still in power despite the ousters of their colleagues around them—pose a new challenge to the United States. In Latin America there still exists a large enough reservoir of good will toward us to relegate to oblivion, sooner or later, the bad taste left by official policies in regard to dictatorships. But the newly freed nations, the public opinion of Latin America that has found its voice, and the new leaders who have emerged from the revolutionary turmoils do expect a wholly new attitude from the United States in all fields—political and moral as well as economic. Washington's actions may determine with a finality never before faced in our hemisphere relations the future of United States' standing in Latin America.

The revolutionary surge against the purely rightist or the supposedly proproletarian Perón-type totalitarianisms in Latin America demonstrated the revulsion of Latin Americans against authoritarian regimes in general. If properly guided and inspired—and this is part and parcel of the new challenge to the United States in the hemisphere—these movements could become a barrier against any further Communist inroads in the region. Curiously, communism thrived better under dictatorships in Latin America than under free governments, and the return of democracy to six of the republics may mean a decrease in Communist growth—if the situation is wisely managed.

In this sense the dictatorial twilight in Latin America has not only constituted the decline of a particular system of government but it has also placed the hemisphere on the threshold of a new era in political development, with immense implications for the interests of the United States in the New World.

4

With the rapid disappearance of dictatorships in the hemisphere, the historical cycle which began in most of Spanish America when the colonial rule of the Iberian conquerors was thrown off in the opening decades of the nineteenth century appears to have run its course. Replacing it are political structures that are more mature and more in tune with the breathtaking materialistic and ideological progress of the continent in the last ten or fifteen years.

Brazil, the colossus of the Western Hemisphere, a nation discovered and colonized by the Portuguese—men more given to compromise than to clear-cut drastic solutions—was alone in almost completely escaping the century-long pattern of Latin America's blood-bathed dictatorships and upheavals. It was the only one of the new American states to enjoy the stabilizing influence of a monarchy for the first sixty-eight years of its sovereign life. Starting out with a Portuguese-born emperor, whom it had gained along with its independence in a singularly smooth and peaceable transfer of power—in sharp contrast to the hard-fought emancipation of the Spanish-dominated countries—Brazil was comparatively orderly in its political development. However, its republican life after 1889 was often marred by disruptive dramatic political strife.

Beginning in 1930 it was plunged into a period of civilian dictatorship that, sweetened by a three-year constitutional interlude, lasted until 1945. It took the form of a deep but distorted social revolution, which in time became a tropical reflection of Europe's political convulsions.

Until World War II most of the Latin-American dictatorships, aside from the notable era of Getúlio Vargas in Brazil, were as devoid of meaningful ideological content as they were rich in naked craving for sheer power. Vargas' rule possessed important elements of an ideology, but in the end it degenerated into pure authoritarianism. True to tradition, the other dictatorships were the product of power clashes and of conflicts staged for the sake of power alone. Occasionally, the personalities of the leaders—men who used the fanatic pull of one or more private ideas as a lever for political achievement—gave these dictatorships a semblance of a purposeful ideological action. But, in virtually every case, it was a disguise for basic power instincts, even if these personal ideas of the dictators may have become temporarily confused or identified with controlled political thought.

One remarkable exception was the rule in Paraguay of Dr. José Gaspar Rodríguez Francia, called El Supremo, early in the last century. A brilliant man whose beliefs bordered on mysticism, he crushed every shred of independent thought among his people as he forged Paraguay into a nation that lived, by design, in splendid isolation from the outside world, eschewing all contacts beyond its borders. It is an objective historical comment on the impact left by Dr. Francia that only during the present decade—and under more modern, if not particularly more benevolent, dictatorial regimes—is Paraguay beginning to make spontaneous gestures to break free from the shackles of the isolation imposed by geography and by El Supremo.

Yet, in 1958, despite democratic trends elsewhere, Paraguay's military dictator, General Alfredo Stroessner, succeeded in re-electing himself as president in a farcical, one-man election. His inauguration for the new term provided an interesting sidelight on the tolerance of Latin-American governments toward dictatorships in the Americas: most of them, including the new revolutionary democracies, sent special delegations to Asunción for the swearing-in ceremonies.

Governments, or systems of government, that nations choose for themselves or allow to be forced upon them are mirrors of their internal problems, pressures, and stresses. Thus, the Latin-American dictatorships of the last century and of the first two or three decades of our century reflected the struggles within privileged, or elite, groups in each country. Sometimes it was money against money, sometimes civilian power versus military power, sometimes the intramural clashes of limited political thought. Occasionally, special features were added, such as the anticlericalism of nineteenth-century and latter-day liberal parties, or the assault on established racial, intellectual, or economic elites by new forces springing from the lower strata. Such was the case of Mexico's Porfirio Díaz; of Venezuela's Juan Vicente Gómez, the half-breed Indian farmer who became the Tyrant of the Andes, and, to some extent, of his old mentor, Cipriano Castro, called the Fighting Lawyer. But no sooner did these men reach power than they made themselves the hubs of new elites, even if it was in the crudest sense of the word, and provided a monotonous repetition of the old story of how power corrupts.

The men who had risen against the wealth and the position of the *criollo* aristocracies—who, in turn, had kept alive the splendor and the grace of a life that began at the viceregal courts of New Spain—channeled their energies and the public funds into frequently grotesque and lavish imitations of this very mode of life. When Cipriano Castro crossed Venezuela from his western Andean strongholds to conquer the capital of Caracas, his self-given rewards were luxury and debauchery of a scope seldom seen before, even in that easygoing city. This, by the way, was a weakness that some modern dictators, such as Trujillo, Perón, and Pérez Jiménez, could not resist either.

The shifting elites had their sprinkling of brilliant European-educated or European-influenced intellectuals. Those with a Machiavellian tinge allied themselves with the men in power, providing at times shrewd political advice and a touch of respectability badly needed by their roughhewn bosses. The modern dictators also used such men: Pérez Jiménez had his political theorist in his minister of interior, Laureano Vallenilla Lanz, and Rojas Pinilla in his minister of government, Lucio Pabón Nuñez. Other intellectuals, steeped in the traditions of the French and American revolutions and later touched by the liberal spirit of the 1848 European movements, formed the gallant, helpless opposition. Gifted polemicists, essayists, or pamphleteers, they were respected but easily silenced voices in the political wilderness.

The constant counterpoint to these clashes of the privileged groups were the economic feudalism, the illiteracy and general lack of education, and the consequent absence of real social and political consciousness in the neglected, backward nations of Latin America. Their political base was extremely narrow—mainly the ever-shifting power groups—and the true interests and desires of the people were seldom if ever expressed or even considered. Actually, what is known as the *pueblo* counted, by and large, for little more than arms and backs to perform labor that brought out the wealth of the countries for the benefit and enjoyment of handfuls of ruling families or men wielding the power of the moment. Sometimes the people could be—and were—drafted into howling mobs incited by skilled leaders to help spill blood on the days and nights of revolution, or into the private armies of the ephemerous *caudillos*. They died but they seldom knew why.

There was no middle class—economically, politically, or socially—to act as a stabilizing force in the perpetual political explosions. Seldom was responsible leadership spawned to call a halt to these convulsions. As a reflection of the whole fabric of forces then at play, Latin America was the perfect breeding ground for dictators—and they were in abundant supply. It bore out with stark accuracy the prediction of Simón Bolívar, the emancipator of South America from Spanish rule, that "our America will fall into the hands of vulgar tyrants."

5

But as times began to change—with the advent of the twentieth century, of two world wars, of the great Depression between them, and the ensuing problems and pressures of economic and social development—the nature of Latin-American dictatorships changed with them. The legitimate cravings of the awakening nations for emancipation from old social and economic systems, the onrush of industrialization, the emergence of the urban proletariat not yet balanced by a middle class, and a tremendous population growth (in Brazil it increases by a million inhabitants annually) were the signs of the fundamental revolution of immense scope that is now occurring in Latin America and will presumably go on for decades to come. The new-style dictator, therefore, was to be a logical historical phenomenon in the rapidly changing and exploding milieu, moving into the vacuum created by the disintegration of feudal-type regimes. He appeared on the scene as part of Latin America's phase of growing pains, but, as the fifth decade of the century is closing and the hemisphere's development is entering a still newer, more advanced stage, he is already becoming an anachronism, a figure of the receding past.

With growing literacy and the expansion of mass communications media, the aspiring dictator could no longer rely on special small power groups but had to lead the nascent public opinion. Newspapers by the hundreds—big and small, good and bad—mushroomed in Latin-American cities, and they were faithful mirrors of the Latin American's love and passion for politics and politickeering. Their impact was enormous. The written word was soon followed by the spoken word, as radio stations, reaching and influencing the illiterate millions as well as newspaper readers, began to blanket with their broadcasts the vastness of Latin America. To this day, radio—now backed by television in seven of the republics—constitutes the most powerful political force in the region south of the Rio Grande. The press and broadcasters are the instruments that can direct and incite urban masses to political movements that have meant the rise and fall of governments—which explains why dictators never fail to turn to censorship and elaborate propaganda machinery once they attain power.

In order to gain favor with public opinion the dictator or

the candidate for dictator had to be a social as well as a political demagogue, had to play upon economic and social difficulties of the day, promise better living conditions, and court the working masses with measures of "social justice." It is significant that among the first acts of Vargas, Perón, and Odría on assuming power was the creation of labor ministries in their countries. Vargas and Perón left behind them highly advanced, if not always practical, labor legislation, and even Odría went out of his way to cultivate labor.

Often the dictator invokes the emerging nationalism of his people. Frequently, as Perón did, he would encourage out-and-out chauvinism, and even now such slogans as "economic colonialism" are bandied about in all seriousness in many of the republics by persons who are not in any way identified with Marxist thinking. This talk of colonialism, usually addressed to United States interests, has been directly or indirectly awakened by the dictatorships and, skillfully pushed by Communists, is the heritage of the new democracies.

The new dictator thus had to court the political forces of the left while combating with police measures the Communists busily making inroads in Latin America and thereby threatening his position as sole dispenser of social betterment. In most cases the Communists could outpromise the dictator. But this avowed opposition to communism—something that Latin-American dictatorships have constantly used to sell themselves to the United States government and public opinion, especially to the Pentagon and local American business communities—has not prevented many of the contemporary dictators from playing with the Communists, openly or otherwise, whenever it suited their immediate interests. Vargas did it in Brazil, Perón in Argentina, Pérez Jiménez in Venezuela, and even that loudest of professional anticommunists, Trujillo, in the Dominican Republic.

Because of these arrangements and because in simultaneous

underground opposition to dictatorships the Communists maintained an organization that other parties could not match, communism prospered under most dictators. The best recent case in point is Venezuela, where the secret police did not persecute the Communists as vigorously as it did members of the Democratic Action Party, and in return many Communists served as police informers. After the revolution, the Venezuelan Communist Party, whose activists often divided their time between police informing and antiregime plotting, particularly when the opposition to Pérez Jiménez became widespread, emerged as a highly influential force in that country. It deeply infiltrated the Caracas press, acquired considerable respectability, and in the December, 1958, elections sent its entire top leadership to Congress.

Modern dictatorial slogans concentrated on economic emancipation and progress and on the urgency of building up the countries. Vargas insisted from the start on economic and social development and had his "March to the West," which urged the opening up of Brazil's vast and unknown interior. Not long before his death he bequeathed to the nation the rabid ultranationalistic and antiprivate-enterprise catchword idea of "Petroleum Is Ours," which continues to have tremendous implications on all Brazil's economic and political thinking. Vargas did little to open up the Brazilian interior, a task that the administration of President Juscelino Kubitschek undertook in earnest many years later. Pérez Jiménez' slogan was the "Transformation of the Physical Environment," and Perón, a disorderly and disorganized administrator, did little besides plastering the Argentine landscape with claims that he is the man who "Fulfills," while his wife Eva operated the politically powerful social-welfare foundation bearing her name.

Not very surprisingly, the dictators' seemingly commendable aims of developing their backward nations degenerated for the most part into excuses for imposing authoritarian rule. A fetish was made of the proposition that economic development is possible only in an atmosphere of political peace and stability, and the obvious corollary to it was the suppression of most, if not all, freedoms. To justify it, some of the dictators cited, a bit out of context, another pessimistic Bolívar prediction that: "only an able despotism can rule America."

This philosophy, if it can be called that, followed the pattern of Porfirio Díaz, Juan Vicente Gómez, and Peru's Augusto B. Leguía, but reached the proportions of a quasi-mystical monstrosity under the regime of General Pérez Jiménez in Venezuela, particularly in the period between 1952 and January, 1958, when his dictatorship was overthrown. The recurring and smug argument has invariably been that the people are "not ready for democracy." The more reasonable view that no nation will ever be ready for democracy unless it practices it daily never made an impression in dictatorial circles, where Western democracy was a bad word. The fact that in almost every instance these dictators were ousted by aroused people who would not live "by bread alone" and seemed to want freedom above all else was the ultimate proof of the fallacy of the dictatorial pseudo philosophies.

And recent events in Latin America demonstrated that even hungry people care for freedom: in Venezuela, for example, the crowds that fought in the streets of Caracas were largely composed of underprivileged men from the hilltop squatters' *ranchos*.

The successors to Díaz, Gómez and Leguía had the relative merit of ending the continuous *caudillo* wars and of bringing to their nations some badly needed peace. Then they evolved more streamlined systems of oppression, borrowing freely, and often with gruesome effects, from such European sources of inspiration as Germany's National Socialism, Italy's Fascism, and Portugal's Corporativism. Allowances were made for local conditions and, without exception, the self-righteous façade of these "socially progressive" dictatorships, to quote from a Venezuelan theoretician, hid from public view the most outrageous practices of corruption, graft, influence peddling, orgies, and personal gain for the dictators and their friends, relatives, and aides. Idolatry and schemes of self-aggrandizement were frequently the key features of these regimes. "Social and economic democracy" became the new dictatorial catchword.

While Latin America's severest modern dictators held in common most of these characteristics, ranging from demagogic bugle calls to a morass of corruption, they were by no means cast from the same mold. They differed in background and personality. Some constructed useful accomplishments before they were finally swept away by the tides of the times. Historians of the future may conclude that some of the dictators meant well in many of their endeavors. And not a few of their triumphant foes, more or less begrudgingly, admit that much even today. The dictators were the product of their day and, negative as the sum total of their impact has been, they were part and parcel of the historical process of transition of Latin America from the old semifeudal period to today's modern age. They may even have rendered a profound service to their nations: because they negated freedom and democracy they stimulated it in the long run, and they taught their people what may be an unforgettable lesson —that democratic unity, though it calls for a selflessness and reasonableness that still are shockingly new to Latin-American politicians, is infinitely preferable to dictatorial oppression. If this is true, then a new political maturity is rising from the rubble of the disintegrated edifices of the dictatorships, and the dictators have fulfilled their historical function.

Chapter Two

THE DICTATORS

1

Five great dictatorships overshadowed the history of South America in the last quarter of a century. Together they formed the main transition phase in the political, economic, and social development of the non-Anglo-Saxon portion of the hemisphere in the modern age. Chronologically staggered over twenty-five years but overlapping in most instances because their heaviest simultaneous concentration came in the late 1940's and lasted until the latter part of the 1950's, they influenced each other and helped to set the political tone for much of Latin America.

This discussion concerns itself with the dictatorships in Brazil, Argentina, Peru, Colombia, and Venezuela; the personalities of their chieftains; and the ultimate impact they had upon their societies—in the measure that it is possible to evaluate them with such a short perspective in time. These five dictatorships and dictators were singled out as subjects for examination because their histories are believed to offer the best insight into the process of basic transformations now occurring in Latin America.

The stories of Trujillo in the Dominican Republic, Somoza in Nicaragua, and Stroessner in Paraguay belong to an earlier dictatorial age, that of absolute domination or ownership of a country by a ruler who, for reasons of locally prevailing conditions, did not need to respond greatly to any of the undercurrents of thought sweeping the hemisphere at the present time. The Dominican Republic continues to be—as Nicaragua was until quite recently—the private estate of its dictator, and until new events occur it cannot be discussed in any other terms. But the death of the aging Trujillo, El Benefactor, which must come to him in a not too distant future even if it is from natural causes, could easily result in a political and social explosion akin to that in Venezuela at the passing of Gómez, the Tyrant of the Andes. Like Gómez, Trujillo, fearing possible rivals, did not allow the emergence of any strong personalities within his regime who could carry on after his death. His relatives seem as inept and ill-suited to dictatorial heritage as were Gómez' sons and brothers.

Paraguay, still stagnant and backward despite the stirrings of new economic activities and a slowly awakening political opposition, is in the hands of an army-backed civilian clique of the Colorado Party, which controls President Stroessner, rather than the other way round.

In terms of the transition that characterized the other South American dictatorships, the Paraguayan authoritarian experience is stationary at best, regressive at worst, even if the Stroessner regime did attract some industry and spread a bit of education. And if it were not for basic United States economic assistance, even these accomplishments would have loomed smaller. In April, 1959, giving in to growing external and internal pressures, Stroessner promised a series of political reforms designed to grant Paraguay at least a semblance of democratic government. The promises were received with natural skepticism, but even these verbal concessions indicated the dictator's uncertainty about his future.

The second Batista period in Cuba was of a hybrid nature, fitting somewhere in between traditional and modern dictatorships. It lacked ideological meaning even more than the Rojas Pinilla regime in Colombia, and, despite many up-to-date trappings, it was more suggestive of the doings of a Trujillo than of a Perón or Pérez Jiménez, who had political ideas of their own, lugubrious as they may have been. It was also distinguished for brutality.

Each of the five South American dictators discussed here has operated under different conditions, under different types of pressures, and in different ways. But one of the important things they had in common, and a revealing one in terms of historical trends in Latin America, was that all five, in varying degrees and in addition to the essential partnership with the military, reached out for alliances with the still politically amorphous working masses. By and large, these alliances were against the intelligentsia, the moderate and fast-growing middle classes, and the traditional elites of money and aristocracy.

In the end, however, this latter group supplied the decisive leadership in ousting the dictatorships and eventually massed behind them the majority of the people in the battles for freedom. In each case at least a large section of the underprivileged working classes turned against the dictators who had set out to woo them, as did the rulers' pampered military allies, who, when the chips were down, preferred to side with the rebelling populations.

Of the five great dictators, four are alive today and none of them has completely surrendered the hope of reconquering

power. The fifth dictator has been dead since 1954, but his
political influence continues to linger, like a voice from the
Great Beyond, over his still-confused nation.

2

This man was Getúlio Dornelles Vargas, the only civilian in
this dictatorial quintet, though he did acquire a home-town
colonelcy in the course of one of the regional civil wars preceding the revolution that elevated him to power in Brazil.
In order of time, Vargas, an outwardly cheerful, deceptively
mild-looking man endowed with much erudition, great personal magnetism, immense toughness, and amazing political
shrewdness, was the first of the remarkable modern South
American dictators. In 1937, after seven years in office, he
formally launched his *Estado Novo* (New State) regime as
the Brazilian version of European fascism and corporativism,
rich in studied demagoguery, political opportunism, and social
appeal. He set himself up as the first contemporary "populist"
president on the continent.

In point of personal and historical interest, Vargas towered
over his more bombastic and superficial dictatorial colleagues
of later days. While functioning as a dictator, he showed
something akin to political brilliance. As a constitutional president, freely elected five years after his ouster from dictatorial
power, he was a dismal failure, a tragic figure who finally
chose suicide as the denouement of his long life. And from his
deathbed he made the parting gesture of demagogic drama
in the form of a political last will in which he proclaimed that
he was giving his life to defend the working people from
rapacious international interests.

Because he led Brazil, perhaps in erroneous fashion but
always with conviction, through her greatest social revolution
since the nineteenth century's abolishment of slavery and the

change from empire to republic; because he was closely associated with the destinies of the largest and potentially the
wealthiest of all the Latin-American nations for well over a
quarter of a century; and because he was a man who commanded as much love as hate among his fellow citizens,
Getúlio Vargas has left a deeper permanent mark on his country than any other modern dictator in his part of the world.

He is best remembered for revolutionizing political thinking in Brazil, fostering economic development, introducing
social legislation, and instilling social consciousness into the
masses that were being transformed from chattel-like farm
hands and unskilled city workers into a fairly articulate rural
and industrial proletariat. His policies and attitudes were
paternalistic, his social legislation was so far ahead of the day
that it often did more harm than good to the country as a
whole, and in his dictatorial heyday he ruled with a constitution faithfully copied after European fascist charters.

Yet, as Latin-American dictatorships go, in spite of his
secret police and his prisons and many attendant abuses and
cruelties, Vargas' regime was not too oppressive. Benevolent
was the word used for it by many observers of that era, and
Vargas' official propaganda machine encouraged the impression.

Proceeding along a tortuous political line, adapting himself
with enormous flexibility to the requirements of the moment,
Vargas presided over the process of transforming Brazil from
an economically feudal and almost completely agricultural
nation into the dynamically expanding, partly industrialized
country of today. Of course, this change was bound to come
sooner or later, but Vargas, appearing on the scene at the
historic moment, quickened it and directed the different forces
at play into channels of his choosing. By centralizing all
national controls in his hands and in the capital of Rio de
Janeiro, he went far toward unifying Brazil politically and

curbing the exaggeratedly autonomous powers of the twenty states forming the federal union.

Looking back at his period from the vantage point of many elapsed years, it is impossible to deny Vargas' many positive accomplishments—some of them fundamental for the development of Brazil—despite the central fact that he was a dictator and often a merciless one. This is a sympathetic judgment that cannot be applied to the other dictators, with the possible exception of General Manuel A. Odría of Peru.

Another fact setting Vargas apart from the other dictators was that he did not enrich himself in office—though most of his friends and relatives did in scandalous fashion and thereby set the stage for the final tragedy of his suicide. His personal life was quiet and unostentatious; he was a devoted husband and a good father. When Vargas died in 1954, he left behind a cash debt of about $40,000. His assets at his death were limited to the family ranch in the south of Brazil and an apartment in Rio de Janeiro. In sharp contrast, such dictators as Perón, Rojas Pinilla, Pérez Jiménez, and Batista amassed fortunes of millions of dollars during their tenures in power.

3

A dictatorship infinitely more outrageous and one almost completely barren of any of the positive aspects of the Vargas era in Brazil was the gift to Argentina of Juan Domingo Perón, army colonel turned politician. Perón rose to the presidency in 1946 through free elections, although some months earlier a mob-supported coup d'état had placed him in a commanding position to capture the votes of millions of workers who had fallen prey to his labor rabble-rousing. Like Vargas, but aping Mussolini's balcony-shouting techniques he had learned during his years in Italy, and which the Brazilian dictator never had to use, Perón presented himself and his wife Eva as the friends—the only friends—of the Argentine workingman. While he also controlled the army, Perón derived most of his power from the labor unions, whose leaders he made and unmade. Despite all abuses, the rank and file gave him their loyalty and support for a long time, perhaps mistaking the disruptive force he had handed them for the dignity and importance they had sought. And, damaging and distorting deeply Argentina's economy, he saw to it they were well off— no matter what was happening to the rest of the country. The loyalty of the Peronista workers did not end with Perón's overthrow in September, 1955. Greatly influencing from exile the political activities in Argentina, he issued instructions to vote for Arturo Frondizi in the February, 1958, elections that were obeyed by two million voters. But Frondizi turned his back on the Peronistas almost immediately after taking office, and the ex-dictator's followers became the worst thorn in his side, as they violently opposed his austere and courageous program of economic rehabilitation for Argentina.

Perón's strength stemmed chiefly from his appearance on the national scene at the psychological moment when he could take advantage of a social explosion resulting from the disintegration of Argentina's cycle of rural semifeudalism. He passed on to the workers and their families the inebriating sensation that they, too, were running the country through something along the lines of a dictatorship of the proletariat, although Perón himself was never known to have used this expression. This approach, heavy on the social aspects of national life, explains why Perón and Vargas were the only ones among the five dictators to have retained a very substantial following for years after their exit from power.

But the decade of Perón's rule left Argentina, a once wealthy country, on the brink of economic ruin. Whereas Vargas had made a fairly serious attempt to find a new basis for the solution of Brazil's emerging social and economic

problems, Perón's ideological contributions were his Justicialismo and Peronismo—two vague doctrines based almost exclusively on demagoguery, chauvinism, and mob rule in the
streets by workers whipped into hysteria by his fascist methods. Vargas had never stooped that low in his dictatorial
days, and, strangely, it took the return of democracy in Brazil
to send him scurrying demagogically after the crowds.

A man of immense personal vanity that even defeat did
not lessen, of highly objectionable morals that included a
palace affair with a teen-age girl, and one of Latin America's
leading exponents of corruption in public office, Juan Perón
loomed as a tragic but probably unavoidable accident in Argentina's history.

4

If one would set out to make a case for an enlightened, benevolent dictatorship that has done a nation some good despite a
denial of liberty, the eight years of the unspectacular regime of
General of Division Manuel A. Odría in Peru could be singled
out as the best modern example in Latin America. It cannot
be put in the same class with the Vargas government because,
while the Brazilian president led a social revolution along
with his political experimentation, General Odría concentrated
merely on sound administration, and, if anything, sociological
transformation in the deep sense was arrested in Peru during
his period. But important progress was made in improving the
lot of the people through the development of the country's
wealth, along with its social welfare and educational programs.

Odría assumed the presidential office in 1948 as the result
of a military revolt designed to end the chaos into which
Peru had been plunged by the attempts of a rabble-rousing
political party, the APRA, to impose quick radical solutions

for the country's deep-seated social problems. The age-old Andean problem of the destitute but stirring Indians—the problem that also is at the root of the revolutionary up-heavals of neighboring Bolivia—was one of them. A dis-orderly and confused social revolution had been in progress in Peru when Odría stepped in at the head of his troops. The process of social ferment was then bottled up for eight years while the military regime successfully worked to restore peace and stability to Peru.

This done, General Odría took a step that became his main achievement and distinction: fulfilling an earlier promise, he allowed the holding of free elections in 1956. When the time came for the inauguration of Manuel Prado y Ugarteche, an old-line civilian politician and former president who emerged as his freely elected successor, Odría bowed out into the wings. Political democracy returned to Peru, and General Odría deserves his share of the credit for it. It was this un-usual, and probably unprecedented, voluntary end of a mili-tary dictatorship that helped to make Odría and his period so worthy of note. It is an objective fact that he had been an efficient and successful administrator who, in eight years, led Peru from abysmal economic and political confusion to rela-tive stability and a prosperous economy.

It may be reasonable to expect that the country's funda-mental social problems will find better and a less painful solution now that Peru stands on a sounder basis. APRA itself, mellower and more mature, has returned to the Peruvian scene as the mainstay of the Prado administration and is making a contribution to its endeavor to develop the country and its people. Political passions, red-hot in 1948, have died down in Peru to a surprising extent but, while deep differences remain among individuals as well as parties and new con-troversies emerge daily, the nation appears to be moving ahead in a more constructive and orderly fashion than ever before.

And this time it is doing so within a free and democratic form of government.

As was to be the case later with Rojas Pinilla in Colombia and Pérez Jiménez in Venezuela, Odría's advent in Peru was greeted with much hope by the conservative classes, who saw in the military revolution a promise of the restoration of political peace and the consequent return of a favorable business and economic climate. This they found in the Odría regime, but they found also repression or denial of most of the freedoms. Thus, these influential but shortsighted people who were willing to go along with Bolívar's "able despotism" formula must share the blame for the initial strengthening of the dictatorship. But in time they learned their lesson and they showed it by helping to establish a public-opinion climate that must have played a key role in leading Odría to keep his word about restoring democracy to Peru.

With all that can be said in his favor, Odría was still a dictator, and in matters of freedom there evidently can be no rationalizations or compromise. He won an earlier election by imprisoning his opponent; he allowed no independent political parties to function in any real sense of the word; he tolerated no freedom of the press, except during the period immediately preceding the 1956 elections; he exiled many of his enemies and imprisoned others. Yet his rule was not characterized by the shocking police excesses of Perón's Argentina, Pérez Jiménez' Venezuela, or even Vargas' Brazil.

A colorless though forceful personality and a quiet, almost timid man, Odría evoked no strong emotions. He was neither hated nor loved. His leave-taking was not celebrated with wild demonstrations of joy, as took place at the fall of the dictators in Argentina, Colombia, Venezuela, and Cuba. Few missed him when he was gone. To the people of Peru, he was an accident of history, accepted while it lasted but forgotten almost immediately when Odría vanished from before the footlights.

5

In sharp contrast to the easygoing but efficient Odría in Peru, neighboring Colombia was run between 1953 and 1957 by an inept and vain military dictator, General Gustavo Rojas Pinilla. As commander in chief of the armed forces, Rojas Pinilla directed a coup d'état that threw out of office Dr. Laureano Gómez, a cantankerous right-wing dictator during whose presidential period the lingering civil war between the Conservatives and Liberals had reached bloody and alarming proportions. When democratic rule returned to Colombia late in 1958, the death toll for the decade of civil war stood near two hundred thousand. The country's population was under twelve million.

Rojas' coup was hailed throughout Colombia as an act of salvation. The general promised a government that would end the internecine strife and bring about the national unity needed to restore Colombia's traditional democracy and allow her to get back on a normal path of progress.

But the bright hopes did not last long. Rojas Pinilla, surrounded by a palace clique of rapacious relatives and friends, soon became a full-fledged dictator, imprisoning his critics, silencing the free press, and erecting a system of self-glorification, special privileges, and corruption. He participated in the latter with complete abandon and immense personal profit, and during his tenure in the presidency he became one of Colombia's biggest cattle owners.

Rojas flooded the country with his portrait in gala army and navy uniforms, with Caesarlike busts, and even with wrist watches bearing his picture on the face. With all this, Rojas Pinilla's performance in terms of being a successful dictator added up to total failure when compared to the records of his colleagues. Despite its opposition to him, the majority of Colombia's public opinion was willing to let him serve out his term ending in 1958, but Rojas, through a series of unnecessary and ill-advised measures, precipitated the 1957 revolt and his own fall. A member of Pérez Jiménez' dictatorial regime in Venezuela, a lethally efficient group, remarked once to this writer that "Rojas is downgrading and cheapening through his stupidities the whole institution of dictatorship." Yet the irony of it was that the Venezuelan dictator repeated some of the very same errors of Rojas and thereby brought doom upon himself.

Unlike Pérez Jiménez, General Rojas left very few important works as a monument to himself—a crucial dictatorial failing even if allowances are made for the fact that Colombia's resources and revenues were not comparable to Venezuela's. Finding a reasonably prosperous land despite years of civil war, Rojas turned it back to its people riddled with internal and external debts—and with precious little to show for them. He did not wreck Colombia's economy as efficiently as Perón did Argentina's—perhaps because he was not very efficient at anything and because he had only four years, against Perón's decade, in which to inflict the damage. To help eradicate all manifestations of independent political life in the nation— always a threat to a dictator—Rojas Pinilla came up with the slogan of "Motherland Above the Parties." Then he proceeded to build around himself a political faction called the Third Force that, in crude and pathetic imitation of Perón's Justicialismo, sought to draw support from organized labor and to do a considerable bit of glorification of the Supreme Chief. In further imitation of the Peróns, General Rojas' daughter Maria Eugenia took over Colombia's social assistance organization, but, having neither the looks, intelligence, nor personality of Evita, she did not extract from these activities important political dividends for her father.

Like Perón before him and Pérez Jiménez afterward, Rojas

Pinilla collided with the powerful Roman Catholic Church, which had just launched its new liberal policy in Latin America and would not tolerate his awkward excursions into the realm of "populist" pseudo social experiments. In May, 1957, Rojas Pinilla, the man who was fully and tragically convinced until the last moment that he was truly beloved by his people, tumbled from power when all of Colombia rose in protest against his arrogant attempt to have his rubber-stamp National Constituent Assembly re-elect him a year ahead of time for another term in office. The democratic government that succeeded the post-Rojas Military Junta allowed him to return to Colombia late in 1958, and the deposed dictator, still dreaming of power, wasted no time in preparing a conspiracy. But so tiny was the support he commanded in the nation that the government had no difficulty breaking up the plot, even before it was actually staged, and arresting Rojas.

Politically, the Rojas Pinilla dictatorship stood for nothing in particular. Although it was conceived as a means of halting the civil war, actually hostilities increased under his rule, and acts of brutal retaliation by his troops, such as the massacre of the civilian population of the town of Chaparral in Tolima department, did nothing to establish peace. The regime was completely lacking in the kind of social content that had been offered as an excuse for Vargas or even Perón. It had tried to capitalize on political—and almost emotional—strife between two sections of the Colombian population, the Liberals and the Conservatives.

Such economic tensions as underlay the conflict were not of a scope to give Rojas Pinilla room or opportunity to contribute anything tangible—not even a sweepingly bad idea—in the social field. While Colombia has a terribly deep social problem in the enormous gulf between the wealthy minority and the utterly destitute rural and urban masses, the civil war was not fought over this issue in any fundamental way. With some exceptions, it was feudal-type civil warfare, but one that in all probability set the stage for new social conflicts already taking shape. Only now that a free government has been created and the old problems are seen in a new and urgent light is Colombia beginning to come to grips with her basic ills.

Thus, caught in a maelstrom he did not fully understand, Rojas was little more than a throwback to the old-fashioned Latin-American military man on horseback. But he, too, performed his historical function: the anti-Rojas revolution united the two warring parties as nothing else could have done. It stopped organized Liberal-Conservative warfare and it has finally put Colombia back on the democratic track after an upheaval-punctured lapse of eleven years. The proof of this new national maturity was the bipartisan support for Dr. Alberto Lleras Camargo in the presidential elections in the spring of 1958 and in the first phase of his administration.

6

The last and the most ludicrous of the South American dictators of mid-century was General of Division Marcos Pérez Jiménez of Venezuela. His was the most ruthless but also the most complex of these dictatorships. It was a bizarre mixture of rule by sheer brutal force and of striking social, economic, and political experimentation that reached all the way back to the beginnings of Venezuelan history, playing on a curious sense of national inferiority of the Venezuelans. Naming his regime the New National Ideal, Pérez Jiménez was, at least in his own eyes, a man with a mission. Like other contemporary Latin-American dictators, he took advantage of the great economic and social pressures in his country. But, deliberately, he ignored the political aspects of the historical transition of a nation that had long been starving while billions of dollars from oil-industry revenues were piling up in its coffers or were being misspent on schemes that were always grandiose but often totally unnecessary.

Pérez Jiménez had a Bolívarian obsession: while Bolívar, the Liberator, had been, nearly a hundred fifty years ago, the political emancipator of his native Venezuela and of much of South America, this intense self-conscious little General from the Andes aspired to the glory of being Venezuela's and, if possible, South America's economic "liberator." Surrounded by a weird cast of characters, some of them brilliant, if intellectually distorted, thinkers, Pérez Jiménez drew many of his basic policies and philosophical ideas from them. But it was his strength of purpose, his immense will power, and his outstanding qualities of cunning and intrigue that held together for nine years this system of total political aberration.

In a way Pérez Jiménez took up where Juan Vicente Gómez had left off at his death in 1935, when one of Latin America's longest personal dictatorships had come to an end after twenty-seven years. And the similarities between the two men were endless and striking. They shared modest beginnings in the Andean state of Tachíra, and both had Indian blood. They both had lust for power, for wealth, and for sensuous pleasure. Both smacked of the nouveau riche. They reacted in similiar fashion to similar situations, they believed in oppression and suppression as basic instruments of power, and both of them made the prison and the torture chamber the grim symbol of their rule—along with achievements of economic development.

It was Gómez who started molding Venezuela into a modern state after nearly a century of civil wars and chaos, and who began to use the country's tremendous oil revenues for relatively constructive purposes. Pérez Jiménez turned the idea of economic development into a mania, particularly when this meant sweeping, spectacular projects with interesting photogenic possibilities and room for profitable financial arrangements for himself and for the members of his personal and official families.

The vast projects—hotels atop mountains, aerial trains, colossal bridges, long tunnels carved through mountains, spectacular highways, and industrial plants much too big for the country's needs—seemed to gladden the soul of this short, dull man born in the dwarfing immensity of the Andes. But where Gómez' approach to his task had been fairly primitive, Pérez Jiménez and his advisers embellished their regime with a *criollo* dialecticism. When he was ousted by the revolution, it became clear that his highly touted accomplishments were largely set off by the damage he left in his wake. Wealthy as Venezuela is, the dictator managed to contract a debt exceeding a half-billion dollars. His impressive highways linked the main cities but left untouched the interior of the country. So few schools were built and so few teachers trained during his decade that the illiteracy level in Venezuela rose instead of declining. Agriculture was sadly neglected. And while he claimed to have solved some of the social problems through the erection of vast housing projects in Caracas and other towns, he created a new social problem by encouraging unplanned and uncontrolled mass immigration from Europe that the country could not absorb smoothly.

Pérez Jiménez' dictatorship was the only modern government in the hemisphere candid enough to come out flatly and publicly against democracy and its bills of rights as an outmoded political system. Even Trujillo in the Dominican Republic has paid lip service to democracy. But the Venezuelan regime spoke only of social and economic democracy and of the conquest of "the physical environment." In the thinking of its leaders, the economic motive was the only one that mattered to men. As it was outspokenly anticommunist, one of the top ministers of the regime once took violent exception when this writer suggested that, essentially, there was little or no ideological difference between the New National Ideal and Marxism.

Borrowing helter-skelter from some of the latter-day ideas of the French Revolution and from Western European and American philosophers of the Industrial Revolution of the nineteenth century, the Venezuelan dictatorship set out to *despolitisar* (rid of politics) the entire nation so that an antiseptic atmosphere of concentration on economics could prevail. When the New York *Times* called the regime a technocracy and meant it disparagingly, official propaganda in Caracas picked it up as a compliment and quoted it in full-page advertisements in United States newspapers.

Pérez Jiménez and his crew capped their theories on the administration of a nation by displaying utter contempt and disregard for the people of Venezuela, their views or opinions. This, in turn, had the advantage of freeing Pérez Jiménez from the necessity of seeking through demagogic tricks the support of public opinion. As his physical appearance and oratorial gifts were particularly unsuited for any attempts at public spellbinding this was probably just as well. Such limited demagogic appeal as the government felt had to be exercised to justify before the nation what was being done to it was carried out through the medium of one or two annual radio-television speeches by the dictator, occasional addresses by one or another of his ministers, and official handouts that the newspapers were forced to publish. And that was another point of resemblance between Pérez Jiménez and Gómez: it is not believed that the old tyrant had ever delivered a coherent, full-fledged speech in public.

The assumption that the lethally efficient secret police, the prisons, the apparent prosperity, and the well-spread corruption were sufficient to control a nation led Pérez Jiménez to the conclusion that he could get away with anything and everything—only because he had got away with it since his first victorious military conspiracy of 1945. Consequently, on December 15, 1957, the regime held a "plebiscite" in which Venezuela was to decide upon the dictator's re-election for five more years. But this was where the assumption went so terribly wrong: within fifteen days of the "plebiscite" the very same people for whom Pérez Jiménez had felt such smug contempt rose in a bloody revolution that swept him out of office and Venezuela.

The political demise of Pérez Jiménez thus completed the cycle of the rise and fall of the great South American dictators of the modern period. Batista's fall in Cuba almost a year later extended to the Caribbean the mounting antidictatorial spirit of the Latin Americans as they broke into a new phase of political history.

Chapter Three

GETÚLIO VARGAS
OF BRAZIL

1

The era of Getúlio Dornelles Vargas, bridging almost a quarter of a century of Brazil's political life and unrolling through his kaleidoscopic succession of roles—as revolutionary provisional president, constitutional president, dictator, senator, again a constitutional president, and, finally, the only modern chief of state to commit suicide while in office—began on a hot November day in 1930.

A junta of generals in Rio de Janeiro, recognizing this smiling, bespectacled little man from the Brazilian deep south as the head of the victorious nationwide rebel movement, had handed him the power over a country of forty-five million inhabitants spread over a territory slightly larger than the continental United States and endowed with immense but as yet untapped wealth. Washington Luiz Pereira de Souza, the deposed president, fled the country under the protection of the cardinal, a provisional regime was established amidst the cheers and hurrahs of the populace, and men said that a new age was dawning over Brazil.

And, indeed, this revolution was Brazil's most important milestone since the advent of the republic forty-one years earlier. It marked the end of the long transition period between the political, economic, and social feudalism of the colonial and imperial days and the emergence of a pattern of unified government and administrative philosophy more in tune with the urgent problems of the twentieth century that were now invading a dormant Latin America.

When Emperor Pedro the Second was forced to abdicate in 1889, Brazilians agreed that although "the monarchy has ended, the republic has not yet begun." And four decades elapsed before it finally did begin with the 1930 revolution, an idealistic and romantic movement of younger people calling itself the Liberal Alliance and promising to meet the nation's demands for new men and new ideas. The rebellion was to end the corruption, the politickeering, and the selfishness of the groups that had ruled Brazil for their own profit and aggrandizement.

In the hour of victory the civilian and military revolutionaries put forth Getúlio Vargas as chief of the provisional government. Already forty-seven years of age and an experienced administrator and politician, he had been their standard-bearer in the presidential elections a few months earlier, but had been defeated by Júlio Prestes, the hand-picked candidate of President Washington Luiz. (Júlio Prestes, incidentally, was no kin of the Communist leader, Luiz Carlos Prestes.) The murder of one of the leaders of the Alliance and charges of electoral fraud triggered the revolution, though Vargas himself had halfheartedly tried to hold the explosion back, as if fearing a premature move. But in less than three weeks of fighting the government was swept from power, and Vargas, commander of the southern rebel armies, made his triumphal entry into Rio to take the reins.

He thus took upon his shoulders the mission that he described as one of giving sense to Brazil's still-haphazard republicanism, of modernizing his country and setting it on a path of real progress—human and material. His admirers claim that he accomplished all these things; his foes insist that by interrupting the constitutional continuity in Brazil and preventing a duly elected president from taking office and then imposing a dictatorship he set the clock back on the country's political development until his own ouster in 1945 permitted the resumption of this advance. In a strange postscript to this controversy Vargas subsequently participated in the democratic restoration of Brazil as the freely elected president five years later.

As seen in perspective, there evidently is truth in both judgments about his first long period in power, and they are not necessarily contradictory. Vargas was a man of contradictions and paradoxes, and so was the Brazil of his time.

In the course of fifteen years of dictatorial rule he saw his vast land transformed from a collection of quarreling states into a unified nation, he rushed its industrialization, advanced its education and health. Under his regime, and for the first time in Brazilian history, the government took an interest in the neglected, miserable workingman. Vargas gave the workers regular vacations and an eight-hour day, sought to eliminate the abuses of child labor, created unions, and left behind a body of social legislation that in itself constituted a major revolution in Brazilian ways.

Unfortunately, however, he did impose a dictatorship, allegedly to enforce his social and political ideas. He rationalized his unquenchable thirst for power in terms of protecting the nation from domestic and foreign dangers. He also lessened considerably the value of his social-legislation achievements by exploiting them for his own political aims through the establishment of captive trade-unions entirely controlled by his labor ministry. By this time, and particularly after he had formalized his one-man rule with the 1937 coup d'état dissolving Congress and canceling elections, Vargas' regime lost its earlier ideological content, betrayed the ardent ideals of the 1930 revolution, and deteriorated into a form of political opportunism that official propaganda insisted on identifying with patriotic reform.

This, then, was the dilemma and the inherent contradiction of the complex personality that was Vargas: his inability to separate his positive ideas and his administrative and political wisdom from his obsession with power. Perhaps in a man such as he, and perhaps in most men who have tasted power, such separation is impossible, so that in the end the good is interred with their bones while the evil lives after them.

However Vargas will be judged ultimately by history, it is undeniable that virtually everything that has been happening in Brazil ever since his appearance on the national political stage—good and evil alike—still bears the imprint of this fascinating and immensely complicated man who commanded as much intense love as intense hatred among his fellow citizens.

2

Few men in contemporary history had prepared themselves so well and so carefully for the task of becoming president— or dictator. While most of the other Latin-American dictators burst rather suddenly into the spotlight from career military positions, Vargas had been a working politician for twenty-one years prior to his grab for power. A quiet and unspectacular man, he had to make up in experience and in a painstakingly acquired political reputation for the fact that he was an essentially dull person.

As a speaker, Vargas was no spellbinder; his speeches sounded grandiloquent, pedantic, and schoolmasterish, and his critics maintained that his talks were noted for saying nothing definite while appearing to be saying plenty. Not to be pinned down on anything was a feature of Vargas' political art.

Yet, particularly after he became president, Vargas displayed something akin to personal magnetism that captivated sophisticated individuals as it did mobs. The secret of his success with people seemed to be his ability to instill confidence and trust in himself as a man and in the wisdom of his policies. This personality trait made him acceptable to hundreds of thousands of Brazilians who, in their deeply rooted individualism, would normally react against a dictatorship. Among those who succumbed to the Vargas magic were distinguished politicians, intellectuals, and professional men.

This wide acceptance of the dictatorial regime, along with the gratitude of the working masses for Vargas' real and alleged achievements on their behalf, goes far in explaining the absence of any serious opposition until the postwar surge of liberalism caused his 1945 overthrow. The only major movement against Vargas, and one of mixed origins, was the 1932 São Paulo revolution. Neither the Communist uprising in 1935 nor the fascist Putsch in 1938 had any popular support.

The pro-Vargas sentiment in Brazil was so strongly entrenched that two months after the army ended his dictatorial government he was elected senator from two states and five years later carried the presidential elections by tremendous pluralities.

His influence continued after his death. Something of a "cult of the cadaver" spread almost immediately following his suicide, as millions of Brazilians seemed to forget overnight the inadequacies and crimes connected with his last administration. Politicians vied for the mantle of being Vargas' successor. João Goulart, the young protégé of the old president and his labor minister, proclaimed himself Vargas' "spiritual heir." Armed with a copy of the farewell letter Vargas had given him a few hours before shooting himself, he assumed the chairmanship of his mentor's Brazilian Labor Party and, riding the wave of emotionalism surrounding what was already becoming the Vargas legend, succeeded in being elected in 1955 as Brazil's vice–president.

Dr. Juscelino Kubitschek ran successfully for the presidency, identifying himself as much as possible with Vargas. His campaign posters depicted him being embraced by the man who had died more than a year earlier.

The principal reason for Vargas' posthumous political life was that no other personality of equal stature emerged in the nation either during or after his era, thus lending credence to the statement of one of his friends in 1930 that "Brazil is a desert of men." It is not too odd, then, that many of the democratic leaders of present-day Brazil are onetime officials of Vargas' dictatorial administration. The country's two principal political parties—Goulart's Brazilian Labor Party and Dr. Kubitschek's Social Democratic Party—were created by Vargas, and the new political generation has not yet come forth with anything new in terms of men or ideas.

Thus, the chairman of the ruling Social Democratic Party, and Dr. Kubitschek's ambassador to the United States throughout 1958, was Vargas' son-in-law, who had served as governor of the state of Rio de Janeiro during the dictatorial period. Vargas' police chief, famous for his ruthlessness and his pro-Axis leanings during the war, emerged as Senate majority leader in the Congress elected in 1955. One of the dictator's top brain trusters and former cabinet minister was the Senate's president pro tem in the same Congress. Several of the men who drafted the fascist constitution for Vargas in 1937 straight-facedly helped to write the 1946 democratic charter. President Kubitschek's key political adviser was the Vargas-appointed governor of Minas Gerais State under the dictatorship. The list is long and it demonstrates that despite his ouster in 1945 and his suicide in 1954 Vargas set up a line of political continuity that is still to be broken. And it also demonstrates that Brazilians are immensely sentimental, tolerant, unvindictive, and highly realistic about politics. As the final touch in the indestructibility of the Vargas legend, Rio de Janeiro's largest thoroughfare is still called Avenida Presidente Vargas.

3

A deliberate, slow-moving man with an extraordinary sense of timing and a remarkable capacity for self-control in time of stress, Getúlio Vargas built his political career on a talent for knowing how to wait for the right moment and then, in his own words, placing himself "at the head of the events." His seeming foot-dragging in the 1930 revolution was a case in point. But on a few occasions rashness and irrationality did explode through the outer casing of his personality, as when he resolved to kill himself, suggesting that fierce fires burned in his soul.

Outwardly a quiet and unemotional person, trusting nothing and nobody, Vargas went through life in a shell of utter loneliness, seeking no counsel and making his own decisions. Short of stature and very tense, he was introspective and secretive. Yet, with his ever-present cigar, a professional smile, and a ready, loud laugh in which he threw his head back in seeming abandon, he succeeded in putting over an image of himself that falsely suggested human warmth and openness.

Vargas wanted to be known as a man of simple habits, which he was, and a radiant smile. But, oddly enough, his official portrait, spread throughout Brazil in hundreds of thousands of copies, showed him glacial and austere, and wearing formal white-tie attire with the green-and-yellow sash of office crossing his shirt front. Brazilians never thought of him that way.

Vargas married early in life, and his wife gave him five children, but in later years they led separate lives under the same roof. Señora Vargas—Doña Darcy—won liking and respect for her quiet good work in the social field. As far as it is known, Getúlio did not engage in extramarital sexual adventures. This was not only in contrast with most of his dictatorial colleagues, but virtually in defiance of the habits of the Brazilian male. When Vargas returned to the presidency in 1950, and was nearly seventy years old, word went around Rio that he had acquired a mistress whom he visited once a week, driving to her apartment in a limousine with drawn curtains. This was the only instance of gossip involving his personal life. Vargas hardly ever drank alcohol. Expensive cigars and good food were his only weaknesses. He detested protocol and ostentation, often strolled almost alone in the streets. He had one curious quirk: that of eating his meals alone.

With so sublimated a personality, the underlying trait of Vargas' character was his craving for power; a Brazilian psychiatrist wrote that Getúlio knew no other love. But, unlike cruder men who reached the pinnacle of dictatorial power, Vargas went after it gradually and almost scientifically, gauging unerringly his own capabilities and those of other men. Very flexible, he knew how to bend with the wind, make concessions, backtrack, or maneuver.

Thus, when São Paulo launched its 1932 revolution demanding the restoration of parliamentary institutions in Brazil and protesting that a Rio-appointed governor had been sent to run the state, Vargas first crushed the rebellion, then announced the elections for a Constituent Assembly, and later

named a Paulista governor. Having toyed at the outset of
World War II with the idea of allying Brazil with the Axis,
he declared war on Germany, Italy, and Japan as a consequence of Pearl Harbor.

In his personal relations Vargas seldom allowed himself the
luxury of permanent vindictiveness: he imprisoned or exiled
his enemies, then often sought to convert them to his cause by
offering them high positions. The granting of amnesty was a
favorite Vargas device. But with the same ease and the same
smile he could and did betray his best and most unsuspecting
collaborators.

True personal friends Vargas never had, except for Oswaldo Aranha, the most devoted to him of all men. But even
Aranha was the target of deliberate humiliations over the
forty years of his political and personal association with
Vargas, who feared him as a potential rival. Yet it was toward
Aranha that Vargas always turned in time of crisis. And it
was the white-haired Aranha, Vargas' Minister of Justice in
1930 and Minister of Finance in 1954, who broke down in
tears at his old chief's funeral. Whenever he could, Vargas
liked to surround himself with old, trusted associates, gen-
erally distrusting political newcomers, with the notable exception of João Goulart.

So great was Vargas' reputation for political maneuvering
that a Brazilian cartoon, published after his overthrow in
1945, depicted him as a smiling circus artist advancing cau-
tiously but surely on a high wire. It was as apt a characteriza-
tion of Getúlio Vargas as was ever made. Actually, the dictatorial propaganda apparatus did encourage, and even plant,
anecdotes showing him as a master of political intrigue. This
appealed to the Brazilian sense of the mischievous, and had
the advantage of diffusing the myth that Vargas could dispose
of any and all opponents. He greeted with delight all the

jokes about him, and one of his strengths was that he never feared humor. In a nation as devoted to political joking as Brazil any other attitude would have been catastrophic.

So long as Vargas could control the situation through his dictatorial powers, his system of political acrobatics functioned smoothly. But it completely collapsed when, as constitutional president elected by a confused and sentimental nation, he soon had to face the mounting opposition of a free congress and press. Perhaps realizing that despite his great electoral victory he was already passé in the new, postwar Brazil, Vargas struck out with desperation and demagoguery in all directions—he encouraged extreme nationalism and even proposed a syndicalist republic of the proletariat and government-controlled labor unions—while his regime foundered in maladministration and corruption.

When the crisis reached its climax and military chiefs demanded his resignation, Vargas, unable to find a way of clinging to power any longer, chose suicide as his final word. Conscious as he was of history, he concluded his farewell letter with the phrase: "Serenely, I take the first step on the road to eternity and I leave life to enter history." Vargas would have loomed greater in it had he been content to retire on his laurels with his election to the Senate and the role of a respected elder statesman. But he could not tolerate the heartbreak of having been deprived of the presidency in 1945, and went after power again—this time rashly, hungrily, and unscientifically—as personal revenge. He won it but, no longer able to govern in his accustomed manner, Vargas, already seventy years old, treated Brazil to the pathetic spectacle of his own personal tragedy and to a government that was called "the sea of mud."

His last three years were a negation of his old method of behavior, the patient but effective method that had guided him through an apprenticeship for power, during which he was briefly a soldier, then a student-politician, a lawyer, a provincial deputy, a federal deputy, a cabinet minister, governor of his state, a defeated presidential candidate, and a victorious revolutionary leader. When, almost inevitably, Vargas reached power in 1930 he began ruling Brazil without hesitation and with the sure hand of a man who had waited all his life for that moment.

4

The quasi-enchanted life of Getúlio Dornelles Vargas began on April 19, 1883, in the ancient town of São Borja, a cattle and trading center on the Uruguay River, which divides Brazil from Argentina. The pampa stretches as far as the eye can see on both sides of the river, and in Brazil its towns, hamlets, and homesteads are inhabited by the tough strain of Gaúchos, now the generic name for the people of the state of Rio Grande do Sul but once descriptive of the men who rode their small, sturdy horses with the cattle herds.

Rio Grande do Sul, and particularly the São Borja region, was a land of open spaces where the people were imbued with the spirit of the frontier and habits of independence and directness. Political and family feuds were commonplace, wealthy ranchers often led their cowboys into battle as improvised fighting corps, and something of an everyday militarism underlay life there. Though they lived on the geographical fringes of the Brazilian republic, the Gaúchos were politically active and conscious, but their influence in national affairs was overshadowed by that of the powerful states of São Paulo and Minas Gerais and of the politicians in the federal capital of Rio de Janeiro. Following the terms in office of two marshals who were Brazil's first presidents—and rather dictatorial ones—after the proclamation of the republic in 1889 São Paulo and Minas Gerais took turns, with only one exception, in providing chief executives for the nation. The presidential elections were little more than formalities: the ruling groups in the two states—the wealthy "oligarchs"— usually agreed on the candidates and these were subsequently imposed on the nation. As soon as a president was chosen and began to hand out his patronage, politicians got down to maneuvers for the ironing out of a candidate from their limited circle for the next term.

Under this system the powerful states of the union could rest assured that the federal government would look after their needs. But the weaker states, particularly the drought-stricken areas of the northeast and the forgotten regions of the Amazonian north, were relegated to continuing oblivion.

Rio Grande do Sul, which was wealthy enough to take care of itself, had also carved out a political individuality all of its own and equipped itself with a constitution that differed from those in the other states forming the Brazilian federal union. The federal constitution of 1891 was modeled after the United States Constitution, and the charters of the Brazilian states copied it fairly faithfully. In Rio Grande, however, a political leader named Júlio de Castilhos, founder of the state's Republican Party, had put through a constitution that gave vast powers to the president of the state and restricted the legislature to budgetary matters exclusively. Castilhos was one of Brazil's foremost disciples of August Comte, the French philosopher, and a top exponent of his Positivism.

Several of Getúlio Vargas' biographers have rightly remarked that Gaúchismo, militarism, and Positivism were the main influences in his formative years. His father, General Manoel do Nascimento Vargas, a veteran of the Paraguayan war of the 1860's, united all these trends in himself. From his earliest years, Getúlio, the third of five brothers, was exposed to seeing them in action. A rancher and a frontier man of iron principles, the old general was the personification of Gaúchismo, a way of life built around strict codes of honor and behavior. Getúlio learned in later years how to play upon the Gaúcho code of honor in his fellow citizens of Rio Grande, though he never bothered to practice it himself. As president he surrounded himself with retinues of Gaúchos, monopolizing to such an extent the federal government that the northernmost state of Pará whimsically inserted a clause in its constitution explicitly barring any Gaúcho from becoming president of the state.

Getúlio was an accomplished horseman at the age of five, and, aside from his craving for power, the love of the Rio Grande ranches and the open spaces was his most marked characteristic. As a grown man Getúlio always returned to the family homestead in São Borja, as if to recharge his life batteries. He was there at most of the crucial moments of his career—when he ran for president in 1930, when the army ousted him in 1945 and he was plotting his return to politics, and in 1954, shortly before his suicide, when the pressures against him had become intolerable.

Militarism came into young Getúlio's life from the wartime stories of his father and from the frequent spectacle of frontier conflicts with the Gaúcho cowboys fashioned into temporary squadrons and regiments. His first ambition was for a military career, and at the age of fifteen he joined the army in São Borja and soon was promoted to sergeant. In 1900, a year later, he entered as a cadet the Preparatory and Tactical School of Rio Pardo, the principal military academy in Rio Grande. He resigned as a result of a dispute and returned to the ranks to complete his military service in Pôrto Alegre, capital of the state.

Vargas' interest in the military was apparently motivated by his realization of the importance of the armed forces in the political affairs of the republic since its inception. Although Marshals Deodoro da Fonseca and Floriano Peixoto,

Brazil's first two presidents, were succeeded in office by civilians, the generals and colonels remained vastly influential in
the game of electing presidents. Somewhere along the line,
however, Vargas must have concluded that if it was good to be
a military man in Brazil, it might even be better to be in a
position to use the military for one's own purposes.

Consequently, Getúlio enrolled in the Pôrto Alegre law
school while still a sergeant. In 1903 he volunteered to participate in the army expedition that was to attack Bolivia. The
dispute was settled peacefully, and all Getúlio extracted from
this additional period of army service was an opportunity to
become acquainted with the remote hinterland of Brazil in
the jungle-bound vastness of the state of Mato Grosso. His
subsequent interest in developing the Brazilian interior and
his resulting March to the West campaign in the late 1930's
may have been in part the fruit of this Bolivian expedition.
Like all of Getúlio's other activities and endeavors, his successive military experiences were not wasted time: he learned
something of tactics, studied the military mind, and made
many friends who later served him in good stead.

Positivism and politics surrounded Getúlio from childhood.
His father was president of the São Borja branch of Castilhos'
Republican Party and intensely interested in political doings
in Rio Grande, in faraway Rio de Janeiro, and in the world
at large. He was a confirmed Positivist, since, oddly enough,
the Gaúchos, like many Brazilians, managed to conciliate Positivism with their Roman Catholic religion. Getúlio Vargas
himself went to the strange extreme of giving the name of
Lutero to one of his sons in an unexplained tribute to the
father of the Protestant Reformation, though personally he
never broke with the Church of Rome. His suicide being a sin
in the eyes of the church, Vargas was denied a religious burial
and no Mass could be said for his soul in Rio Grande.

Castilhos was something of a domestic deity around the

Vargas home—although Getúlio's maternal uncle, Dinarte Dornelles, led the local anti-Castilhos faction—and his ideas about a strong government and parliament serving as a mere ornament were held sacred. This is doubtless how Getúlio's own political thoughts began to germinate to become translated decades later into his own form of dictatorial strong government. Castilhos had insisted on the preservation of the greatest personal liberty for citizens, and the system worked in Rio Grande. But when later Vargas, a disciple of Castilhos, conquered the presidency of Brazil, it became increasingly difficult for him to conciliate in his own mind the concept of a strong executive with civil liberties, and the 1937 dictatorship came as the result.

Both Castilhos and his successor as president of Rio Grande do Sul, a politician named Antonio Augusto Borges de Medeiros, were living examples of the theory that power is not something to be lightly abandoned, and in this Vargas emulated them to the end. When rebel chieftains once presented Castilhos with an ultimatum to quit or be ousted, he stepped down with the remark that he was leaving only temporarily and that, "I shall return here, recalled by yourselves." He was right in his prediction: a few months later another rebellion and a bloody civil war restored him to the presidency of Rio Grande.

Getúlio Vargas, like Castilhos, preferring to bend with the wind rather than resist it at the wrong time, used similar words when the military ousted him in 1945, and, again like Castilhos, return he did, five years later. Faced with military pressure for his resignation in 1954, Vargas tried the same technique a second time: he agreed to take a leave of absence without actually giving up the presidency. When the generals, in effect, turned him down, he killed himself.

It was from Borges de Medeiros, the man who launched him politically, that Vargas learned how to hold on to power.

Succeeding Castilhos, Borges de Medeiros served on and off for twenty-five years as president of Rio Grande, finally making room for Getúlio.

6

The opening years of the twentieth century found Getúlio in Pôrto Alegre, studying law, busy in student politics, and devoting his nights to self-imposed intellectual homework that ranged from Nietzsche to Baudelaire. Although his father's ranch in São Borja prospered, and his older brothers, Viriato and Protásio, were doing well there, Getúlio lived modestly in a boarding house in the capital. He spent his small allowance on books. His luxuries were cigars and billiards; he was addicted to both. Occasionally he indulged in writing and reciting poetry.

Vargas' reading pursuits gave him considerable erudition, particularly in politics, philosophy, and literature; equipped him mentally for his future career; and made him the only intellectually outstanding South American dictator of the century. His special kind of vanity took advantage of this fact in ensuing years: upon publication of his speeches in book form, he quietly got the Brazilian Academy of Letters to violate its own rules and elect him as a member—thus "immortalizing" him—although there were no vacancies at the time. His fellow "immortals"—Brazil's most famous literary men—did not protest.

But Getúlio did not neglect the practical side of politics in favor of theories. He was an active member of the Castilhos Academicians' Bloc and a contributor to *O Debate*, the newspaper of the student wing of the Republican Party which sought to spread throughout Brazil Castilhos' authoritarian ideas. He befriended other politically active students, who were impressed with his quiet demeanor, his ability to listen, to speak only when he had something to say, and with his clear judgment. The contemplative young man, charming and polite, also began to attract the attention of the party's leadership.

In 1906 Vargas received his first opportunity to appear in public, representing the student organizations in greeting Brazil's President Affonso Penna on his visit to Pôrto Alegre. In this first public speech, the forerunner of uncounted hundreds that followed in latter years, he set forth his views with a naïveté of youth mixed with a foretaste of his singleness of purpose and of the ideas he would one day put into practice. "We still are," he said, "mere observers of the facts of the present, but we shall be the judges of the future." Then: "Democracy is the common aspiration of civilized peoples . . . but only through education can we have a nation truly capable of a democratic government." Thirty-one years later Vargas decided that Brazil was not sufficiently educated for democracy and, therefore, he brought it to an abrupt halt.

Vargas made another speech in São Borja in 1907, this time greeting Senator Pinheiro Machado, one of the powers of the republic. A great admirer of the Senator, Getúlio told him: "Your attitude has been to await the march of events, placing yourself at their head, to direct them." He thereby stated his own credo of what a successful political technique should be.

Back in Pôrto Alegre Getúlio became involved in his first political campaign on behalf of a Borges de Medeiros candidate for the state's presidency. He traveled extensively through Rio Grande, receiving his baptism in grass-roots politics, drafting a students' manifesto that was said to have done great harm to the opposition's candidate, and finally being credited with staging a harmless shooting affray that broke up in a stampede the latter's biggest mass rally.

The Vargas-backed candidate won, and a month later, in

December, 1907, Getúlio graduated with honors from the
law school, delivering the farewell address on behalf of his
class. Ignoring an offer to teach philosophy of law at the
Pôrto Alegre university, he returned to São Borja, where his
father had just been elected mayor. He considered practicing
law in his home town, but when the opportunity came, Getúlio preferred to accept a post as assistant district attorney in
the state capital. He was twenty-six years old, and the appointment was considered a great distinction.

After a year, however, he tired of the petty cases he was
trying and, upon his father's insistence, agreed to return home
and open a law office. A lawyer's work in São Borja was far
from exciting—a succession of routine land disputes—and
Getúlio used his spare time to write an essay on Epicure and
to continue dabbling in politics.

This latter activity paid off: he caught the attention of
Borges de Medeiros and, supported by his politically influential father, he was nominated as one of the Republican
Party's candidates for state deputy in the 1909 elections.
Running from São Borja and again helped by his father, the
mayor, Getúlio won handily. His political career had begun
in earnest, but twenty-one years were to elapse before it
reached its culmination.

7

The first four years of this career, until Getúlio suddenly resigned his seat in the State Assembly and went back to full-
time practice of law in São Borja in 1913, were dull and unspectacular. The legislature met only three months of the
year and, under the provisions of the Castilhos constitution,
was not allowed to vote on anything except budget matters.
The deputies were free to deliver speeches on general themes

and, for all practical purposes, they were a debating society rather than a working state parliament. Some of the members had been there for twenty years and had no greater ambition than to remain for another twenty, if they lived that long. The circumstances were, then, hardly propitious for a young politician to make an impact on public opinion. Since there was little else he could do, Vargas began to study the state's budget in detail. The knowledge he thus acquired, along with a reputation as a financial expert, became a sound foundation for the continuation of his political career in ensuing years. As usual, the patient young man was not wasting his time.

During the nine months of the Assembly's annual recess, Vargas sat behind his lawyer's desk in São Borja, earning a comfortable living and making political friendships. In 1911 he married Senhorita Darci Sarmanho, daughter of a São Borja bank manager and granddaughter of a Rio Grande revolutionary general. His quiet, uneventful existence was enlivened only by political feuds and intrigues involving the leading families of the frontier region, which included the Vargas clan.

Getúlio was re-elected to the Assembly in 1913, but decided not to take his seat in protest against a write-in voting procedure used by the leadership of the Republican Party. His resignation, offered in a speech before the legislature, gained him greater notoriety than he could have hoped to win in four more years as a deputy.

While World War I was being fought in Europe, the Gaúchos of Rio Grande went on with their private political wars, sometimes reflecting national political conflicts, sometimes being merely the result of local problems. Vargas was active in these situations, but principally as mediator. When his older brother, Viriato, was charged with the murder of

a hostile politician, Getúlio's efforts at conciliation averted a
São Borja civil war that could have spread to other parts of
the state.

Possibly in recognition of his mediatory talents, Dr. Borges
de Medeiros, still president of Rio Grande in 1916, offered
Getúlio the post of police chief of the state. Vargas, who
had an eye on other things, turned down the appointment,
but accepted the nomination to run again for State Assembly.
This time he was promised the job of majority leader, and
was duly elected in 1917.

Combining the position of majority leader with that of
rapporteur of the Assembly's finance committee, Vargas devoted his time and best efforts to the self-appointed task of
bringing about a truce between his Republican Party and the
Federalist opposition. But Rio Grande was not yet ready for
pacification, and neither was the rest of Brazil, moving as it
did from one political crisis to another.

While in Rio Grande the running controversy was between
the advocates and the foes of Castilhos' system of strong government—and it was Vargas' job to defend it in the Assembly
—the national crises as usual had to do with battles for the
presidency among the big states and powerful economic and
political groups. Presidents were still being nominated and
elected in smoke-filled caucus rooms, with the voters being
given little choice beyond the endorsement of preselected
candidates.

But, partly as a result of World War I, which had accelerated the country's economic development and with it
spread new ideas, Brazilians were becoming increasingly resentful of the old-fashioned political practices. The 1922
election of Arthur Bernardes, carried out in classical style, led
to an abortive rebellion by the young officers of Copacabana
Fort in Rio de Janeiro. This movement of the "Lieutenants"
was the first of a series of military and civilian revolts against

the old order that was to climax in the 1930 revolution and Getúlio's conquest of power.

At the time, however, Vargas, then serving his second term as majority leader in the Assembly, had little sympathy for the Copacabana uprising. Rio Grande, already considered politically as the third-most-important state in the union, had been expected to join in the rebellion. But old Dr. Borges de Medeiros decided against it, and Vargas rose in the Assembly to explain that while his chief had been under pressure to "throw the destinies of the state to the risks of a revolution, he followed a superior line that separates a movement within the constitutional order from one that degenerates in revolutionary anarchy."

This was the first recorded gem of Vargas' double talk and his genius for confusing issues.

The following year, in 1923, Dr. Borges de Medeiros was re-elected once more president of Rio Grande. However, Dr. Assis Brasil, the defeated candidate, was not prepared to accept the situation and began preparing a revolution. He marshaled ten thousand armed men against the two thousand soldiers of the state's military brigade loyal to the government. To restore the balance, Dr. Borges de Medeiros ordered the creation of the Provisional Corps made up of his own followers. Vargas was named commander of the São Borja detachment and commissioned a lieutenant colonel.

But the new colonel never had a chance to lead his men in the field. Instead, he went to Rio as federal deputy for Rio Grande do Sul. Borges de Medeiros felt that he needed a trusted representative in the Brazilian capital to dissuade the central government from any ideas about federal intervention in his state. He arranged for Vargas' nomination, and the election was a formality. Getúlio was forty years old when he thus rose from the provincial to the national political scene.

8

The Rio Grande civil war could not be settled, even though Dr. Borges de Medeiros agreed to revise the state constitution prohibiting the re-election of the president. And the following year, in 1924, as Getúlio himself was elected to a second term in the Federal Chamber of Deputies, the civil war spread to the rest of the nation.

Again, young officers and civilian idealists rose against the regime of President Bernardes. The movement began in São Paulo, and at once the warring Rio Grande factions took sides in the national revolution. The ruling Republican Party rose in defense of the embattled Bernardes, and in São Borja the Vargas clan fought the revolutionaries tooth and nail. In Rio, Getúlio Vargas served on a special commission created to study a revision of the federal constitution so that Bernardes and "the public powers" could gain greater executive force.

Vargas now stood squarely on the side of those demanding the scrapping of the 1891 constitution, patterned after the United States Constitution, and the establishment of a strong government in Brazil. He was never to deviate again from this political line, although, for expediencies of the moment, he often paid lip service to liberalism. While President Bernardes, forced by circumstances, governed most of the time with the special powers he enjoyed under a modified martial law then in effect, Vargas lectured his congressional commission on the advantages of the strong-executive constitution of Rio Grande. In it, he said, "authority and liberty are admirably wedded."

The 1924 revolution was eventually quelled—in Rio Grande, however, the fighting went on for two more years— and the idea of revising the constitution was dropped by the government, though not necessarily by Vargas. The notion that the Brazilian constitution was inadequate, because of its exaggerated liberalism and the great degree of autonomy it gave the individual states, continued to fascinate him for years to come—until he was in a position to do something about it.

Actually, the fathers of the Brazilian republic in 1891 were somewhat impractical in seeking to fit the constitution of a nation as developed as the United States already was when its Constitution was written to the country of political chaos and administrative disorganization that they inherited at the demise of the empire. The conception of states' rights that may have made a certain sense in the United States made virtually none in Brazil. It led to abuses, to regionalisms, and resulted in the confusions and upheavals that marked the opening decades of Brazilian republicanism. Vargas was, then, evidently right in looking forward to a change in the system and the fact that, as president, he did unify Brazil politically was one of his principal accomplishments in office. Having entered parliament in 1923 insisting that Rio Grande "demands respect for its autonomy," he did modify his ideas on the subject in the short time of two years. But he never wavered in his conviction that what the country needed was a strong government.

As leader of the Rio Grande congressional delegation, Vargas befriended opposition deputies from his state—though these men often went home to fight Vargas' kin and friends in the state's bloodied fields—and established politically profitable relations with congressmen from other states. Rising from his recent obscurity of just another provincial politician, Getúlio rapidly gained the spotlight as a highly influential deputy—and the man to be watched. He worked hard—he sat on the Finance Commission of the House in addition to his duties on the constitutional reform group—and made it his business to learn as much as he could about the affairs of the

other states as well as of the republic as a whole. He spoke
little, but when he did he made an impression. Quiet, amiable,
and always willing to listen, he gradually won the trust of
different political groups in Congress, and his counsel was
sought in many quarters. He lived modestly, his two elder
sons were in college, and when he was not engaged in political homework he allowed himself the recreation of the
cinema. As usual, Vargas was marking time and preparing
for the next step upward.

This step came in 1926, when Washington Luiz Pereira de
Souza, the new president of Brazil, named him finance minister, one of the most powerful positions in the goverment.
The election of Washington Luiz, as he was commonly
known, created no problems. The nation was tired of civil
war; many of the military leaders of the 1924 revolt were still
in prison, others exiled. One of the latter, incidentally, was
the army captain named Luiz Carlos Prestes, a fellow Gaúcho,
who later became head of the Brazilian Communist Party and
whose path later was to cross Vargas' many times. Prestes'
forces defeated the army of the Vargas clan in Rio Grande,
then wrote a page for themselves in Brazilian history by
dodging for two years the victorious federal troops in an epic
two-thousand-mile march along the jungle-infested western
frontier.

But in 1926 Brazil was calm once more, and Vargas felt
he could accept the cabinet post without compromising his
political future. His immediate task was to carry out the
monetary reform planned by President Washington Luiz, and
this touched upon a study of the fundamentals of the Brazilian economy, traditionally monocultural and in those days, as
now, dependent to an awesome degree on its coffee production and exports. Along with many economists Vargas felt
that the nation's future hinged upon the development of other
sources of wealth, such as cocoa, cotton, and minerals.

But as finance minister, Vargas never had a chance to reform either the currency or the economy of Brazil. Within a year Dr. Borges de Medeiros offered him the nomination for the presidency of Rio Grande, as his successor. Getúlio did not hesitate. The finance ministry under an unspectacular administration gave him temporary prestige but sidetracked him from further political advancement and by then his sights were set high. The country was full of ex-ministers, while the presidency of a powerful state such as Rio Grande put him in the running for greater things. Yet his one-year tenure in the ministry had not been wasted time: it had given Getúlio an opportunity to learn from inside the workings of the central government.

In making Vargas president of Rio Grande, old Borges de Medeiros assumed that his protégé would do his bidding. But he soon found out that Vargas had other ideas: he rejected Borges de Medeiros' list of state secretaries and named his own men. Oswaldo Aranha, his college friend, became secretary of the interior.

Beginning in 1928, peace was finally restored in Rio Grande, and the credit does go to Vargas. Dropping the partisan habits of his predecessor, he appointed opposition leaders to state jobs. And this was the end of the opposition. Administratively Vargas also inaugurated a new approach to government. His emphasis was on economic development and the solution of social problems. He helped cattlemen by opening a special credit department in the state bank, reformed the education system and built new schools, encouraged experiments with the planting of rice and wheat. Interestingly, Vargas insisted on reading every night the galley proofs of his party's newspaper, suggesting changes of all kinds. This censorial preoccupation may have been a forerunner of what eventually became a virtual propaganda ministry under Vargas' dictatorship.

In 1929, a year after Vargas took over the government of Rio Grande, Brazil was plunged into the quadrennial excitement of the presidential election. As a successor, Washington Luiz made it known that he would support the São Paulo politician, Júlio Prestes. Vargas, who had been sounded out by some friends as to his own availability, wrote Washington Luiz on May 10, 1929, that the Republican Party of Rio Grande would support Prestes at the right time. He declared flatly that he was not interested in being a candidate himself.

Faithful to his principles and his technique Vargas refused to be rushed prematurely into anything. He was biding his time, waiting for the "march of events." Shortly after Getúlio's letter to Washington Luiz, João Neves da Fontoura, a friend of Vargas, was told by Francisco Campos, Secretary of Interior of Minas Gerais, that Minas would not go along with the Prestes candidacy but would instead support a Rio Grande candidate. Secret conferences were held among politicians of the two states, a pact was signed, and it was agreed that Getúlio Vargas would be the opposition candidate for the presidency of Brazil.

9

The 1930 presidential campaign, pitting Getúlio Vargas against Júlio Prestes, soon developed into the most frenetic, no-holds-barred contest in the history of the Brazilian republic. Prestes, the official candidate, had the support of the governments of all the states except Rio Grande, Minas Gerais, and tiny Paraíba in the country's parched northeast. But the Vargas candidacy, presented as a movement of political and moral restoration to the nation, appealed to the imagination and the emotionalism of Brazilians. Thousands began to rally under its banner. The Liberal Alliance was formed by Vargas, President Antonio Carlos Ribeiro de Andrada of Minas, and

João Pessôa, president of Paraíba, to sponsor the campaign. The revolutionary officers and civilians of 1922 and 1924 joined the movement, as did students, workers, and young professional people throughout Brazil. It was youthful idealism against the entrenched interests of stale old politicians.

The great Depression, which had an immediate impact on Brazil, gave Vargas added strength. Coffee, produced in great overabundance before 1929, could no longer be sold on world markets. The country's finances neared collapse and official banks could no longer advance money to producers, thus throwing the coffee industry into a severe crisis that immediately affected all other activities in Brazil. The poor became poorer; the nascent middle class could not hold its own. Social problems, always acute, were aggravated to a point of explosion.

Prestes had no convincing answers to any of these issues. Vargas and the Alliance campaigners, on the other hand, unrolled a comprehensive and scintillating program of reforms that made the heads of the voters swim. There would be an amnesty for former rebels, a new elections' law, reorganization of courts, a new education system, a new approach to basic economic problems, and, above all else, legal protection for the working masses and measures to better their lot. When the Washington Luiz government prevented Vargas from making a campaign speech at an appropriate indoor location in Rio de Janeiro, Getúlio spoke in a city plaza. Tens of thousands of persons turned out to hear him in the biggest alfresco rally Brazil had seen until then.

But when election day came on March 1, 1930 it was Prestes who was declared the winner. The Alliance immediately charged fraud—the presidents of the pro-Prestes states had promised to "fill the ballot boxes" and there was little doubt that they had kept their word. Oswaldo Aranha, acting president of Rio Grande since his friend Getúlio stepped

down to run for office, fired off a cable to Washington Luiz
protesting fraudulent practices. João Pessôa, whose winning
congressional candidates in Paraíba were refused seats in Rio,
voiced more protests. Getúlio Vargas sat quietly in São Borja,
then returned to Pôrto Alegre to resume the presidency of
Rio Grande. He was awaiting the events.

With Aranha and Pessôa in command of these events, it became clear that a revolutionary spirit was spreading in Brazil
and that there would be hard-fought opposition to Prestes'
office-taking. Even Vargas committed himself: in an address
to Brazilians, he promised that the time was not far when the
results of the elections would be "rectified."

But the act which shifted the revolutionary planning into
high gear was the murder on July 26 of João Pessôa by thugs
in the service of the government. An explosion was unavoidable, and in Rio Grande Aranha took over the preparations
for a rebel movement. With the co-operation of politicians in
Minas and in Rio he carefully laid his plans. Hundreds of
young officers offered their services to the new cause. Arms
and munitions were secretly manufactured. The state police
force, a military organization, was pledged to the revolution.
The over-all military planning was in the hands of Colonel
Pedro Aurelio de Goes Monteiro, a Vargas colleague from
military academy days, who, fifteen years later, led the army
in ousting Vargas from office.

All was ready for the revolution, but Vargas was still reluctant to give the word. Some of his friends said that he was
hoping until the last moment for a solution that would obviate
violence. Others said that he did not want to move until he
was absolutely certain of success. But even when Goes Monteiro informed him early in September that preparations had
reached the point where the coup could not possibly fail,
Vargas still insisted on more time. He wanted assurances from

military commanders in Rio that they would join the revolution.

Finally, Vargas agreed to set the date: October 3. Pedantic as he was, Getúlio earlier went to the trouble of withdrawing ten thousand milreis from his bank account to pay for a trip to Rio. But when the revolution erupted, he waited a full week in Pôrto Alegre before moving north, just to be sure.

The rebellion broke out simultaneously in Rio Grande, Minas, and Paraíba. In Pôrto Alegre the fighting was brief; the local army commander surrendered to Aranha, who again took over the state's presidency. Troops in Paraná and Santa Catarina went over to the side of the revolution. But in Rio the garrison remained faithful to President Washington Luiz, who, despite all indications to the contrary, had refused all along to believe that a revolt was in the making. Prestes was visiting the United States.

As commander in chief of the Rio Grande revolutionary armies Vargas began his slow trip to Rio when it appeared reasonably certain that the movement had succeeded. Having reached Paraná on October 24, Getúlio received word that the military chiefs in Rio had at last bowed to the inevitable and forced Washington Luiz out of office. Two generals and an admiral formed the Junta of Government.

For a whole week the Junta gave indications that it would like to stay in power rather than turn it over to Vargas. Police Chief Bertoldo Klinger, a colonel, was the mainstay in this plan. With Getúlio still awaiting developments in Paraná, Aranha traveled to Rio to inform the Junta that the revolutionary armies recognized only Vargas as their supreme chief and intimated that they would attack Rio, if needed, to make their will prevail.

The Junta capitulated. On October 31 Vargas entered Rio to the cheers of the capital's inhabitants, a short, smiling man

in an open-neck khaki shirt. On November 3, 1930, in a
ceremony at the gray Catete Palace, once the home of barons
of the empire, he was sworn in as Provisional President of
Brazil.

10

Once in power Vargas turned to the task of running Brazil
with the zeal of a fanatic reformer. Inheriting the government
of the country in the midst of a general depression that came
on top of a traditionally distorted economy and faced by
explosive social pressures, the new president wasted no time
in putting his "New Deal" into practice.

Working in an atmosphere of postrevolutionary exhilara-
tion and excitement, Vargas made his first period in office—
the nearly four years of his tenure as Provisional President—
by far the most positive and productive of all his government
periods. By concentrating on administration and not worrying
unduly about politics—his craving for power had just been so
splendidly gratified and his first official act was to declare
an amnesty—he was able to lay the foundations for the transformation of Brazil into the modern state that it is today.
Whatever his subsequent errors and faults Vargas established
in these first four years a solid basis for the country's development, and his successors have been building upon it ever since.

As dictator, in fact if not in name, Vargas ruled by decree,
but he made no serious attempt to curtail public liberties.
True enough, there was no congress and the states were run
by Vargas-appointed Federal Interventors, most of them military officers, but otherwise there was nothing oppressive
about the regime. Getúlio spoke vaguely of elections and an
eventual return to a constitutional regime, but he set no date
and seemingly gave the problem little thought.

All of his attentions were devoted to administrative problems and the reforms he had promised during his election campaign. And, alongside economic questions, labor matters were his pet projects. Because of their explosive potential, they were just as urgent as fighting the perils of the deepening depression.

Less than a month after assuming the presidency Vargas created the Ministry of Labor, Industry and Commerce, which became known as the "Ministry of the Revolution." Lindolfo Collor, one of the Minas Gerais founders of the Liberal Alliance, was put in charge of it, and the stage was set for a veritable revolution in Brazil's approach to social problems.

Until 1930 the country had no social legislation to speak of, and the little there was was enforced haphazardly or not at all. A few laws had been passed in the 1920's but, in the phrase current during the Washington Luiz administration, "the social problem was a police problem." The abolition of slavery in 1888 had disrupted the feudal economic and labor force situations in Brazil and nothing had come to replace them. Rural workers lived in conditions approaching those of serfdom, shifting from one plantation to another, seeking, but not finding, betterment of their fate. The industrialization of Brazil that had begun gradually around 1914 and the exodus from the countryside to the cities combined to spawn a great, miserable, and restless urban proletariat exploited to the fullest because there was nothing or no one to protect them.

Vargas and Collor thereupon set about changing all that. A series of decrees established a system of tutelage for the workers and for the first time in Brazilian history gave the country a comprehensive body of social labor legislation.

The workday was limited to eight hours and the work week to six days. Theretofore, men often worked twelve, fourteen, sixteen, or twenty hours a day, often seven days a week, to eke out a living from their miserable wages. Children under fourteen were no longer permitted to work in industry. Women gained the right to be paid as much as men for the same work performed; in the old days a woman, working alongside her husband, was sometimes paid one-half his wages. Pregnant women were not allowed to work for four weeks before and four weeks after childbirth. For the first time workers were legally entitled to two weeks of paid annual vacation if they had been employed for a full year. A minimal salary was decreed so that workers could receive basic wages that had some relation to living costs. Prior to that employers paid as little as they could get away with—which was easy in those days of unemployment and a growing idle labor force.

All of these measures, accepted many years earlier in most civilized nations, were new to Brazil, and they marked the beginning of the long, painful process of bridging the gulf between the country's immensely rich minority and its immensely poor majority. A quarter of a century later this process is still under way, but impressive progress, its roots in the early Vargas legislation, has been made.

These preliminary steps were followed by others. To enforce workers' protection laws, regional labor offices were set up in every state in Brazil, and inspectors had the task of seeing to it that the laws were obeyed by employers. Special juntas were organized to decide labor disputes, forerunners of a system of regular labor courts that Vargas was to create in 1939.

To provide for workers when they could no longer earn a living, Vargas established Retirement and Pensions Institutes for public employees. These were subsequently extended to all federal employees, bank and commerce workers. Hospitals and clinics were added to the Institutes, where workers and their families could receive free treatment and medicine. Both employers and workers had to contribute monthly to these institutes, in addition to the funds provided by the gov-

ernment, and thus Vargas came up with something of a welfare state in Brazil long before the system was tried elsewhere.
Vargas had no Socialist ideas and made no effort to interfere
with the capitalistic system in Brazil; but this welfare-state
policy was essential in a country as backward as Brazil, where
private retirement plans were unknown and commercial in-
surance was altogether out of the reach of working people.
In time the social-security institutes, controlling vast funds,
became plums of political patronage, and they remain so to
this day.

Another series of Vargas decrees introduced trade-unionism in Brazil and machinery for collective bargaining. Here,
however, the President polluted his social ideas by his political
ideas. The labor ministry was given full control over the
nascent unions and the law stipulated that "no more than one
union will be recognized for each profession." In a step
toward corporativism of the Portuguese dictatorial model,
Vargas ordered the unions to elect from their membership
representatives to the 1934 Constitutional Assembly.

In other fields Vargas reorganized the Ministry of Education and Health; reformed the whole educational system
along modern lines; stressed the construction of schools, a
vital measure in a country of illiteracy as high as Brazil; ear-
marked funds for fighting killer malaria in the far north of
the country and in the steamy lowlands outside of Rio; and
launched irrigation projects in the drought-plagued northeast
of Brazil.

Simultaneously with this social "New Deal"—and compari-
sons with Franklin Delano Roosevelt later became inevitable
—Vargas worked hard to straighten out Brazil's economy. A
National Coffee Council was organized to oversee the problems of the industry. In a bold step designed to save it from
ruin the government began purchasing the unsold coffee,
and when it became necessary because of the inability of

depression-hit world markets to absorb it, to throw it into the ocean or burn it in furnaces of factories and locomotives. A parallel attempt was made to control coffee acreage but it was not any more successful in those days than it is at the present time.

The Vargas government sought to encourage agricultural and industrial production. In the case of sugar and alcohol it established a special institute to deal with the problems. The trend was toward increasing state intervention in the economy, but, under the circumstances, there was no choice. In a move in another direction the government leased thousands of hectares of jungle land to Henry Ford, hoping that rubber planting, once the source of Brazil's wealth, could be revived. That the plan failed was nobody's fault.

The Vargas administration succeeded in curtailing public expenditures without halting development plans and did much to restore international confidence in the long-term soundness of Brazil.

11

In the midst of all his reformist endeavors Vargas had to face a three-month-long revolution, a virtual civil war that nearly toppled him from power.

While the movement avowedly was aimed at the restoration of constitutional rule in Brazil and the end of the provisional government that by its very definition was dictatorial, the interests at play were vastly diversified. The conspiracy against Vargas began in Rio Grande, where the seemingly eternal Dr. Borges de Medeiros felt bitter that his onetime disciple, Getúlio, no longer paid heed to his suggestions. It was joined by a number of Vargas' political friends, who sincerely believed that the new president had betrayed the ideals of the 1930 revolution in refusing to set a date for elections.

The plotting spread to São Paulo which had its own list of complaints against Vargas. There were people who were honestly disturbed by his increasingly dictatorial turn of mind; others resented that the state was run by a military interventor who was not a Paulista, and they spoke of military occupation; there were still others to whom an anti-Vargas revolution would be a revenge for 1930 and the coup against their fellow politician, Júlio Prestes. There were powerful economic interests that disliked Vargas' social policies, and finally there were officers who preferred to see a military rule. Significantly, General Bertoldo Klinger, who had wanted the 1930 Junta of Government to keep power indefinitely, was named the supreme military commander of the rebellion.

The seat of the revolution was in São Paulo, which wholeheartedly supported the Constitutionalist movement. In Rio Grande, again traditionally divided, State President Flores da Cunha remained loyal to Vargas, turning against the forces led by Borges de Medeiros.

The revolution broke out on July 9, 1932, as the rebels launched their march on Rio, which was defended by loyal troops commanded by General Goes Monteiro, chief of staff. Getúlio remained at the Catete Palace, with two revolvers in his desk drawer. He told a visitor that he would not let "the Cardinal take me out of here," an allusion to the fate of his predecessor, Washington Luiz.

General Klinger commanded nearly 25,000 well-armed troops, while the São Paulo industrial complex worked around the clock to produce weapons and munitions. People of São Paulo displayed an emotional fervor, and thousands came forth with financial contributions: the poor gave their wedding rings and the rich made donations running into millions of milreis.

But Goes Monteiro's troops stopped the rebels at the frontier of Rio de Janeiro State, and Flores da Cunha defeated the revolution forces in Rio Grande. Old Borges de Medeiros was arrested, and early in October most rebel commanders in São Paulo entered into negotiations with General Goes. The revolution collapsed.

Vargas survived the rebellion, but he immediately realized that once more he had to bend with the wind to avoid a repetition of what had just happened. Consequently, he announced that elections for a Constituent Assembly would be held on May 5, 1933. The country was obviously unprepared to accept his views on a strong government, and Vargas could wait for a more propitious occasion.

Although he announced that bygones were to be bygones Getúlio indulged in a few acts of personal vengeance: he temporarily exiled some of the leaders of the rebellion, notably Borges de Medeiros, the man to whom he owed much of his political career. Loyalties, indeed, Vargas did not have. Ten days before the elections for the Constituent Assembly a rock crashed atop his car near the mountain summer resort of Petropolis crushing Getúlio's legs, seriously injuring his wife, and killing his aide-de-camp. The physician who possibly saved the life of Mrs. Vargas and brought the president back to health was Dr. Pedro Ernesto. But when he later became Vargas' political opponent, the dictator showed no gratitude nor any mercy in persecuting him.

While the Constituent Assembly toiled in Rio over a new constitution for Brazil Vargas showed himself singularly unconcerned with the whole problem. After spending two months in bed recovering from his accident he took a long flying trip to the north and northeast of Brazil studying local problems and possible measures for improving conditions in those backward areas. Back in Rio he received the visit of the President of Argentina and went on unrolling his program of social and economic reforms.

On July 16, 1934, the Assembly approved the new constitution and elected Vargas to a four-year term as president. Having made no effort to influence the deputies in drafting the charter, Getúlio did not hide his contempt for the result of their deliberations. He told a few trusted friends that the new constitution failed to give the government the means and the power for conducting an effective administrative program. Then he made a prediction strange coming from a man who had just been chosen a democratic president: "I think I shall be the first to revise the Constitution." He also allowed as how he had agreed to stay in office, despite his dislike for power, only to complete his program.

In retrospect, Vargas' strange behavior indicates that he was embarking upon a long, complicated political play ultimately designed to hand him complete dictatorial power on his own terms. It required patience, but Vargas had always had plenty of it; he also knew his people well and was aware of the ease with which political sentiment could be shifted in Brazil. As constitutional president he met all the immediate demands of a nation just emerging from a bloody civil war and craving for a democratic regime, and this gave him time to develop his long-range scheme. He accepted a constitution he knew to be unworkable, and whenever he could he helped it to become more so. In sum, Vargas concluded that by giving democracy enough rope it would hang itself.

Brazilian politicians and their mania for plotting and politickeering pushed the process along. And so did the Communists. Many of the former busied themselves launching a defamatory campaign against Vargas, while Congress, often losing itself in sterile debates, delayed the passage of government legislation. Getúlio, on the other hand, did all he could to shine as a progressive and efficient administrator. Subtly the notion was diffused that Vargas was an irreplaceable man and that if it were not for Congress always throwing monkey wrenches into his plans the President could do magnificent things for the nation. The terrain was thus being prepared for Getúlio's next step.

The Communists' unwitting contribution to Vargas' plans was their uprising on November 27, 1935. At dawn of that day they struck at the Rio barracks of an infantry regiment, at the air force school on the outskirts of the city, and in Natal in the northeast. Many officers and men were killed in the surprise attack, but by evening the government had the situation in hand.

Luiz Carlos Prestes, hero of the 1924 epic march, who had returned to Brazil as secretary-general of the Communist Party, led the movement, which was camouflaged as the National Liberating Alliance. Despite the misery prevailing in the country Brazilian workers did not support the Red revolt: communism had limited appeal among them and they were apparently satisfied with Vargas' efforts on their behalf. Prestes was eventually arrested and sent to prison for nine years. His pregnant, German-born wife, also a Communist, was turned over by Vargas' police to the Gestapo in an act of rare cruelty. She was killed in a concentration camp after the birth of her daughter. The girl, incidentally, rejoined her father in Brazil in 1958, after having lived in Russia since the end of the war.

The abortive Communist uprising gave a new impetus to arguments that to defend itself from this kind of danger Brazil needed a strong government. The activities of the fascist Brazilian Integralist Action, an organization of roughs in green shirts given to raised-arm salutes and other Hitlerlike symbols, provided further fuel for the advocates of the strengthening of the regime.

The Integralistas, who jumped on the anticommunist band wagon following the 1935 Red uprising, were led by a slim, mustachioed politician named Plinio Salgado who fancied himself as the Brazilian Fuehrer. The party received assistance and funds from Germany and Italy and was dangerously influential among the large German communities in the south of Brazil. There, German was taught in schools, German newspapers were published, and the Nazi influence was growing alarmingly.

Nazi policy in those days was to attract Brazil to its side, and efforts were made to drive a wedge between Rio and Washington. Vargas, who at the time was active in promoting inter-American co-operation, gave these maneuvers a cold shoulder. To make the point even more strongly, he sent Oswaldo Aranha, his closest friend and collaborator, as ambassador to the United States. The following year Roosevelt visited Rio on his way to the inter-American conference in Buenos Aires, and the two presidents exchanged pledges of devotion to democracy.

But shortly thereafter Vargas wrote Aranha in Washington —hinting at what was developing in his mind—that Brazil was poor in political ideas that would stimulate the nation morally and ideologically and neutralize the "seduction of exotic and subversive doctrines."

12

Early in 1937 the political parties launched their activities aimed at the presidential elections of the following year and, as usual, pressures rose and talk of still another civil war was revived.

As was his custom Vargas gave no indication of his own plans. Although he described as "silly" in private conversations the growing agitation in certain circles to extend his term, he made no move to halt it. On another level he made special efforts to assure himself of the backing of the military, come what may. General Eurico Gaspar Dutra, another of his colleagues from military academy days, was named Minister of War. Goes Monteiro continued as Chief of Staff. The army and navy were being modernized, their air arms were expanded, and officers were receiving preferential treatment. The internal situation in Brazil and international pressures made these moves appear reasonable.

The announced candidates for the presidency were Armando Sales de Oliveira, the Vargas-appointed Interventor of São Paulo, who had the backing of Flores da Cunha in Rio Grande and of all the opposition elements; José Américo de Almeida, former Minister of Communications, who was given to understand that he would be the official candidate; and the Integralistas' Plinio Salgado. But, again, Vargas was helped by the events.

First, José Américo delivered a series of rather unfortunate campaign speeches that went far to discredit him with his government backers. With Vargas' quiet blessing, the official support for his candidacy was withdrawn. Next, the administration obtained evidence, or claimed it did, that Flores da Cunha was plotting a revolution, even without waiting for the elections. Army reinforcements were sent to Rio Grande, where Vargas' younger brother, Benjamin, was already gathering his own forces against Flores da Cunha. On October 16, Flores was persuaded to give up the state presidency and exile himself in Uruguay. This helped to weaken the Sales candidacy. To fight Salgado the government moved in force against all the Axis organizations, suppressed foreign-language newspapers, and closed German, Italian, and Japanese schools.

Getúlio Vargas, therefore, was left as the only possible solution in the political impasse, which was where he wanted to be all along. The atmosphere in Brazil had become such that public opinion was receptive to the reasoning, spewed forth by the pro-Vargas press, that the moment was too critical to risk an electoral battle and that emergency measures were essential. Military chiefs announced that order in the country could be maintained only if Vargas, the reluctant dragon, agreed to stay in power. Only the continuation of his rule could guarantee the defense of Brazil.

Vargas was not only agreeable to these "suggestions," but he had also carefully prepared for the perpetuation of his regime. For several months Justice Minister Francisco Campos, the man who had helped to launch Vargas' candidacy in 1930, had been working on a new constitution that was practically a carbon copy of the authoritarian constitution of Poland.

On the rainy morning of November 10, 1937, the inhabitants of Rio awoke to find the congressional buildings surrounded by troops and were informed that Vargas had carried out a coup d'état. Not a shot was fired; there was no opposition.

The dictatorship that was to last almost eight years had thus been launched. Armed with his constitution, Vargas proclaimed the regime of Estado Novo that was to usher in another new era in Brazilian history. All political parties were dissolved, the autonomy of the states was abolished and their flags burned in a public ceremony. Skillfully guided by Vargas democracy had indeed hung itself in Brazil.

The nation was told that the new political status quo would prevail indefinitely—as long as Brazil was in danger from domestic and foreign enemies. It was explained that, while on the one hand the Vargas coup was necessary to defend democracy from totalitarian inroads, on the other hand Western democracy could not serve the interests of Brazil, which lacked sufficient education to practice it properly. Henceforth,

Brazilians were to forget politics and concentrate on development and education. The Vargas constitution made ample provisions for such matters.

The dictatorship brought all the customary trappings. Press censorship was established. A powerful Department of Press and Propaganda (DIP) was set up, of all places, in the building that until recently housed the Chamber of Deputies. Its chief was an intellectual with violently uncombed hair, named Lourival Fontes. In the bizarre ways of Brazilian politics he was elected to the Senate when democracy was restored in Brazil in the next decade, even though his ministrylike department had been one of the most exasperating instruments of dictatorship.

For the eight years of Vargas' autocratic reign DIP worked day and night to build the legend of Getúlio and his achievements. The degree of Vargas' acceptance was a measure of its success. A special news agency was created to distribute official information, every evening all the radio stations broadcast the department's *Hour of Brazil,* and the cinemas were flooded with government newsreels showing a smiling Vargas doing this and doing that, going here and going there. Laudatory books about Vargas and Estado Novo were subsidized by the regime, and some extremely reputable men found no conflict of conscience in writing them.

The police force was vastly expanded, the country was filled with plain-clothes men specializing in political work, and Colonel João Alberto Lins de Barros, one of the military leaders of the 1930 revolution, organized a riot force of brutal, red-capped policemen to repress any antiregime demonstrations. The prisons began to fill, police interrogations turned to tortures, and a mild terror got under way. Some of Vargas' opponents had been exiled even before the November coup and many of the congressmen had to seek asylum in foreign embassies.

Vargas had finally reached his lifetime goal of imposing a strong government upon Brazil, but he conveniently omitted Júlio de Castilhos' precept about the maintenance of civil liberties.

Having solved his domestic problems, Vargas devoted himself to a complicated game in foreign relations. At the outset of his dictatorship he deceived whatever hopes there may have been in Berlin or Rome that the new regime would cooperate directly with them. Not wanting a political party of his own Vargas ordered the dissolution of Salgado's Integralista Party as well. At the same time he went on breaking up German and Italian organizations in the country.

On May 10, 1938, Salgado, apparently encouraged by the Axis governments, attempted an uprising designed to murder Vargas and capture power in Brazil. Late at night Integralista shock troopers, some disguised as members of the presidential guard, attacked the palm-bordered Guanabara Palace where Vargas and his family lived. The assault, a complete surprise, almost succeeded, since the loyal soldiers were vastly outnumbered by the Integralistas. Vargas, his daughter Alzira, his son Lutero, his brother Benjamin, and an aide-de-camp fought back from the top of a staircase, firing from submachine guns until they ran out of bullets. In the end Vargas was saved by the arrival of army reinforcements led by General Dutra.

Salgado was exiled to Portugal—he returned after the war to run unsuccessfully for president in 1955, and in 1958 was re-elected to Congress—and an investigation showed that the conspiracy had been organized by the German ambassador, who was forthwith expelled.

To keep Vargas from edging too close to the Nazis then engaged in a major effort to infiltrate South America, the United States maintained a cordial relationship with him. Oswaldo Aranha, a friend of the United States, was appointed

Foreign Minister after the 1937 coup, indicating that Brazil would maintain its Pan-American loyalties.

But Getúlio was still playing both ends against the middle. Between the beginning of World War II in Europe in 1939 and Pearl Harbor, when it still looked like the Germans could win the war, he conducted a policy of studied neutralism. Temporarily forgotten were his earlier protestations of devotion to freedom.

During the long battle between the *Graf von Spee* and the three British cruisers in South Atlantic waters in 1939, Brazil, carefully observing her nonbelligerency, refused to let the British men-of-war come into her ports to obtain supplies. To the despair of British intelligence, Brazilian police tolerated the activities of Nazi spies who infested Rio and Santos, reporting on the movements of Allied shipping. Many of the sinkings of these ships by Nazi submarines were attributable to the guidance of spies working in Brazil. Colonel Flinto Muller, the police chief, acquired a reputation for refusing to arrest spies spotted for him by Allied agents. Muller is now a senator.

On June 11, 1941, Vargas went aboard a Brazilian warship in Rio Bay to declare that the Western democracies were "anachronisms." The possibility of Brazil declaring war on the Allies was seriously considered at that time in high government circles. German and Italian news agencies worked freely in Brazil, and newspapers subsidized by the Axis disseminated its propaganda at will.

But Pearl Harbor changed everything overnight. With the United States in the war, Brazil could not afford to side with the Axis. And, in a typical shift of position, Vargas threw Brazil fully behind the free world. An emergency conference of American foreign ministers was held in Rio in January, 1942, and shortly thereafter Brazil declared war on the Axis powers. Brazilians, whose sympathies all along had been with the Allies, enthusiastically greeted their entry into the conflict.

13

Brazil—and Getúlio Vargas—prospered in the war years. The nation, participating in the "battle of raw materials" that streamed uninterruptedly to the war plants in the United States, repaired its shaky finances and built a healthy bankroll. For the first time in more than a decade Brazil had no trouble selling her coffee. Because most of her prewar sources of essential imports had dried up for the duration, Brazil's own industry grew by leaps and bounds. The United States Export-Import Bank lent money to begin the erection of the Volta Redonda steel mills, the first major steel plant on the continent. Employment in the country rose, living standards improved, and a foretaste of prosperity came for the first time to the Brazilian workingman. The government went on streamlining social legislation to keep pace with expanding industry and the expanding proletariat.

The stimulus of the war, combined with the earlier planning of the Vargas government, resulted in unprecedented development for Brazil during that period. Rio and São Paulo were among the world's fastest-growing cities. The long-neglected Brazilian hinterland began to open up; Vargas' interest in aviation, which included the creation of the air ministry and the launching of an airport-building program, helped to lay the groundwork for the eventual bridging by air of the country's enormous distances. Today, Brazil has the second largest commercial aviation network in the Western world.

But the war effort and the conquest of the hinterland also saw tragedy. Thousands of men, nobody knows exactly how many, died of hunger, thirst, fatigue, and disease when the

government embarked upon the fantastic scheme of transport-
ing a vast labor force from the drought areas of the northeast
to the jungles of the Amazon to produce rubber for victory.
In the absence of roads and all other facilities this migration
collapsed in an awesome human drama.

Militarily, Brazil gave the Allies all possible support. Air
and naval bases were made available to the United States along
the thousands of miles of Brazilian coast. They played an outstanding part in the logistics of the African and Mediterranean
campaigns. Brazilian planes and warships joined United States
forces in fighting the menace of German U-boats infesting the
south Atlantic and the Caribbean. Brazilian merchantmen were
sunk. A Brazilian infantry division and an air squadron went
to Italy to battle the Nazis.

Brazil was thus wholeheartedly committed to the cause of
democracy and freedom in the world. But this commitment
brought domestic implications: if Brazilian soldiers went overseas to fight dictators, what excuse was there for the maintenance of a dictatorship in Brazil?

While the war ran its course this question was not raised
too seriously, and Getúlio Vargas was able to enjoy power
without challenge. He kept DIP and the secret police busy,
letting it be known that any talk of restoring constitutional
rule in Brazil was premature.

But with the end of the war and the wave of liberalism that
was sweeping the noncommunist world, the dictatorial status
quo could not be maintained. To the protesting voices of
public opinion at home were added those of officers and soldiers returning from Italy. The people were insisting that
democracy be re-established. A Rio newspaper defied DIP
and published an interview with José Américo, the 1937 presidential candidate, urging elections. A group of outstanding
citizens of Minas Gerais circulated a manifesto along similar
lines.

This was the turning point in the history of Vargas' dictatorship. Getúlio could no longer ignore the growing impatience of the nation with his regime; sentiment for democracy ran high in the armed forces and he could think of no way to repress the awakening movement.

His answer, therefore, was to temporize, maneuver, and see how he could best use Brazil's yearnings for democracy for his own purposes. Starting out by lifting censorship from the press, Vargas encouraged political debate. He then promised elections for president and for a new Constituent Assembly. As usual, he announced that he had no desire to stay in power —but he failed to set a date for the elections.

The next step was the formation of a government political party: the Social Democratic Party. Overnight, many of Vargas' ministers and state Interventors became ardent democrats as the official electoral machine was set in motion. Vargas also allowed his opponents to become organized in the National Democratic Union and proclaimed an amnesty.

The principal beneficiary of this amnesty was Luiz Carlos Prestes, the Communist leader. Vargas had a place for him in his blueprint for keeping power. Because it suited his own purposes, Prestes, overlooking his nine years in prison and his wife's fate, allied himself with the dictator. The result of this pact was a Communist-engineered campaign for "Constituent Assembly with Vargas." The idea was that an Assembly could be elected and allowed to redraft the constitution but Vargas would stay on as president.

This was too much for most Brazilians, who by then were accustomed to Getúlio's talent for political acrobatics. War Minister Dutra, who was to be the official candidate for president, was among those increasingly resentful of Vargas' tactics. The unhappiness spread deep among the military, including some of Getúlio's oldest associates. A speech by American Ambassador Adolph Berle, hinting that the time for dictatorships was gone, helped to inflame the atmosphere. Anti-Vargas demonstrations erupted in Rio. The dictator decided to act to regain control of the situation. His first step, which was to be his last, was the appointment on October 29, 1945, of his younger brother, Benjamin, as Rio police chief. He could not have made a worst mistake. Benjamin, known as "Beijo" (the Kiss), was a playboy with a reputation for loose morals, a penchant for casino gambling, and brutality. As was the case with many of Getúlio's relatives Benjamin had enriched himself considerably during the dictatorial era. Up to this time he had been chief of Vargas' personal outfit of tough bodyguards.

Getúlio misjudged the situation badly. The military took Benjamin's appointment as an insult and a provocation. Hurried meetings were held among generals and admirals during the day of the twenty-ninth, and it was decided that Vargas must go. Leading the military coup was General Goes Monteiro, the officer who had the military command of Vargas' 1930 revolution. He had remained loyal to his chief for fifteen years, but now could read the writing on the wall. General Dutra also went along with the revolt.

Early in the evening tanks rumbled out of army barracks and moved downtown. Troops occupied strategic spots in the city. Emissaries from the war ministry went to Guanabara Palace, then the presidential residence, to offer Vargas the choice of stepping down voluntarily or being forced out.

The sixty-two-year-old dictator knew when he was beaten —at least temporarily. After a rather feeble attempt to talk the generals out of their plan he agreed to resign. The next day, October 30, 1945, a special air force plane took him to São Borja and political exile. On his way out, however, Vargas was allowed to issue a manifesto to the nation, stressing his good qualities and promising to return.

14

The extraordinary thing happened five weeks later: Vargas did make a political return. In the general elections held on December 2, Getúlio was chosen senator by two states and deputy by several others. General Dutra, who inherited the dictatorship's nationwide political machine, was elected president. Scores of Vargas' ministers and Interventors were sent to Congress. Having suddenly won democracy, Brazilians were not quite sure what to do with it. And, evidently, they had not been too unhappy with Vargas and his administrations.

In the days following Vargas' deposition demands were made to deprive him of political rights and keep him as isolated as possible from the outside world. But José Linhares, Chief Justice of the Supreme Court, who became Provisional President pending elections, and the military chiefs felt it would be undemocratic to do so. And, after all, their loyalties to Vargas were not altogether dead, despite his ouster.

In São Borja, where he was greeted as a hero, and at his near-by ranch Vargas was all smiles and charm. He inspected his cattle, drank *chimarrão*, the pungent tea of the Gaúchos made of maté herb, and talked to the many politicians who flew south to see him. They quickly realized that, notwithstanding the Rio contretemps of October 29, Vargas' star had not yet lost its glitter. Getúlio did not actively seek election to Congress but he did not oppose the presentation of his name to the voters.

The bulk of his votes came from São Paulo, the state with the heaviest proletarian concentration tied to its industrial complex. The workers, old and new generations alike, obviously remembered Getúlio's gift to them of Brazil's social legislation. The other candidates stood for little that interested the workers and, in São Paulo as elsewhere, the old Vargas magic still worked. There was even a feeling of guilt about his deposition. The interesting thing was that Vargas was elected without the Communist vote because they had presented their own candidates in São Paulo. But the Communist candidate for president, an unimpressive waterworks engineer named Yedo Fiuza, received nearly ten percent of the national vote—another indication of how communism grows under dictatorships.

As senator, Vargas lived quietly in an apartment overlooking Guanabara Bay and did not take his congressional duties too seriously. While the Constituent Assembly gave Brazil still another constitution—a liberal charter incorporating the new social and economic principles born during the Vargas era but specifically barring a president from succeeding himself in office—Getúlio was busy with his political future.

He organized the Brazilian Labor Party, an amorphous catchall of left-wingers, right-wingers, and opportunists that devoted itself to pro-labor demagoguery—and waited for the 1950 elections. Having been elected a senator was not enough to placate his ego, so terribly wounded by the 1945 military coup. Getúlio had to return to power "on the shoulders of the people."

The unspectacular and not particularly successful Dutra administration helped to create a climate propitious to Vargas' latest bid for power. In the rapid postwar economic expansion most of Brazil's foreign balances were spent on essential and nonessential imports. Dutra's development program was slow in getting started. Inflation was on the upswing and workers had difficulties making ends meet. The President, an unimaginative military man, did not know how to attract them either to himself or to his party, entirely dominated by old-line politicians, industrialists, and businessmen. Meanwhile, social pressures and agitations were rising again.

In the absence of any exciting new figure on the Brazilian political scene the field was by default left to Getúlio. He made the best of it. To his demagogic courtship of the masses, hitting hard on social problems and on nationalism, he added the pull of his own personality. The cry of "Queremismo"— a word coined from the Portuguese verb *querer*, meaning to want, and applied to Vargas in the 1945 elections—was revived as a campaign slogan. His old nickname of "Gê-Gê" came back into use. Several smaller parties, including the Communist, which had lost its legality in 1947, and the Social Progressive, supported his candidacy. The latter even provided a candidate for vice-president to run on Getúlio's ticket. He was João Café Filho, whom Vargas had persecuted and exiled in 1937. His alliance with Getúlio was one of the big political sensations of the year.

When the elections rolled along late in 1950 Vargas and Café Filho were chosen for the five-year term beginning in 1951. Getúlio failed to capture an absolute majority, but his plurality was impressive. Some members of the Democratic National Union, whose candidate, Air Brigadier Eduardo Gomes, was defeated by him, sought to prevent Vargas' inauguration on the grounds that he lacked this absolute majority. The objections were overcome and on January 31, 1951, Getúlio Vargas, sixty-eight years old but not showing his age, moved into the Catete Palace for his fourth presidential period in little over twenty years.

15

In contrast with the many positive accomplishments of Vargas' previous governments his latest administration was a disaster. This was largely because Getúlio had lost touch with the facts and the reality of Brazil. His entourage of greedy relatives and officials composing the palace clique isolated him from the outside world and he no longer made the effort to find out for himself what went on.

The same tired old faces of the dictatorial days assisted him in running the country. Lourival Fontes, ex-propaganda "minister," was Chief of the Civilian Household at the palace. Gustavo Capanema, former Minister of Education, was majority leader in Congress. Nereu Ramos, onetime Interventor in Santa Catarina, was speaker of the Chamber of Deputies. Vargas' son-in-law, Ernani de Amraral Peixoto, was back as governor of the state of Rio de Janeiro and wielded great power. The ever-faithful Oswaldo Aranha was finance minister. José Américo returned to the fold as communications minister. Benjamin "the Kiss" Vargas spent his days at the palace.

Meanwhile the economic and financial situation of Brazil was deteriorating alarmingly: budgets were unbalanced, new money had to be printed constantly, income from coffee exports was decreasing at an alarming rate, and inflation was getting out of control. Since in Brazil economic crises have always led to political explosions—Vargas' earlier popularity was greatly helped by his successes in the economic sphere—Getúlio, completely disoriented, now sought to make up for it with political measures.

He turned to more and more demagoguery, attempted to play on the nationalistic feelings that his Communist allies were busily exploiting. He attacked foreign capital, pushed through Congress a bill setting up a national oil monopoly (the opposition National Democratic Union, also vying for popular support, made this law even more restrictive than originally proposed), and submitted another one providing for a state electric power monopoly.

Enviously eying Juan Perón's labor-based regime in neighboring Argentina, Vargas began talking of a syndicalist republic for Brazil. His young friend from São Borja, João Goulart, was made Minister of Labor in an apparent move toward the organization of such a proletarian republic, presumably with himself as semidictator.

To make matters worse, Vargas' relatives and aides began to indulge in practices of corruption and influence-peddling on a gigantic scale. The President himself remained above suspicion and unbelievably oblivious of what was happening around him.

Attacks of the opposition on Vargas and his government picked up momentum with the approach of the October, 1954, congressional mid-term elections. Getúlio sought a truce with the National Democratic Union, which, however, met with rebuff. The Union had tried earlier in the year to get Congress to impeach him, but had failed to win enough support.

Getúlio's loudest and most bitter critic was a young newspaper publisher and congressional candidate named Carlos Lacerda. Writing daily inflammatory articles in his *Tribuna da Imprensa*, he berated the president and his aides for maladministration and corruption. Lacerda had many friends in the air force, where anti-Vargas sentiment was also building up, and, when threats were made against the publisher's life, a group of officers took it upon themselves to protect him around the clock.

Shortly after midnight on August 5, 1954, Lacerda, his young son, and Air Force Major Rubens Florentino Vaz, his escort that evening, returned to the publisher's home on a quiet street in the residential Copacabana district of Rio. As they were getting out of the car a man fired at them across the street, killing the major and wounding Lacerda in the foot.

These shots, and Major Vaz's murder, were to be to Vargas what the assassination of João Pessôa in 1930 by government thugs was to President Washington Luiz. They set off the fatal revolutionary crisis.

The testimony of the driver of the gunman's getaway car

led to the revelation that the fatal bullet was intended for
Lacerda and that it was fired by a hired murderer on instructions from Lieutenant Gregório Fortunato, chief of Vargas'
personal guard. When Getúlio learned about it his remark
was: "Lacerda was wounded in the foot, but I was stabbed in
the back."

Still underestimating the depth of the crisis Vargas may not
have realized how right he was. The murder shocked public
opinion and had an immense impact on the armed forces. Demands were shouted for the president's resignation. Vargas
was not accused of ordering the murder of Lacerda, but his
son Lutero, a deputy, was implicated in the plot. However,
Getúlio, again trying to temporize, did little beyond promising
that the guilty would be punished. Refusing to take responsibility for the actions of his aides he flew to Belo Horizonte
to strike in a speech at those who "are insulting me."

But, whether he knew it or not, Getúlio no longer had any
control over the situation. As events developed with dramatic
speed it became known that Gregório had arranged for the
escape of an aide who had actually hired the gunman and provided him with a large sum of money.

The air force took matters into its own hands, directing the
investigation from Rio's air base of Galeão. Air force troops
flushed out and arrested several members of the presidential
guard involved in the assassination. An air force team searched
Catete Palace for evidence, a supreme humiliation for Vargas,
and came upon a small arsenal in Gregório's room, hundreds
of thousands of cruzeiros, and a secret file incriminating high
government figures in fantastic schemes of corruption and
influence-peddling. It turned out that Gregório, an almost illiterate Negro, was one of the most powerful men of Brazil,
arranging Bank of Brazil loans that ran into millions, being
feared and courted by some of the nation's most distinguished
figures. Vargas' private secretary was revealed as a participant

in a huge illegal loan transaction. Other aides were implicated in currency counterfeiting.

The lid was off and the ax was about to fall. Yet Vargas still refused to capitulate. He rejected Vice-President Café Filho's proposal that they resign jointly, and kept repeating to all comers that as constitutional president he could not be forced to step down. "From here I'll leave dead," he said.

But Vargas' position had become untenable in this "sea of mud." The war minister, General Zenobio da Costa, insisted that the army could keep Vargas in power, and the President believed him. But when all the air force generals and one-half of the army generals stationed in Rio signed a manifesto demanding Vargas' resignation as the only constitutional solution for the crisis, the minister had to face reality.

"I can maintain order," he told Vargas, "but it will cost much blood, a lot of bloodshed."

Army and air force generals were in constant conferences, aviation and naval units stood alerted. Army police troops surrounded Catete Palace. The tension was intolerable. Finally, succumbing to pressure, Vargas called a cabinet meeting to decide his fate.

He ate a late dinner alone, as was his custom, and signed some papers that he stuck in his pocket. About three o'clock in the morning of Tuesday, August 24, 1954, the meeting got under way. After two hours of discussion Vargas announced his decision: if the armed forces would keep public order, he would agree to ask Congress for a leave of absence. As Getúlio interpreted this formula it made his commitment rather vague and left him free to talk his way out of it later, when the pressures died down.

But this was not the way the War Minister understood Vargas' stand. At a 7:00 A.M. meeting with his fellow generals, he told them that Vargas' leave of absence was to be immediate and permanent, that it was a face-saving device for resignation.

One of the generals drove to Catete Palace and informed Benjamin Vargas that his brother had been betrayed by the war minister.

Benjamin went to Getúlio's bedroom, woke him up, and repeated what he had heard. Vargas sat up in bed. "This means I'm deposed?" he asked.

"I don't know," Benjamin replied. "But this is the end."

A few minutes before eight o'clock Vargas walked to his office in his pajamas, then returned to his bedroom. A small group of relatives and friends, including his daughter Alzira and Oswaldo Aranha, waited outside. They had pledged themselves to fight to the end alongside Vargas if the palace was attacked by the army. Each person had a submachine gun.

About 8:15 A.M. they heard a pistol shot in Vargas' room. Rushing in they found him stretched on the bed in a pool of blood, his head pierced by a Colt .32 bullet. Getúlio's son Lutero, a physician, pronounced him dead. Vargas could not live through the dishonor of a second ouster.

On the bedstand someone found a white envelope. It was Vargas' farewell letter and political testament. It was an extraordinary document, almost incoherent, rambling, full of hate, recriminations, accusations, and pathos. It bared a new, emotion-racked Getúlio Vargas, a man nobody had known. In part, it read:

> Once again, the forces that are coordinated by the interests [that are] against the people have anew unleashed themselves over me. They do not accuse me, they insult me; they do not combat me, they slander me; they do not give me the right of defense. They need to gag my voice and prevent my action, so that I will not continue to defend the people, as I have always defended them, principally the humble ones. I follow the destiny that is imposed on me. After decades of domination and exploitation by interna-

tional economic-financial groups, I made myself the chief of a revolution, and I won. I initiated the work of liberation and I inaugurated a regime of social liberty. I had to resign. I returned to the government on the arms of the people. The underground campaign of the international groups became allied with national groups revolted against the regime of guarantee to the worker. . . . They do not want the worker to be free. They do not want that the people be independent. . . . The coffee crisis came, our principal product became valorized. We attempted to defend its price and the answer was violent pressure on our economy to the point of our being forced to surrender.

I have fought from month to month, from day to day, from hour to hour, resisting a constant aggression, accepting everything in silence, forgetting everything, renouncing myself to defend the people that now is left unprotected. I can give nothing further but my blood. If the birds of prey want the blood of somebody, want to continue sucking the Brazilian people, I offer my life in sacrifice. I choose this way to be always with you. When they humiliate you, you shall feel my soul suffering at your side. When hunger beats at your door, you shall feel in your breasts the energy for the struggle for yourselves and your sons. When they slander you, you shall feel in my thoughts the strength for reaction. My sacrifice will maintain you united and my blood shall be your banner of struggle. Each drop of my blood shall be an immortal flame for your conscience and shall maintain the sacred vibration for resistance. To hatred, I answer with my forgiveness. To those who think they have defeated me, I answer with my victory. I was the slave of the people and today I free myself for eternal life. But this nation of whom I was the slave, shall no more be the slave of anyone. My sacrifice shall remain forever in your soul and my blood shall be the price of your redeeming.

I fought against the exploitation of Brazil. I fought against the exploitation of the people. I have fought with a bared breast. Hate, infamies, slander, did not destroy my spirit. I gave you my life. Now I offer my death. I fear nothing. Serenely, I take the first step on the road to eternity and I leave life to enter history.

Chapter Four

JUAN PERÓN

OF ARGENTINA

1

Between 1945 and 1955, a decade more hectic and agitated than anything it had experienced in its entire history, Argentina lived through the sustained shock of the Peronista regime and its self-styled social revolution.

And the shock did not altogether wear off when Juan Domingo Perón, deposed by a four-day military revolt in September of the latter year, hid aboard a Paraguayan gunboat in Buenos Aires harbor on his way to exile. From successive havens in five Latin-American countries, this gaudy and stubborn ex-dictator and ex-general has been directing hundreds of thousands of his ever-loyal followers at home in deeds of multifarious mischief ranging from strikes to sabotage and terrorism, as well as determining the casting of their votes in elections. While he has never ceased to threaten from afar eventual reconquest of his lost power, Argentina, economically prostrate and socially disoriented and confused, has been desperately trying to recover and convalesce from the immense damage that Perón's megalomaniac policies have wrought.

In the years of rule by Perón and his remarkable second wife Eva, the attractive and astute actress without whom he may have remained just another second-rate contender for power, Argentina suffered and panted through an extraordinary and spectacular chain of events. Forced into major social and economic upheaval, it witnessed at the same time an exciting demagogic pageant, a frustrated dream of international greatness, the illusion of having spawned a new world ideology, and, not least, a reign of terror, brutality, and intimidation.

There were other ingredients in this amazing regime that Juan and Eva Perón claimed they set up for the salvation of the downtrodden "humble ones" of Argentina and the establishment of "true social justice." A cult of their personalities, aiming at the sublime but achieving the ridiculous, was implanted, and millions of Argentines straight-facedly heard Eva compare her husband to Jesus Christ, and Juan proclaim a day of Saint Evita while she was still alive. Corruption and graft in government were standard occurrences. The Peróns themselves lived in nabobesque luxury—he with sixteen custombuilt automobiles and two hundred forty motor scooters, she with three hundred dresses, most of them Paris imports, and a fortune in jewels and furs. Perón's personal wealth after the revolution has been estimated at several hundred million dollars which were said to be deposited in numbered accounts at Swiss banks and to have financed the Peronista underground activities in Argentina after his overthrow.

So long as Eva lived—she died of cancer in 1952—Perón's own excesses, political and personal, were kept reasonably in check. Cool, calculating, and a master politician in her own right she knew how to guide her often irresponsible husband along the path that spelled success for both of them, though her own ambitions antagonized and alienated many of their supporters, notably the military. After she passed away Perón floundered in political errors and personal immorality that shocked the nation and finally caused his downfall. While displaying his public grief over Eva's death, he took a fourteen-year-old girl student for his mistress and showered her with his late wife's jewelry. He became embroiled in disputes with the Roman Catholic Church that climaxed in the burning of churches in Buenos Aires. He encouraged open terrorism against his enemies.

After ten years of his nightmarish government Argentina neared national collapse. And if in the end it did survive Perón and Peronismo, it was thanks to the immense courage, determination, and patriotism of its best citizens. The long, painful, and patient trek back to order, reality, and normality began during the thirty months of provisional government of President Pedro E. Aramburu, the man whom Argentina owes an eternal debt of gratitude. It was continued in the constitutional administration of Arturo Frondizi, who took office on May 1, 1958, as the first completely freely elected president of his country in almost thirty years.

Frondizi's inauguration under such distinctive auspices may well have marked the end of the cycle of conflicts, distortions, and crises that formed Argentine history since the late 1920's. The twin phenomena of Perón's emergence on the scene and his relatively long demagogic sway over the destinies of a nation as advanced by Latin-American standards as is Argentina were the culmination of the power struggles of the preceding years and of deepening social and economic problems of that period. Thus, in 1945, Argentina was as ripe for Perón and his promises of a glorious new age as Brazil had been ripe for Vargas and his promises fifteen years earlier.

2

In the early 1940's Argentina seethed with the discontent of rural workers and even more with that of the fast-expanding urban proletariat. Argentina's industrialization, combined with the heavy prewar and wartime influx of Italian and Spanish immigrants, had created a mass of restless men and women rapidly acquiring a political consciousness and a distaste for the status quo, under which the country was dominated economically and socially by a group of moneyed families. The system of this oligarchic rule, as it was called, had been successful for the long decades when Argentina was predominantly an agricultural nation living in reasonable prosperity from the meat and the wheat it sold the world. But the economic problems, the whole fabric of Argentine society, and attendant pressures had been shifting and changing ever since the days of the great depression. The influence of the Radical and Socialist parties on political and social thinking had also been considerable. In short, all the elements were at hand for the outbreak of a social revolution and, with it, Argentina's entry into the vast movement that, in fits and starts, had been sweeping Latin America since the advent of Porfirio Díaz in Mexico earlier in the century.

This classical situation was complicated in Argentina by the cravings of the military for power. By 1943 many of these army men also became involved in a campaign to bring Argentina closer to the Axis in the world war then in progress. While President Ramón S. Castillo, a right-winger but not necessarily a Nazi enthusiast, had kept Argentina from joining most of the other Latin-American republics in declaring war on the Axis or at least breaking relations in the wake of the Pearl Harbor attack, he was just as reluctant to commit himself in the opposite direction. The Argentine military clique, often subsidized and invariably encouraged from Berlin and Rome, was thus becoming impatient with Castillo's neutrality.

This, then, was one of the motives behind the coup d'état of June 4, 1943, carried out by a secret society of officers whose leaders included Juan Perón, the forty-seven-year-old army colonel who had spent some time in Italy training with fascist troops and studying and admiring the techniques of Benito Mussolini. Subsequently, Perón was to refer to Castillo's ouster as the Glorious Revolution. For a variety of reasons the military regime that ran Argentina for the next three years took no formal steps to join the Axis camp, but until the end of the war that country remained a haven for Nazi spies and agents as well as a convenient spot for the resupplying of Hitler's submarines operating in the South Atlantic. After the collapse of Germany, Argentina opened its doors to Nazi war criminals and officials from all over Europe.

A figurehead general served as president while Perón established himself as Undersecretary of War and head of the Secretariat of Welfare and Labor. In time, he also became vice-president of Argentina. But as his military colleagues jockeyed for power in the traditional manner of garrison politics, Perón turned his attentions and favors to the labor movement, never before a factor in national tests of strength. It was the support of the unions, mobilized by blond Eva Duarte at a crucial moment in October, 1945, that won the day for him and made Perón the unofficial dictator of Argentina.

The following year, and again in 1951, his control of the labor movement led to his election as president, thus providing a mantle of legality for what had become one of the worst Latin-American dictatorships of the modern age. Perón enjoyed the backing of the armed forces for a long time, but this military support would have waned completely long before the 1955 revolution if it were not for the Peróns' skillful direction of the unions and the street-fighting mobs.

During his ten years in power, Perón gave Argentina the nearest thing to a proletarian dictatorship in a noncommunist nation. Along with Eva, he harangued the poor into hating the rich, and came forth with a pseudo ideology called Justicialismo, derived from the word justice, that blandly proclaimed that instead of the struggle of classes there should be only one class of people—the working people. Ruling with the backing of union leaders personally faithful to him and with the blind following of the mesmerized—and pampered —labor rank and file, Perón, with Eva's aid, was able to stage one of the most astounding demagogic performances of the century.

Controlling the machinery of government through the octopus arms of the Peronista Party that reached to the lowest levels of administration, destroying all free thought in Argentina through his secret police and the domination of all media of communication and education, operating a vast propaganda apparatus, vying for mass popularity through the immense giveaway schemes of Fundación Eva Perón, and imposing the state's direction over all the key economic activities in the country, Perón for a decade held in his hands absolute power over his nation.

The extent of his misuse of this power became evident only when the 1955 revolutionary government could take time to survey and audit the damage. Agriculture, once Argentina's mainstay, was on the brink of ruin; the national treasury was empty as a result of fantastic and unworkable undertakings and catastrophic mismanagement of domestic and foreign finances; inflation was eating into wages and salaries; and the economic structure of the country became so distorted that

Getúlio Dornelles Vargas, President of Brazil, during his last term in office, 1950–1954

Getúlio Dornelles Vargas; Ernesto Dornelles, his cousin; and João Goulart, Minister of Labor 1950–1954, currently Vice-president under Dr. Juscelino Kubitschek, President of Brazil

Juan Perón, President of Argentina, 1945–1955

Juan Perón of Argentina salutes as he drives past cheering throngs in Buenos Aires shortly after he was sworn in as President of Argentina for his second term in 1952. Waving at his side is his wife, Eva

President Manuel Odría of Peru salutes the colors during a parade in Lima, 1955

Lieutenant General Gustavo Rojas Pinilla takes office as President of Colombia for a new term, 1958

Pérez Jiménez addresses Congress in November, 1957, announcing plans for a plebiscite designed to reëlect him as President of Venezuela

Pérez Jiménez talks to a Venezuelan reporter

it could no longer provide a sound basis for the livelihood of most Argentines.

There can be no question that the Argentine worker never had it so good as under Perón. His income, in wages and bonuses of all kinds, shot up. He was protected to such a degree that private employers trembled before him. He received low-cost housing, hospitals, schools, swimming pools, restaurants, clubs, summer resorts, and presents of cash and goods whenever it pleased Eva to send a windfall his way. He gained standing in society—and a modicum of dignity—that defied his wildest dreams. All he had to do was to support Perón; the moment he abandoned the party line, retribution was swift and terrible. When a strike against the government was attempted by the railroad workers, it was smashed with a brutality that Perón's propaganda normally associated with the hated oligarchs.

The trouble with Perón's social program, aside from the fact that it was politically inspired in the most barefaced way, was that it introduced artificial living standards that Argentina, wealthy as it was, simply could not afford overnight. The bubble had to burst. When it did, Perón went off with the vanishing of the great illusion. But the love and gratitude of thousands of Argentine workers survived his fall. They were not economic analysts, but simple men and women, and to them the Perón prosperity, the excitement and the circus-like pageantry of his days were the real thing in a golden era. It is not surprising, therefore, that two-and-a-half years after his ouster over two million Argentines were willing to accept Perón's orders on how to vote in the elections.

With all its ills and aberrations, the Perón decade did constitute a deep revolution in Argentine ways. The clock cannot and should not be turned back on the legitimate conquests of the workers that came along with Peronismo. The challenge

to the new democratic government and its successors is how
to fit them into an orderly scheme of things and how to resume the nation's progress along healthier lines than those en-
visioned by Perón's ambition-distorted imagination.

3

Before June 4, 1943, very few Argentines outside a small military circle had ever heard of Juan Domingo Perón. A career
army officer with the rank of colonel, he enjoyed a sound
professional reputation built in almost thirty years of service.
Himself a graduate of the Argentine Military College, he had
taught at military schools, written competent military history
papers, and, like many officers, on occasions dabbled in politics. There had been interesting episodes in his career such as
his expulsion from Chile, where he had served as military
attaché; his sojourn in Italy and his friendship with Nazi army
missions in Argentina before the war; but there was no reason
during these thirty years why the general public should have
noticed him.

He was born on October 8, 1895, in the town of Lobos in
the province of Buenos Aires, not too far from the national
capital, the son of a farmer of mixed luck and, allegedly, the
grandson of a physician. At the turn of the century Perón's
father took the family to Patagonia, the wind-swept, almost
uninhabited extreme south of Argentina, to take over a sheep
ranch there. It is not known just how the ten years spent by
Perón in the cold bleakness of Patagonia influenced the formation of his personality; but if nothing else it gave him many
years later the idea of sending political prisoners there. There
was a Peronista prison in Río Gallegos, the town where Juan
was brought up, and another one, the worst of all of them, at
Ushuaia on Tierra del Fuego, on the far side of the Straits of
Magellan.

When Perón was fifteen the family returned to Buenos Aires province and the boy entered the International School at Olivos. He then moved to pre-engineering college and at the age of sixteen became a cadet at the military college. Two-and-a-half years later, in December, 1913, Perón had the insignia of an infantry second lieutenant pinned on his uniform, and was thus launched on a military career that ended formally in 1955 when a court-martial expelled him from the army for behavior not befitting an officer.

Young Lieutenant Perón was a tall, sturdily built, and handsome man. His face, surmounted by a massive nose that hinted of Indian blood, was strong, though it easily broke into smiles. And, indeed, Perón was already a charmer in those days. A hail-fellow-well-met type he was a ladies' man as well as a man's man. He was well liked and admired for his athletic prowess: he had been the best fencer in military school and later held for a long time the army's fencing championship; he was an expert rifleman, rode well, swam, boxed, and played tennis. Sustaining his interest and participation in sports in later years, he did much for their development in Argentina, and one of his many titles was First Sportsman.

At the age of twenty Perón made full lieutenant and was assigned to an infantry regiment. For nine years he led an obscure garrison life, and in 1924 was promoted to captain. In 1926 Perón was brought to Buenos Aires and appointed to the general staff of the army. He made enough friends there to win a job as private secretary to the Minister of War, then a full professorship at Argentina's Superior War School. There he immersed himself in military history and wrote studies of the great campaigns. He was partial to Caesar and Hannibal and Napoleon, but Alexander the Great was his special hero. On a more modern level, Perón specialized in the doctrine of Von Clausewitz and in the strategy and tactics of the German Imperial Army in World War I.

Late in 1929 Captain Perón was back at the general staff, this time in the operations section. He had a hand in planning the army's revolt against President Hipólito Irigoyen, the last Argentine chief executive chosen in a completely untrammeled election until 1958, and subsequently described these events in a book entitled *What I Saw in the Preparation and the Revolution Itself*. General José Uriburu won the power and Captain Perón his first experience in the overthrow of governments, an art that was to come in handy for him.

Between 1930 and 1936 Perón was again out of the limelight but steadfastly pursuing the development of his career. He taught again at the Superior War School and continued to attract the attention of senior officers of the Argentine army and of members of the Nazi military mission that was schooling Argentine troops. He earned his promotion to major, and finally was sent to Chile as military attaché. Somewhere along the line he was married, but few details are available about his first matrimonial venture. His wife died in 1936.

The Chileans did not take kindly to Major Perón; in fact, they expelled him in 1937 on charges of espionage. It was reported at the time that the dashing Argentine officer also misbehaved with young girls and boys, an early foretaste of his latter-day sexual inclinations.

Back in Argentina, far from being disgraced, Perón put in a tour of duty with mountain troops, lectured at the Naval War School, and served briefly as Director General of Civil Aviation. He was well thought of in high military circles, soon was raised to lieutenant colonel, and in 1938 was named military attaché in Italy. This was an important appointment from the viewpoint of the bosses of the Argentine armed forces. An intense flirtation and co-operation between them and the governments of Italy and Germany had been in progress for several years. German and Italian instructors had infiltrated the Argentine army, vast sums were spent to buy the loyalty and friendship of Argentine officers. The Axis had long hoped to establish in Argentina a base of operations against the United States in the event of a new world war. Nazi and fascist influence was considerable, and five or more pro-Axis organizations functioned freely in the country.

With Argentina holding such an important place in the over-all Axis scheme it was natural that a trusted officer such as Perón, for years enjoying the friendship of Axis military missions in Buenos Aires, would be sent to Rome in a top liaison capacity. For Colonel Perón, his three years in Italy were important from a military as well as political standpoint. As an officer he studied assiduously the organization of Italian mountain and ski troops, and even served with regiments in the Alps and Tyrol after Italy was already in World War II. As an aspiring politician he absorbed the lessons of Mussolini and the Fascist regime, and was to remark later that while Il Duce "was the greatest man of our century," he, Perón, with the advantage of hindsight would avoid Mussolini's "certain disastrous errors."

From his observations of Mussolini at work Perón drew two major lessons. One was the use of organized labor, held captive in government-controlled unions, as a political prop. The second was the value of social-justice demagoguery in winning the allegiance of the masses. Perón also heard Mussolini's balcony speeches, and in time transplanted the technique to the balconies of the Government House in Buenos Aires. While in Rome Perón also learned from fascism how to put together a political party—the Peronista Party was a fair imitation of it—how to operate the secret police, and how to run a huge propaganda machine. In fact, aside from local variations and Eva Perón's contributions to his regime, Perón did little to depart from the Mussolini model of a dictatorship.

And in the end his own mistakes were more foolish than Il Duce's.

Despite his well-advertised penchant for humble people fun-loving Perón's friends in Italy included Prince Umberto, later king of Italy, and outstanding members of the Italian oligarchy.

In 1941 Perón flew back to Argentina and a succession of commands of mountain troops as he imparted to his Andean soldiers the lessons he had learned in the Italian Alps. But for the next two years the Colonel's principal activity was the organization of Grupo de Oficiales Unidos (GOU), the secret fraternity of pro-fascist officers which included all ranks from second lieutenant to general. Freshly returned from Italy and basking in the glory of friendships with top fascist personalities he was the natural leader of the new military movement. While German and Italian banks in Buenos Aires pressed loans on Argentine officers to guarantee their devotion to the cause, Perón collected their undated letters of resignation, a powerful weapon for controlling their behavior and loyalties.

The aim of Perón and his GOU was the overthrow of President Castillo. The motive was to align Argentina with the Axis when the time came and, meanwhile, to put the military in charge of the government. The official excuse for this revolution was the tired classic of so many Latin-American revolutions: to secure national renovation, elevate the international standing of the republic, and end corruption, which was as accepted under Castillo in Argentina as it was almost everywhere else in Latin America.

4

The "Glorious Revolution" of June 4, 1943, turned out to be the easiest thing in the world. President Castillo, an ailing man, threw in the sponge as fast as troops from Campo de Mayo, the king-making army barracks outside the city, marched up to Casa Rosada, the pink-colored building housing the presidential offices, the control of which has always meant the control of Argentina. The only momentary complication in an otherwise perfectly planned blueprint of the coup was that the wrong man beat his GOU colleague to the presidential job. He was General Arturo Rawson, head of the cavalry school, whose soldiers reached the palace before everybody else. But this was soon remedied: Rawson was gently pushed out the next day and replaced with General Pedro Ramírez, the war minister, who was supposed to have taken over the presidency in the first place.

Although Colonel Perón had been the chief plotter of the revolt there had been no thought of making him president at that time. He still was an officer of field rank and not sufficiently well known in the country. He was given the post of Undersecretary of War, but with considerably more power than the title suggested. This suited him for the time being; no sooner had President Ramírez assumed office than Perón began planning his overthrow. In actual fact the June, 1943, revolution launched Perón on his vertical climb to power.

His assault developed simultaneously along two fronts. While filling all key positions in the war ministry with GOU officers who were personally loyal to him rather than to President Ramírez, Perón at once began to roll up labor support, thus putting in practice the lessons of Mussolini. In October he asked Ramírez to let him take over the National Department of Labor, then an inactive government agency of little consequence. The President, not knowing what Perón had up his sleeve, agreed immediately. He made no objections either, when the cunning Colonel proposed a month later to transform the Department into the Secretariat of Labor and Welfare, practically a full-fledged labor ministry. This was the start of Perón's policies of wholesale social demagoguery that ultimately catapulted him into absolute power. Appropriately enough, November 27, the date the new Secretariat was created, became later one of the three great annual Peronista holidays.

At about this juncture of events the path of Juan Perón crossed the path of Maria Eva Duarte, twenty-four-year-old radio and theatre actress who was making her way in the big city after a depressing provincial childhood as one of five illegitimate offspring of a tenant farmer. Perón was nearing forty-eight when they met.

They were introduced to each other at a party just as Perón, already Undersecretary of War, was also becoming Secretary of Labor and Welfare. Their encounter marked the beginning of a political partnership, strengthened two years later, in 1945, by bonds of marriage, that helped Perón reach the presidency and dictatorial powers, and made Eva into the most powerful woman in modern history.

In her autobiography *The Reason of My Life*, Eva described her meeting with Perón as "my marvelous day." She explained, in that odd mixture of false humility and crusading fervor forming her propaganda-angled prose, how Perón inspired her with the realization that social justice in Argentina was attainable under his guidance. Offering her considerable talents to assist him in his campaign to fashion Argentina's workers into a political weapon she quoted herself as telling Perón: "If it is as you say, the cause of the people is my own cause; however great the sacrifice, I will not leave your side until I faint."

The offer was accepted. It was sealed a few days later by a secluded weekend at a resort near Buenos Aires, and Eva, who meanwhile had moved to an apartment adjoining Perón's, lost no time going to work for him. As Perón endeavored to

attract organized labor to his side—a precedent-breaking undertaking for an army officer—Eva backed him with radio
broadcasts in which she described him as a "new genius who
will become a father to our poor." She was said to have introduced him to labor leaders of her acquaintance and was
credited with turning the Railroaders' Union, one of Argentina's biggest unions, into the first Peronista labor group. She
taught him how to speak effectively over the radio, polishing
his early imitations of Mussolini.

Perón's opening salvo in his courtship of labor was a speech
barely a week after he organized his Secretariat. In it, he
announced that "the Revolution wishes to impress upon the
spirit of the Argentine worker the pride of belonging to a
powerful and generous country, where justice and equality
reign supreme and where the fear of spurious influences cannot warp the job of living and creating."

On New Year's Eve of 1943 Perón delivered another
speech, this time hinting obliquely that Argentina should declare itself on the side of the Axis. "It would be suicidal," he
said, "to remain passive and persist in an attitude of wait and
see." But President Ramírez not only refused to ally Argentina with the Nazis, but acting under United States pressure
broke relations with Germany and Japan four weeks later.

In the eyes of the pro-Nazi GOU officers who had put
Ramírez in office seven months earlier, this was a breach of
faith. Actually this was a Perón play, because he had the
sense to realize Germany no longer stood a chance of winning the war and that the truly "suicidal" thing for Argentina would be to join Hitler so late in the game. Although
Perón went on giving the Nazis all possible help until the
bitter end—as the *Blue Book* of the United States Department of State made clear in abundant detail—he never again
talked of entering the war on the losing side. Besides, Argen-

tina earned good money selling her meat and wheat to the Allies at top prices. But the issue supplied Perón with the lever he needer to unseat the president.

While Ramírez' prestige was sagging because of his dispute with the army and of general political and labor difficulties, Perón's own popularity had soared with an immense stroke of good luck. Early in January, 1944, an earthquake had destroyed the town of San Juan. Knowing a good thing when he saw one, Perón immediately mobilized the resources of his Labor and Welfare Secretariat to bring aid to San Juan and followed it up by setting up a fund for the town's reconstruction.

It was a masterly touch. With Evita's radio assistance and the gullibility of the Argentine press Perón gained instantaneous national fame as the Saviour of San Juan. That most of the reconstruction funds found their way to his own pocket did not become publicly known until it was much too late, and Argentines could only whisper that the San Juan Relief Fund had become the "San Juan Perón Relief Fund."

In February, as Perón increased his pressure against Ramírez, the President decided to hit back. He dissolved the GOU and sent a few loyal officers to the Ministry of War to demand Perón's resignation. But the Colonel, now sure of his own strength, retorted with a rude word. A few days later six pro-Perón officers visited Ramírez with guns in their hands. The result of this visit was his resignation.

5

The new president was General Edelmiro Farrell. For all practical purposes he was a puppet of Perón. The Colonel was not yet ready for the final jump, feeling that more preparation was required. This included having Farrell appoint him acting Minister of War so that he could control the army.

He retained, of course, the Secretariat of Labor and Welfare. The next period in Perón's activities was principally directed at Argentina's working masses, although he did not neglect other matters in his endeavor to strengthen his overall position. Thus, by the middle of 1944, he was Argentina's vice-president and full war minister, and loomed as the most powerful man in the nation. The new effort, meanwhile, was twofold: to gain control of the unions through pro-labor policies and to endear himself personally to the rank and file of the workers.

To achieve the first goal, Perón promised the workers that soldiers would never again be used to break strikes, that the state would sponsor legislation covering everything from social security to low-cost housing, and that the labor movement would be given an undreamed degree of autonomy. He befriended powerful labor leaders and made a practice of attending union meetings and haranguing the workers with speeches about social justice.

His plan, and it was working smoothly, was to capture individual unions, form new ones where it was necessary, and then weld them into a monolithic labor movement that he could control at will. To do so Perón set his sights on the old, 500,000-member General Confederation of Labor (CGT) and dissolved a rival Communist-dominated confederation. He made no bones about quietly imprisoning labor leaders who would not go along with him.

Eva Duarte was Perón's closest collaborator in these endeavors, attending meetings with him, talking to union chiefs and individual workers. And she worked with him in the allied field of winning the affections of individual citizens. The locale for this effort was Perón's office at the Secretariat of Labor and Welfare where he spent many hours every week receiving everybody who wanted to see him and handing out money and jobs with regal generosity. Eva, who subsequently dispensed this kind of largesse on an incomparably vaster scale, wrote in her autobiography that in those early days she often saw him "listening to the humble workingmen of the country, speaking to them of their problems, giving them the explanations they had been craving for many years."

And then: "What happened in Bethlehem nearly two thousand years ago was repeated here. The first to believe were not the rich, not the wise, not the powerful, but the humble."

The Perón technique with needy cases was doubtless convincing, and the following story throws light on its workings. A woman with five small children entered his office one day and immediately proceeded to weep. Perón produced candy from his desk and asked her what was the matter. She said, "My Colonel, I'm without work with my five children. They are about to throw me out of the house because I owe seven months' rent."

Perón asked, "But where is your husband, Señora?"

She replied, "He cannot get work because he was just released from prison."

"But why was he in prison?" Perón asked. When the woman did not answer but wept instead, Perón said, "Well, what can a man do with five children and no job but be a thief?" Forthwith he wrote a check for three hundred fifty pesos to pay the woman's rent, gave her two thousand pesos in cash, each child five hundred pesos in brand-new bills, found the husband a job as a gardener, and placed her as a hospital charwoman.

Repeated with enough frequency, such gestures could not fail to spread across the land Perón's reputation as the benefactor and protector of the poor and downtrodden at a time when nobody else seemed to care about them. Simultaneously, Juan and Eva, this amazing twosome, hit upon the inspired slogan and symbol of the "Descamisados," which swept Argentina like a prairie fire. Meaning the "Shirtless Ones," the word was applied to the poor workers who presumably could not afford a shirt. Perón and Eva glorified this poverty and parlayed it into the unifying theme of their movement, a modern above-the-waist version of the sans-culottes of the French Revolution. In dramatic gestures at political rallies Perón often shed his jacket and rolled up his sleeves, at times even tore off his shirt. Eva never went quite that far, though she would tell how she offered Perón her life, "burning it up with love for his descamisados."

Day after day Perón would shout that "my country's workers . . . follow me almost as though I were a banner," while Eva would proclaim that to atone for a century of exploitation of the poor, "another century is needed during which the privileged class will be the worker." Indeed, they were preaching an irresistible doctrine and not missing a single trick in the demagogue's handbook in so doing. Falling on receptive and grateful ears, their exhortations eventually produced the essential political and physical support that brought success to Perón's desperate gamble for absolute power.

6

The full measure of this gratitude became frighteningly clear in October, 1945, when Perón seemed to totter on the edge of defeat. By rescuing him all may have been lost. Argentina's civilian masses demonstrated that the military was no longer the only controlling force in the country's politics. A new precedent was thereby set in Latin America.

The great crisis developed gradually in the middle of 1945, after Perón, the nation's vice-president, war minister, and Secretary of Labor and Welfare for over a year, indicated

his intention of running for president in the forthcoming elections. Despite his vast powers Perón's current policies and his
presidential aspirations faced tough opposition.

Powerful business and landowning interests were openly
against him because of his labor agitation and his ideas on
the state's intervention in the national economy. In a 1944
speech he had declared that the principle of economic liberty
"cannot prevent the state from exercising its proper tutelary
action to co-ordinate private activities toward a collective
national purpose, subject to certain precepts which are innate
thereto." When Perón finally became president, this "tutelary
action" became the government's iron hold over all Argentine economic activities. By June, 1945, when the Colonel's
campaign for power was in full swing, hundreds of business
organizations issued a manifesto condemning Perón.

Liberal currents of Argentine opinion—which included
the press, the universities, and the students—saw in Perón
the continuation in their country of the Nazism and fascism
that had just been defeated in Europe. The certainty of Allied victory had greatly embarrassed the Farrell-Perón regime
and, on March 27, 1945, the government had no choice but
to go through the motions of declaring war on Germany and
Japan so that Argentina could be represented at the United
Nations conference in San Francisco. But this gesture did not
deceive anyone, and the anti-Perón sentiment gained momentum.

The army itself had become wary of the slick Colonel and
there were ominous rumblings against him among the officers. Independent labor unions took up arms against him when,
after the initial period of courting them, Perón in 1945 proclaimed a new policy that, in effect, killed free trade-unionism in Argentina. He announced that henceforth the state
would control the unions and elect its leaders, that they could
no longer engage in political activities (unless it was to back

Peronismo), and that the government would settle all labor-management disputes, thus ruling out strikes. This was the very negation of the glittering promises Perón had made so recently, but by now his power over the leadership of the big unions was so firmly entrenched that he could afford to take off his gloves. And to hundreds of thousands of humble workers he was still the hero.

When August, 1945, came along Argentina was in a state of extraordinary turmoil and chaos. After Farrell lifted a modified form of martial law to allow pre-election campaigns, all the anti-Perón parties united in demanding that the supreme court of Argentina take over the government. On September 19, liberal forces marshaled 500,000 people for a "March of the Constitution and Liberty" in Buenos Aires. While many political experts were betting that Perón was finished, the Colonel turned to demagoguery and brutality to fight the adverse tide.

In tearful radio speeches he portrayed himself as a victim of the workers' enemies. "If through having tried to defend the workers my name is to be execrated by those who used to live happily through the unhappiness of all those who made their fortunes for them, I bless God for having made me deserving of such a curse," he said on one occasion.

At the same time Perón's police went after the opposition with all the means at its disposal. The huge Buenos Aires university was closed and dozens of faculty members and students were imprisoned, as were many politicians. Anti-Perón newspapers were prevented from publishing. In the streets policemen beat and shot demonstrators and in prison cells the most atrocious tortures were practiced on the foes of the regime. In October over 30,000 students went on strike in six universities across Argentina, and it took the police six days to dislodge them from the campuses. Thousands of new arrests were made.

In addition to all his other problems Perón at that point had to face the fact that the Argentine constitution of 1853 barred a vice-president from running for the presidency. The next major crisis helped him overcome this obstacle.

It began on October 5, when Farrell named a friend of Eva's family to be acting director of the national post office and telegraph. The man, a career official, probably deserved the appointment, but anti-Perón officers seized upon it as an issue to try and topple the Colonel. On October 7 General Eduardo Avalos, commander of the Campo de Mayo garrison, informed Perón that the army resented the post office appointment. According to his memoirs, Perón told Avalos that, having been forced by the military to accept the responsibilities of his various offices, he must insist on his own choice of officials. He said that since the officers were trying to dictate his behavior he was ready to resign.

The next two days witnessed a contest of wills between Perón and the army chiefs. Finally, President Farrell, persuaded that the majority of officers were determined to get rid of Perón at all costs, asked him through intermediaries to live up to his earlier threat and, indeed, resign. Perón, who had toyed with the idea of starting a civil war by throwing regiments loyal to him against the rest of the army, changed his mind and resigned from all his posts.

Between October 9 and 11 Perón remained at home in downtown Buenos Aires in urgent and heated conferences with friendly officers and labor leaders—and with Eva. He was getting ready for the next move. On October 12 events took an unfavorable turn for him. Farrell's cabinet resigned and Perón's enemies, led by General Avalos, occupied the key spots in the government, although the President was allowed to keep his job. The following day Perón and Eva went by motor launch to a friend's private island near the El Tigre resort. He wrote later that he had informed General Avalos of his whereabouts but that he did not want them to be made public.

At one o'clock in the morning of October 14 Perón's fortunes appeared to have hit rock bottom. Colonel Aristóbulo Mittelbach, the new chief of police, came to the island to arrest him—in fact if not in name. Mittelbach had just replaced Colonel Filomeno Velazco, a friend of Perón's and one of the most brutal men to emerge during the Peronista decade.

Mittelbach had orders, issued in Farrell's name, immediately to take Perón to the gunboat *Independencia*, pending his transfer to another site of detention. While Perón, in full uniform, stood on his dignity and insisted with Mittelbach that he "had not expected any such affront," Eva became hysterical and struggled with the arresting officers to prevent her man's detention. In the end Perón was removed to the gunboat and Eva rushed to Buenos Aires. To leave her in liberty, as it presently developed, was the army's worst mistake.

Later in the day Perón was taken to the naval prison on the island of Martín García, far in the estuary of River Plate. According to his own account he was placed "in a cell allotted to military prisoners, with two guards and a servant to wait on me." The Avalos faction of the army was still not sufficiently confident of its own strength to take such measures against Perón as may have effectively neutralized him.

His enemies in Buenos Aires were having their brief moment of joy over what they believed to be Perón's downfall, although the government would not confirm the fact of his arrest. Radio Belgrano, which for months had had to meet most of Eva's wishes, celebrated by firing her. But it turned out to be a short-lived triumph for Radio Belgrano and all those who so happily hailed the end of Perón. Both the Colonel and his lady friend were extremely active, and their efforts soon bore fruit.

From the island of Martín García, Perón bombarded his

friend Farrell and his foe Avalos with letters and telegrams demanding that he be charged with whatever crimes he was supposed to have committed. He insisted on either a public trial or immediate freedom. He forwarded instructions to Eva telling her, "to you I entrust my workers." Then he blandly informed Farrell that he had contracted pleurisy and that his life would be in danger if he were not moved to a hospital.

It was as elementary a subterfuge as anyone could have conceived under the circumstances, but, amazingly enough, it worked. For one thing, the army still underestimated Juan and Eva. For another thing, the army itself was divided. And for still another thing, Eva's counteroffensive on Perón's behalf was gaining thrust.

From the very moment of her return to Buenos Aires on October 14 she frantically began to rouse all the pro-Perón labor leaders for a mass movement that would set him free. The unions responded as she had hoped they would; Perón and Eva had not worked in vain for the past two years. In her book Eva thus described these feverish days:

> From the time that Perón went (to prison) until the people recovered him for itself—and for me!—my days were filled with pain and fever. I rushed into the streets looking for friends who might still be able to do something for him. Thus I went from door to door. . . .

This figurative bell-ringing brought out Peronista workers in droves. Two days later, on October 16, thousands of meat-workers, Perón's staunchest and toughest friends, started streaming into Buenos Aires from the suburb of Avellaneda, from the meat-packing town of Berizo, and from other near-by strongholds. Without interference from the army or the police they virtually occupied the city, and their ranks swelled from hour to hour with reinforcements from other unions as well as workers at large.

At dawn of October 17 Perón's military enemies dug their own grave. They allowed Farrell to order his transfer from Martín García to the Central Military Hospital in Buenos Aires. Acting on cue, armed squads of union goons raided the factories and stores in the city, forcing them to close down for the day. As tens of thousands of shouting men and women staged demonstrations and riots in front of the hospital and the Government House demanding Perón's liberation, a full-fledged revolution was in progress. At least a half-million participated in it in the capital's streets.

By noon the army chiefs recognized their defeat. Perón was set free, and fighting his way through hysterical mobs of his supporters drove to Casa Rosada. Farrell received him like a long-lost brother and beamed at his side as the sweating Perón, speaking from the balcony overlooking the tightly packed Plaza de Mayo, hoarsely delivered a speech in the best Mussolini tradition.

He announced his resignation from the army "to put on the coat of the civil servant, and to mingle with the suffering and powerful masses which build up with their work the greatness of the nation. . . . I wish to press all of you closely to my heart, as I might my mother."

Some of his listeners may have missed the point in the heat of the excitement, but Perón was merely announcing his determination to conquer soon the presidency of Argentina. The constitutional ban on a vice-president no longer applied to him and he was no longer a soldier. And in the crescendo of that day's popular explosion of emotions, he had come to the threshold of ultimate power.

7

Between his day of triumph on October 17, 1945, and the elections of February 24, 1946, Juan Perón technically was nothing more than a private citizen and a candidate for the presidency. But, in reality, he wielded complete control over the government of General Farrell, that pliant puppet he had installed in office early in 1944. And, consequently, he was able to command all the resources of the regime for his electoral campaign.

Before officially launching this campaign Perón took care of an important item of personal business: on October 21, he married in a secret civil ceremony Señorita Eva Maria Duarte, the woman who had saved him four days earlier and who had been his closest collaborator for the past two years. He was fifty years old, she was twenty-six. It is not clear why they kept their marriage a secret; not a word was breathed publicly either of their church wedding ceremony, which took place on December 9. Only a month later, in the course of a political rally, did Perón make the announcement.

Although their union in wedlock cemented an immensely profitable political partnership Evita took angry exception to any suggestion that it was a "political marriage." In her autobiography she insisted that:

> . . . we got married because we loved one another, and we loved one another because we loved the same thing . . . we married even before the decisive battle for the liberty of our people, with the absolute certainty that neither triumph nor defeat, neither glory nor failure, could destroy the unity of our hearts. . . . And it was natural for a woman to give herself, to surrender herself, for love; for in that surrender is her glory, her salvation, her eternity.

Now, as his wife, Evita emerged as Perón's best, most effective, and most devoted campaigner and propagandist. In uncounted radio and mass-rally speeches this pretty, intense girl, with her blond hair austerely tied in a bun over her neck, praised him to the heavens in accents so admiring and submissive as to border on religious mysticism. In real life a proud, hard, vindictive, cool, and calculating woman, Evita's public technique was to present herself as modesty and humility personified, speaking in awe of Perón, to whom, incidentally, she always referred by his last name.

In her book, as in her speeches, she compared Perón to a condor and herself to a sparrow. He had intelligence, she had heart; he was cultured, she was simple; "he was great and I small, he was the master and I pupil, he was the figure and I the shadow." The approach was successful with men and women alike: to the men she was the adoring little woman, to their wives she was one of them.

Perón entered the campaign as the candidate of the Labor Party, organized in November, 1945, by his union friends. His running mate was Juan Hortensio Quijano, a lackluster, sad-looking man with a drooping mustache whose main credential was that he was a congressman of the traditional Radical Party. The Radicals led an anti-Perón coalition of leftist parties and their candidates for president and vice-president were, respectively, Dr. José P. Tamborini and Dr. Enrique M. Mosca. Quijano represented a small, Peronista splinter group of the Radicals, and Perón picked him in the hopes of garnering some Radical votes. The first Peronista candidate for vice-president, Colonel Domingo Mercante, stepped aside for Quijano but was later rewarded with the important job of governor of the Buenos Aires province.

The platform of Perón and his Labor Party was one of extreme economic nationalism and of social demagoguery. It called for the nationalization of foreign-owned utilities and

railroads, war on foreign trusts, a reasonable program of social welfare but also profit sharing by workers in all enterprises, and the vote for women.

Perón himself chose nationalism and hatred of foreign interests as his main election theme. As he explained it:

> The country was alone. It was off its course, unguided,
> and without a compass. All had to be handed to foreigners.
> The people, lacking justice, were oppressed and incapable.
> Foreign countries and international forces submitted them
> to a domination not far removed from colonial oppression.

His favorite foreign target was United States Ambassador
Spruille Braden, who, in turn, fought him as hard as he could.
Braden left Argentina even before the October 17 vindica-
tion of Perón, but during his five months in Buenos Aires the
two men had engaged in open warfare, with the prestige of
the two countries dragged into the fray. American newspa-
permen were beaten and Braden's life was threatened.

Braden's tenure as ambassador to Argentina was the only
postwar instance of the United States taking a clear, unequiv-
ocal stand against a dictatorship in Latin America, for the
Farrell-Perón government could not be described in any other
way. Unfortunately, however, this commendable policy was
not carried out in a sufficiently subtle or imaginative manner.
Openly seeking to prevent Perón's election it backfired because too many nationalistic-minded Argentines, even if they
were anti-Perón, saw in it the dreaded threat of Yankee intervention. After the State Department issued its Blue Book
on Argentina, listing in documented detail Perón's wartime
Nazi and fascist connections, the totalitarian character of his
techniques, and the practices of brutality and intimidation
during the election campaign, the Colonel managed to turn it
to his advantage. Plastering the walls of Argentine cities with

posters asking "Braden or Perón?" he probably won more votes than he lost as a result of his dispute with Braden.

In the light of all these events, it is strange how the State Department soon after the election was able to transform its policy toward Perón into one of cordiality and friendship. Perón's supporters broadened the antiforeign campaign to include Argentina's Jews, and for months Buenos Aires and other cities in the country were the scene of brutal anti-Semitic persecutions reminiscent of Hitler's days in Germany. While Perón himself disavowed and condemned the attacks on Jews, his police did nothing to protect them.

What the police did during that period was to concentrate with all its might on the anti-Perón opposition. With sadistic Colonel Velazco again running the federal police, a reign of terror swept Argentina. Arrests mounted into the thousands: the most prominent Argentine citizens could not escape Velazco's plain-clothes men if they were even remotely identified with the opposition. Hundreds of Argentines fled the country. Tamborini's and Mosca's rallies were broken up by police-protected hoodlums, and candidates were beaten. The police used sabers, tear gas, and bullets to cope with demonstrators. Throughout the campaign Buenos Aires was the stage of continuous riot.

While Perón thus battled his enemies he courted the workers with skillful measures calculated to win their votes. On December 20, President Farrell, as usual doing his bidding, signed a law, drafted by Perón before he quit the Secretariat of Labor, establishing a compulsory Christmas bonus for all workers corresponding to a full month's salary. Wage increases were decreed at the same time. Shortly thereafter, managements struck back by shutting down most of Argentina's industry and locking out the workers. But this Strike of Employers did not last long. Acting under the protection of police and troops, union strong-arm squads herded the workers back to the plants and forced them to resume production. The only law in Argentina was the word of Juan Perón, private citizen and candidate for president.

Tamborini and Mosca, who conducted a fairly ineffectual campaign against Perón, never had a chance against the overwhelming power marshaled by him. Even the Roman Catholic Church, which later had cause to regret bitterly its attitude, supported the Perón ticket, presumably because the Radicals were anticlerical and happened to have the small Communist Party on its side in this election.

Perón and the Farrell government did not bother to interfere in any way with the voting and counting of returns on February 24, 1946. The election was free and honest, and to nobody's great surprise Perón won it by the reasonably comfortable margin of 1,527,000 to 1,207,000 votes. Argentines thus cleared the way for the first six years of a legal dictatorship in their unhappy country.

8

On June 24, 1946, Juan Perón formally became constitutional president and with great gusto and immense reformist zeal proceeded to reshape his country in accordance with his megalomaniac recipe for government. Vargas had named his 1937 fascistoid regime the New State, and Perón, without much nomenclatural imagination, came up with New Argentina to describe his experiment.

To this task Perón brought the conviction that he was a man of destiny. Whereas many rulers undoubtedly think they are, few come right out and say it as Perón did in his memoirs that were published a few years later.

I am at the head of my people not only by a decree of destiny. I am there because, without knowing it perhaps,

I prepared myself for it as though I had known that some-day this responsibility and privilege would be my lot. . . . I was prepared by life itself: my parents' home, my child-hood in wild Patagonia, my military career, my life in the mountains, my journeys to Europe. . . . All these had ac-customed me to conquer. To conquer Nature is more diffi-cult than to lead and control men, and it had often fallen to my lot to struggle with the forces of Nature and overcome them.

Having pledged himself before the elections to a program of economic and political nationalism, Perón wasted no time in carrying it out. Two days after his inauguration he an-nounced that "national economy must be based on the fact that all fundamental components be controlled by the State." And as soon as the details could be worked out, he busied himself turning these "fundamental components" over to the government. In some instances it took a lot of time and a lot of doing; in many instances it was downright harmful to the economy of the nation, which could not digest the huge chunks that Perón was trying to force down its throat. But he had committed himself to chase the foreign interests and the domestic oligarchs out of Argentina, and half-measures evidently would not do.

To co-ordinate his nationalization and development schemes, Perón devised a Five-Year Plan that he laid before Congress in October, or less than four months after assuming the pres-idency. Actually, working from an office at Casa Rosada in the months before his election, Perón was ready to unroll his program the moment he was sworn in. A rotund economist named Miguel Miranda was put in charge of the Five-Year Plan, and as Argentina's "economic czar" supervised it until a dispute with Perón several years later sent him scurrying to Uruguay.

The first major nationalization was that of the Central Bank. Undertaken while Farrell was serving out his last months in the presidency, it was a wise step, for a government can hardly direct a country's finances without fully controlling the principal financial organ. But what ensued under Perón had little relationship to the realities of Argentina and, in the end, resulted in its economic ruin.

In February, 1948, after protracted negotiations, Argentina bought from Britain, as part of the Andes Agreement, twenty-seven thousand miles of British-owned railroads and seventeen thousand adjoining properties. The cost was $420,-000,000 and it was to be paid in meat and wheat exports. Perón also contracted to exchange another $112,000,000 worth of his exports for British coal, oil, and machines. Thus, in one fell swoop, he committed most of Argentina's foreign earnings for some years to come.

Earlier, Perón had expropriated the Argentine telephone service operated by a subsidiary of the International Telephone and Telegraph Company, at a cost of over $90,000,000. Hundreds of additional millions went into the purchase of other utilities, harbor facilities, and grain silos and elevators. A state merchant marine was organized so that Argentina's exports and imports could be carried in Argentine bottoms, and it presently became one of the world's important merchant fleets. First Perón took over former Axis ships detained in Argentine harbors, then began ordering the building of passenger liners and freighters in Western European yards.

A crash program was undertaken to introduce heavy industry into Argentina, with steel mills, a tinplate plant, and an aircraft industry spectacularly leading the way. When a refugee Austrian scientist, Ronald Richter, sold Perón in 1951 on the fantastic scheme of extracting nuclear energy from the sun, the gullible President-Dictator spent many millions of dollars equipping a laboratory for him on Huemel Island in one of the southern Argentine lakes. This enterprise, advertised to the world with the full backing of the Peronista propaganda machine, in the end exposed Perón to painful ridicule. Richter was arrested when his hoax was proved.

In the first three years of his regime Perón paid virtually all of Argentina's foreign debt. When, on July 9, 1949, he issued in Tucumán the "Declaration of Economic Independence," Perón could brag about all these impressive achievements. But his cheering listeners hardly suspected that their leader was already pushing Argentina toward the brink of bankruptcy.

Argentina now owned everything on her territory and paid all her debts. But the war-amassed reserves of gold dollars and pounds sterling were being exhausted or nearing exhaustion in the wake of these proud gestures. Massive imports of industrial goods and of luxuries for the privileged Peronista clique were emptying the treasury. The nationalized railways were losing money heavily. Millions of dollars of imported machinery rotted at pierheads because nobody knew where to take it or what to do with it. The new industries could not get on their feet. And a new, great foreign debt was in the making.

Perón could thus declare on that July day of 1949 that Argentines were breaking "the dominating chains which have bound them to foreign capitalism" and "recovering their right to govern their own sources of national wealth." Yet six years later, when Perón was deposed and the well-hidden truth of his machinations became known, it turned out that the nation neared ruin, and it took the United States aid that he had scorned so long to keep Argentina from foundering.

To gratify his megalomania Perón did not hesitate to put the squeeze on Argentina's agriculture, the country's mainstay. As part of the Five-Year Plan, the government created IAPI, a powerful organization whose Spanish initials stood for Argentine Institute of Trade Promotion. The Institute purchased grain and meat from the producers at the lowest possible prices and sold them abroad for as much as the traffic would bear, with the government keeping the profit.

While the postwar world faced hunger, Perón refused to sell his food even at world prices, cold-bloodedly taking advantage of a sellers' market. When, years later, wheat and beef again became plentiful and Perón had trouble unloading his stocks even at bargain rates, he spoke darkly of capitalist conspiracies against New Argentina.

The low prices IAPI paid the producers naturally discouraged planting and cattle raising. When Perón fell, Argentina's agricultural production was at a record low point; meat production was inadequate to feed the beef-loving Argentines and still maintain exports. In 1958 President Frondizi had to take the unbelievable step of ordering meat rationing in the country.

Privately owned industries were harassed by taxes, extra bonuses, and holidays for workers, and by the government's attempts to dictate their policies. Productivity declined, while between 1943 and 1947 wages rose by one hundred twenty-one per cent. The obvious result was inflation, the bogey that plagued Perón until his last day at Casa Rosada, and by the end of 1947 he was forced to admit that in the past four years the cost of living had increased by eighty-five per cent. The actual figure may have been higher, but Perón controlled statistics as he did everything else.

Unquestionably, Argentina was in dire need of a comprehensive plan of economic development and industrialization which would raise the living standards of her citizens and enable her to make a mark in the postwar world. But, as history itself has demonstrated, Perón's way was not the proper way of going about it.

9

While putting a strait jacket on Argentine economy, Perón set out to do the same for the nation's political life. If earlier there had been any doubts about Perón's dictatorial proclivities, the new President disposed of them with dispatch. During his first six-year term, however, he allowed, of necessity, some vestiges of democracy to linger on. He had to tolerate them until he could broaden his political base and achieve full control of all means of expression. It must be remembered that, like many Latin-American dictators, Perón was always preoccupied with legality.

But the concept of legality, when handled in the right manner, can be made flexible, and in time Perón saw to that also. Early in 1949, after a few false starts, Congress approved a new constitution, replacing the 1853 charter. The new document vested immense powers in the person of the president and removed the traditional ban on a second term. Perón, of course, had assured the Congressmen—seventy-odd per cent of whom were Peronistas—that he had no intention of seeking re-election. So it was the tired, old story all over again: a new constitution was trotted out to put a legal stamp of approval upon the acts of a dictator. Trujillo had done it long before in the Dominican Republic, Vargas had done it in Brazil, and after Perón, Pérez Jiménez was to do it in Venezuela.

The Radical opposition in Congress, reduced in the March, 1948, elections, had the courage to stand up against the constitution, but it could not amount to more than a moral gesture. A deputy who openly criticized the Peróns was expelled from the House by his Peronista colleagues, and forty-two Radicals in Congress resigned their seats. Those who remained hung in the Radical caucus room a sheet of directions on "How to Proceed in Case of Arrest."

For arrests had now become a routine activity for Colonel Velazco's men. And arrests meant lengthy detention without charges, tortures, frame-up trials, and long prison sentences. Armed with the new law of Desacato (Disrespect), Perón could and did put in jail anybody who dared to criticize him, his wife, or his regime.

The judges obliged with sentences when prisoners accused by Perón's government were brought before them; they, too, were Peronistas. Between 1946 and 1947, Congress impeached the entire Supreme Court of Argentina, and gradually all the federal judges and local magistrates were fired and replaced with Perón's trusted followers.

The press still enjoyed some freedom, particularly because the great newspapers like *La Nación* and *La Prensa* refused to buckle under dictatorial pressure. It took Perón several years to get up enough courage to confiscate *La Prensa*. Meanwhile, the Peróns began acquiring newspapers and radio stations to spread the Peronista gospel. Perón occasionally wrote commentaries on international affairs and signed them Descartes. Foreign embassies, trying to follow the vagaries of Perón's foreign policy, carefully read the Descartes articles as a clue to the dictator's thinking. This foreign policy included playing with neutralism, occasionally courting the Soviet Union, often attempting to force a quarrel between the United States and Britain, and always plotting for the creation of a Peronista South American bloc.

Evita took over the newspaper *Democracia*. She either praised Perón in it herself or had the editors praise her. The over-all propaganda effort was directed by the Subsecretariat of Information, known simply as Subsec, which had all the attributes and powers of a regular propaganda ministry. It was reminiscent of Vargas' DIP, with the difference that the

Brazilians had too much sense of humor and proportion to engage in the kind of ridiculous deification of the regime at which Subsec excelled.

In short order, Perón (who, in the meantime, had promoted himself to brigadier general) became Argentina's First Soldier, First Worker, First Descamisado, First Patriot, and a long list of other Firsts. The lovely Argentine landscape became clogged with signs and posters proclaiming that "Perón Fulfills" and "Evita Dignifies."

Copying Hitler and Mussolini, the Argentine dictator formed his personal political party and, with his usual modesty, called it the Peronista Party. Eva followed up with the organization of a Women's Peronista Party. By then women had been given the right to vote and were therefore a prime target for Peronista propaganda, with an eye on the approaching 1951 presidential elections. Someone wrote a hymn titled *Muchachos Peronistas* and the streets of Argentine cities echoed with the song, just as Germany had echoed with the sound of *Horst Wessel* and Italy with *Giovinezza*. Membership in the Peronista Party became a condition for a government job. Anti-Perón elements were purged from the foreign service and other ministries, and from the labor movement. The regime now had all the classical fascist dictatorial trappings. As it happened, Perón was the only one of the five modern South American dictators to have his own political party. All the others, before and after him, subscribed to the theory that politics were harmful to the development of their nations. The way Perón had it set up, it certainly was true of Argentina.

The General, who promptly established himself as Argentina's worst dictator since the days of Juan Manuel de Rosas between 1835 and 1852 (after Perón's overthrow a secret Peronista group circulated leaflets flatteringly comparing him to Rosas), made no bones about his sympathies for the defunct European dictatorships. In fact, Argentina became a haven for hordes of refugee officials and scores were given top jobs by Perón.

Otto Skorzeny, the SS paratroop general who rescued Mussolini from prison, became a close friend of Perón's. Perón made a point of being photographed with him. Dino Grandi, once Mussolini's foreign minister, prospered in Argentina after the war. Ante Pavelich, former head of the Nazi puppet Croatian regime in Yugoslavia and a hated war criminal, was another Perón guest. In 1958, after recovering from wounds resulting from an attack near Buenos Aires, Pavelich moved to Paraguay to advise President Stroessner on repression techniques. Luftwaffe ex-generals Hans Rudel and Adolph Galland came over to help with the reorganization of the Argentine air force (which Perón began equipping with British-built jets), and Dr. Kurt Tank, of Focke-Wulf fame, advised Perón's nascent (and very inefficient) aircraft industry. At least seven top Gestapo officers aided Colonel Velazco in his police work. The offices of the National Economic Council were filled with outstanding Nazi economists.

10

Although he had the nation practically in the palm of his hand Perón, like most vain men, preferred popular support and adulation to mere police-induced obedience. To preserve the support he had gained in the 1946 elections and to expand it for 1951 he and Evita turned the old spectacle of their social justice demagoguery into a truly grand production.

The main piece in this endeavor was the doctrine, or ideology, of Justicialismo, derived from the Spanish word *justicia* but actually indistinguishable from Peronismo, derived from Perón. The Peróns presented it as one of the world's great ideologies and as a Third Force answer to capitalistic democracy on the one side and to communism on the other. In her book Eva defined it as the end of class war and the advent of "co-operation between capital and labor." She wrote:

Capitalism—to give everything to capital—exploits the workers. Communism . . . proposes a system of strife. . . . Justicialism, on the other hand, also wishes to arrive at a single class: those who work. . . . It wishes to achieve this end by co-operation rather than strife. We do not want a single proletarian class, but a single class of former proletarians who will live and work worthily.

The Peróns expressed the expectation that Justicialismo would eventually spread throughout the world and Eva wrote that "a new day for humanity is about to dawn: the day of Justicialismo." To help this process along, at least on the initially modest scale of Latin America, Perón combined a neutralist position in the cold war—Argentina's votes in the United Nations were a sample of this policy—with deliberate efforts to spread the Peronista faith and Argentine political influence on the continent.

The generation-old idea of an anti-United States ABC bloc (Argentina, Brazil, Chile) under Argentina's direction was carefully revived by him. The problem was that within the context of South America's internal rivalries, countries like Brazil took a dim view of any thought of Argentina's hegemony. But the plan made some headway. Getúlio Vargas toyed with the idea of a closer alliance with Perón before he committed suicide in 1954. Chile, governed by ex-dictator Carlos Ibañez del Campo, and Paraguay, run by Dictator Stroessner, entered into Economic Union pacts with Argentina. Attempts were made to bring Bolivia into the arrangement. Special labor attachés, with considerable funds at their disposal, were added to many Argentine embassies abroad, notably in Latin America. Their mission was to infiltrate into local labor movements and preach Peronismo. In Rio de Janeiro at least one newspaper was financed by Perón. Finally, Perón launched his own Latin-American labor confederation, an outfit called ATLAS, but it made very little progress. Its only ally was the procommunist CTAL organization in Mexico (shortly after the 1946 elections, the Communists had jumped on the Peronista band wagon). In short, Perón was aping Nazi and fascist—and Communist—infiltration techniques.

But before Justicialismo could become a profitable article of export, the Peróns concentrated on making it a full success at home. Propaganda in every shape and form led the Justicialismo assault on the consciences and allegiances of Argentines. Perón and Eva wrote and spoke about it incessantly, striving to make their doctrine something of a religion. The General-Dictator enriched his fiery oratory with an almost Biblical turn of phrase, as when he declared that "only the humble will save the humble."

Social protection laws á l'outrance were promulgated in a hard-sell promotion of Justicialismo. Some were probably sound sociologically, others were absurd. Thus, the legal distinction between legitimate and illegitimate children was abolished. The hand of Eva, herself an illegitimate child, loomed behind this law. Another law automatically added a twenty-four per cent compulsory tip to every restaurant and hotel bill in Argentina. No further tipping was legally permitted, but no patron ever neglected to throw a few extra pesos on the waiter's tray if he expected decent service again.

The government spent great sums on workers' housing and other facilities, such as vacation resorts, and, regardless of the motivations, this was one of the positive accomplishments of the Perón regime.

Perón himself continued his pep-talk and favor-granting

audiences once a week. This had considerable political value and, since in the process he did remedy thousands of personal tragedies of little people, another point would be scored for Justicialismo. On another day of the week he conferred with labor leaders on issues that ranged from basic policies to trivialities. Since the labor movement was his principal prop these sessions formed an actual part of the business of government.

Eva held her own labor audiences at the Secretariat of Labor and Welfare, handling many union problems and acting as intermediary between workers' leaders and her husband whenever necessary. She was often instrumental in arranging wage rises that were completely out of reality with the situation prevailing in a given industry. Eva, who insisted on calling herself Evita in her public appearances, held no official position in the government, but for all practical purposes was La Presidenta, as many people called her. She wielded immense power, could and did make and break ministers and ambassadors. When Foreign Minister Juan Atilio Bramuglia, one of her early labor friends, incurred her displeasure because his performance as president of the United Nations Security Council during the 1948 Berlin crisis gave material for more headlines than could be earned by the Peróns, she arranged to fire him.

But the most spectacular Justicialismo undertaking, and Evita's greatest own show, was her social aid project known as Fundacíon Eva Maria Duarte de Perón. Without any question it was the world's greatest extortion and giveaway racket. Between 1947 and 1952, the foundation extracted an estimated $150,000,000 from industry, commerce, labor unions, and individuals. As no books were kept by the foundation and Evita had full control over it, nobody knows actually just how much was collected, how much was spent on good works, or how much went into other channels.

The foundation occupied a seven-story building especially

constructed for it, and Evita's personal staff of assistants to-
taled over one hundred persons. A veritable charity assembly
line, it handed out millions of pesos to needy, and not so
needy, people who came to ask for help. Evita herself did
much of the handing out. As a deliberately soft-touch organization it bought homes for poor families, sent sewing
machines and appliances for the asking. It built excellent modern hospitals and luxurious orphanages and homes for the aged.

No businessman or industrialist in his right mind who
wanted to stay in business ever turned down a foundation
request. To say "no" was to ask for persecution and ruin. On
the other hand voluntary donations could be parlayed into
government favors. Labor unions turned huge checks over to
Evita for her charities, and workers "voluntarily" assessed
themselves for donations whenever a good excuse presented
itself. Colossal graft was attached to this operation and, undoubtedly, Eva and Juan profited from it. The presidential
salary could not possibly have paid for the luxury of their
lives, their several homes (one with a private zoo), her hundreds of dresses, her furs and jewels.

Actually, Evita made no secret of her opulence, and with
a curious insight into the psychology of Argentine women
insisted on mixing with the Descamisados wrapped in her most
expensive furs and sporting her costliest jewels. She explained
it in her book, saying that like every Argentine wife and
mother, "I am, after all, a woman.

"I like the same things that she does: jewels and furs,
dresses and shoes. . . . Like them, I like looking nice more
among my own than before strangers. And that is why I wear
my best finery when I come to my 'Descamisados,'" she
wrote. And the women of Buenos Aires slums, seeing her as a
Cinderella, as a woman of the people who had made good,
loved her for it.

Calculated as it must have been for the greater glory of

Juan and Eva Perón, Justicialismo nonetheless filled a real need, emotional as well as material, for the masses of Argentine workers. It created an unreal world in Argentina, but at the same time it performed an historical function as a bridge between the old and the new social orders. Perhaps it was unavoidable in the context of Argentine history.

11

Evita's ambition was boundless, and this was her greatest tragedy. As Argentina's First Lady and commanding an immense power over the lives and destinies of her husband's subjects, she still knew heart-rending frustrations that could not be alleviated at any price.

The first frustration, and it was responsible for most of her subsequent actions and attitudes leading in turn to other frustrations, was the refusal of traditional Argentine society to accept her. To the ladies of the exclusive clubs and famous Rural Societies Eva was a parvenue actress, and her husband's conquest of supreme power did not alter the fact.

When these ladies, who, incidentally, represented the least-progressive forces in Argentina, failed to name her honorary chairman of their own philanthropic organization Eva took it as a slap in the face. She never recovered from it and she never forgot it. When she spouted fury against the oligarchs and demanded "a century" of privilege for workers she was hitting back at the stubborn society ladies. Her ultimate destruction of their charity group and the creation of Fundación Eva Perón were acts of vengeance. Perhaps Justicialismo itself would not have been born if it were not for Eva's rejection. Because, above all, Eva was a woman. In her autobiography she devoted pages to bitter insistence that she could not have cared less what the society ladies thought of her or whether they accepted her or not.

In June, 1947, Evita embarked on a European tour as spectacular as it was pathetic, with the evident aim of making the grade socially at home. On this "Rainbow Tour," as Perón called it, she was received and honored by heads of governments in three countries. Spain's dictator Francisco Franco awarded her the cross of Isabel la Católica. Pope Pius XII granted her a half-hour audience and decorated her with the Grand Cross of the Order of Pius XII. These initial triumphs were followed by mixed popular receptions in Italy and France. She had hoped for an invitation from the King and Queen of England to come and stay at Buckingham Palace, but all she received was an invitation to take tea with the Queen. Mortified, she cut London out of her schedule and rushed home. On the way to Buenos Aires she stopped off in Rio de Janeiro, where a conference of American foreign ministers was under way, attended by President Truman. If Eva had expected to make a splash in Rio that, too, was a failure. And, home in Buenos Aires, the society ladies still looked the other way.

For the next four years Evita sought compensation for her frustrations in her work and her steadily growing power. She was her husband's chief political fixer, his chief propagandist, and, in practice, the chief overseer of Justicialismo. And it was killing work. Eva went daily to her own office, often to the Labor Secretariat. She inspected her hospitals, housing projects, and orphanages in a whirlwind of frenzied energy. Frequently she sat up most of the night, either at her office or at political or labor meetings and conferences. She related in her autobiography that it was not unusual for her to get home as Perón was getting ready to leave for work in the morning.

When the railroaders' union, once Perón's closest ally, struck for higher wages late in 1950 in an ugly walkout that went into the new year, Eva risked her life by going unescorted to yards and stations to harangue the men into returning to work. There she was no longer among adoring descamisados but in the midst of angry and disillusioned men. Inflation was getting out of hand, the mirage of the Justicialista heaven was beginning to pale. In the end, when Evita's persuasion failed, her husband broke the strike with police and troops, imprisoning and torturing the railroaders' leaders.

In 1951, as Perón's first term was drawing to a close, Eva published her autobiography, *The Reason of My Life*. It was an almost metaphysical cry of devotion to Perón. Larded as it was with pathos and propaganda, it had a certain poignancy and offered much insight into the thinking and reactions of Eva as both woman and politician. Near the end of the book, she wrote with a touch of prophecy:

> Perhaps someday when I am gone for good, someone will say of me what so many children of the people are wont to say when their mothers have gone, also for good: "Only now do we realize that she loved us so much."

Throughout that curious book Eva played on the theme of being the mother to orphans and to the whole nation. It seemed to bring to the surface her regret at never having had children of her own. Tough and hard as she was, Evita loved children and her reaction to them was probably the only unstudied and unrehearsed of her public attitudes. This, then, may have been, consciously or not, another of Eva's deep frustrations.

The autobiography immediately became a best seller in Argentina, partly because it was compulsory reading. It was published in English as *My Mission in Life*. The copyright was in the name of Juan Perón, and after his overthrow he blandly claimed that the book's royalties were the only money he had.

While in her autobiography Eva insisted that she had no
ambitions for an official government position ("If I became
a functionary, I should stop being part of the people"), that
same year, in 1951, she launched her candidacy for Argentina's vice-presidency on a Perón-Perón ticket for the November elections. By then, Perón had conveniently forgotten
his 1949 pledge not to seek re-election and was an official
candidate. In February, 1951, Eva had led a delegation of
Peronista women who called on Perón and asked him to serve
a second term. The dictator had readily agreed and told the
women that, to him, Eva was worth "more than five ministers." This was the first hint of her forthcoming bid for the
vice-presidency.

On August 22 hundreds of thousands of Peronistas were
rounded up in downtown Buenos Aires for a mass demonstration in which they demanded the formation of a Perón-Perón
ticket. The turnout was not quite as large as the Peróns had
expected, but Eva promptly let it be known that she was willing to sacrifice herself and be vice-president to her husband.
It looked briefly as though the Peróns were going to have
their way again. The army, however, pampered and modernized as it was by the regime, put its foot down. Argentina,
Justicialista or not, was still a nation of men, and the idea of a
former actress in her early thirties as commander in chief of
the armed forces, should anything happen to Perón, was more
than the generals were ready to accept.

Consequently, word was sent to Perón that Eva would have
to be made to forget her vice-presidential ambitions. Perón
was enough of an army man himself to understand at once
that it was useless to insist. And on September 2 the ruling
family staged a face-saving operation. Eva presided over a
mass rally, and in tones that bordered on hysteria announced
that she was withdrawing from the race as an act of personal
renunciation. Perón's propaganda made the best of her abne-

gation, but nothing could prevent the idea from spreading that Juan and Eva had finally suffered a defeat and that, therefore, they were vulnerable.

On September 28 a group of officers took their cue from it and staged an anti-Perón revolt, the first one since he had grabbed power in 1945. The rebellion was headed by General Benjamin Menendez, but it had only the support of a few units of the air force and navy. Apparently forewarned, Perón had taken all available precautions, including assuring himself of the loyalty of the ground forces. He capped the occasion by a "loyalty" demonstration of Peronista workers, and the movement ended the same day it was begun. Perón's vengeance, in part revenge for the earlier rebuff to Eva, was to imprison many officers, including General Rawson, the man who had been president for a day back in 1943.

Since elections were approaching and it was time to revive the antiforeign bogeyman, Perón also charged that the United States had had a hand in the revolt. Only the year before Washington had granted him a $150,000,000 loan to help bail him out of his growing economic difficulties. The loan was part of a dogged policy of cultivating Perón despite all his excesses and outrages, a policy that continued until his ouster.

Meanwhile, Eva, this time frustrated in her political ambitions, was beginning the losing battle for her life. Early in November, after weeks in bed at home, she entered a Buenos Aires hospital for an operation. Word soon spread that exploratory surgery had revealed the presence of cancer. Already in her book she had hinted at her deteriorating health: "I am stronger than I appear to be," she wrote, "and my health is better than the doctors think." But the ravages of cancer and of her exhausting life (she starved herself for years to keep her figure) were showing as Perón prepared to face the polls.

On October 17, the anniversary of their 1945 coup, Perón proclaimed the Day of Saint Evita; with broadcasts from her sickbed Eva did her best until election day to help her man win again.

The elections were held on November 11, 1951—Perón had advanced the date by nearly three months because of growing economic pressures—and he was re-elected for a second six-year term. His running mate was Rear Admiral Alberto Tessaire, a figurehead. They defeated the Radical slate of Ricardo Balbin and Arturo Frondizi. As in 1946 it was not necessary to tamper with the ballot boxes: the opposition had been smashed long before the Argentines voted.

Balbin had spent ten months in prison on a Desacato sentence, while Frondizi had served several shorter terms. Martial law was in force. A constitutional amendment had banned coalitions between opposition parties. Not a single newspaper was permitted to open its pages to Balbin. As before, Radical rallies were broken up by Peronista hoodlums and police. Campaign literature was destroyed. No access to the radio was given to Balbin and his fellow candidates. Under the circumstances Balbin and Frondizi were making nothing more than a courageous moral gesture of defiance. Thus once more the Perón dictatorship received legal sanction at the ballot boxes.

12

With the 1951 re-election Perón reached the last high point of his phenomenal career. The decline set in from that time on, though it took nearly four years before it resulted in his ultimate fall.

The Argentine economic situation had been deteriorating since long before the elections as the years of grandiose mismanagement, inefficiency, graft, and impossible schemes fatally sapped the national structure. The country, liberated from external debt only four years earlier, now owed over a billion dollars abroad and new debts were accumulating daily. A sharp decrease in agricultural production, largely due to the operations of the IAPI monopoly, made it impossible for Argentina to keep up the required level of her beef and wheat exports under commitments to Britain and other countries. The rise in world commodity prices following the Korean war helped a little, but not enough to make a marked difference in Argentina's balance of payments.

At home inflation was worsening, there were more and more "illegal" strikes, and the constant, Perón-decreed pay hikes no longer silenced popular outcry. Prices were always ahead of incomes. Promised hydroelectric plants were not built in time, fuel imports had to be curtailed, and by 1950 power rationing had to be imposed in Buenos Aires.

Discontent was appearing throughout Argentina and the early glow of Justicialista euphoria was beginning to vanish. New broadsides of demagoguery and propaganda had to be fired with growing frequency to counter the adverse tide. As usual, the giveaway programs of Fundación Eva Perón led the parade. She was candid enough to admit that "my work helps to consolidate the enormous political prestige enjoyed by the general," and the Peronista momentum, combined with the atrocious acts of intimidation, sufficed to carry the day for him. Women, elated over having the vote for the first time in Argentine history and more frantically pro-Perón than their men, gave the dictator a powerful assist.

But Perón had already deeply antagonized other important segments of Argentine and foreign public opinion, and the seeds of unforgiving opposition were sown in many minds. The murder of *La Prensa* was perhaps the turning point in the patient tolerance accorded Perón by so many of his fellow citizens.

La Prensa, a fearless and outspoken antidictatorial news-paper and a power in its own right, was forced to discontinue publication on January 26, 1951, as the climax of years of persecution. It was the last free voice in Argentina, since all other opposition newspapers had been effectively silenced, shut down or purchased by the Peróns between 1949 and 1950. Denied newsprint and advertising, prevented by Peronista news vendor unions from circulating, it finally had to stop publishing. Its publisher, Dr. Alberto Gainza Paz, fled the country to escape arrest. A few months later Perón expro-priated the newspaper for one-eighteenth of the assessed value and turned it over to his General Labor Confederation (CGT).

The rape of *La Prensa* was the final nail Perón had driven to complete his dictatorial edifice. The handful of Radical deputies in Congress served as a showcase and were not per-mitted to be heard or sometimes even to be seen. They were arrested whenever they displeased the dictator.

On June 24, 1952, Perón was inaugurated for his second term, which was to last until 1958. Eva could not attend the ceremony; she was dying. She passed away on a July evening at the age of thirty-three, and Juan Perón was left alone to do more mischief—and to ruin himself.

Having so heavily leaned on her in life Perón now shame-lessly proceeded to extract maximum mileage from her death. His propaganda machine built a religious myth around her person and the government formally requested the Vatican to initiate steps to canonize her. She was called the Spiritual Guide of the Nation, or simply SHE in capital letters and hushed tones. An order of lay Sisters of Evita was called into being. A huge monument to her was to be built in Buenos Aires. The city of La Plata was renamed Eva Perón for her. One of the two new Argentine provinces already bore her name; the other had been called President Perón. To squeeze the last drop out of his late wife's prestige Perón acquired the title of First Widower, though he did not quite live up to it, while Eva's body was preserved for eternity and laid in state at the labor confederation's headquarters.

With Evita and her political wisdom gone Perón had to rely on himself and his closest associates. The really good men who had assisted him in the opening days of his rule had vanished: some fell from grace, others just had had enough of Peronismo. What was left in human potential around Perón was, at best, unimpressive. His top labor aide was José Espejo, onetime janitor at his apartment building. His political advisers included Carlos Aloé, governor of Buenos Aires province and head of the regime's publishing chain. He had been Perón's army orderly and his whispered nickname was "the ass." After the 1955 revolution the Buenos Aires joke was that Aloé had been sentenced to "six years of grammar school." Perón's business partner was Jorge Antonio, who had risen to a position of fortune and influence from his pre-Peronista beginnings as a guard in an insane asylum. In charge of terrorism was Guillermo Patrick Kelly, a professional thug who led the strong-arm Nationalist Alliance.

Perón started his second term by launching a new Five-Year Plan of economic development. With the Argentine economy foundering under him, he turned again to the United States, conveniently forgetting his very recent denunciations of America, capitalism, and Yankee imperialism. With its blindness concerning dictators, Washington was ready as ever to oblige. Dr. Milton Eisenhower, the President's brother, came to Buenos Aires in 1953, spent several cordial days with Perón, attended a soccer game with him, and opened negotiations for a $60,000,000 loan for a new steel mill and other forms of assistance.

On the domestic front Perón pushed Justicialismo with new fervor as though to make the nation forget its mounting daily problems. Late in 1951, he unveiled the concept of a syndicalist state as the logical consequence of Justicialismo. The idea was that labor unions would elect directly representatives to Congress and provincial legislatures, thus ending even the pretense of a democratic system in Argentina. In December, President Perón Province (the former El Chaco) did actually equip itself with a syndicalist constitution and held an election on the fascist corporate model.

13

In 1953 Perón, no longer restrained by Eva, embarked on a series of personal excesses and political tomfooleries that ultimately led to his downfall.

Less than a year after her death he abandoned all pretense of grief and began acting the "merry widower" fully. His public display of gaiety included a great and renewed devotion to sports. He sponsored, at the state's expense, Argentine teams that competed internationally. He missed no important soccer game. He took to motor scooters with passion, and one day this fifty-eight-year-old head of state led a parade of scooter riders through the streets of Buenos Aires. Foreign beauty queens were invited to visit Argentina to meet the president.

If Argentines took all this in stride, they developed objections to Perón's love life, particularly when it became known that his mistress was a fourteen-year-old girl named Nélida Rivas. Her nickname was Nelly, and she was a student at a high school in Buenos Aires. The dictator met her at a party at his former residence of Olivos which he had turned over to the girls of the High School Students Union.

In time, Perón was spending more and more time with the teen-age girls, directing their sports activities, taking his meals with them. Lecherously, he insisted that the girls call him by his nickname, "Pocho," as his mother had done, and once encouraged a table of girls to chant, "Pocho, eat your soup," as he sat chain-smoking and grinning. One of Perón's favorite amusements was to stuff a wallet full of money in a pocket of his trousers and award it to the girl who could first locate it. But Nelly was his favorite: he gave her Eva's jewels, a house, and a bank account.

Peronista women who had loved Evita bristled with indignation when gossip spread about the dictator's pastimes. The army took an even sterner view. When, after the revolution, a court-martial formally expelled Perón from the army and stripped him of his general's rank, it declared that his conduct had been "unworthy of an officer and a gentleman."

"Cohabitation with a minor, aged fourteen, falls under the sanctions of the penal code," the court said. "It is superfluous to stress the stupor of the court at the proof of such a crime committed by one who has always claimed that the 'only privileged in the land were children.' "

While Perón was thus demoralizing the presidential office, Buenos Aires was engulfed in a wave of regime-backed terrorism. It all started on April 15, 1953, as the dictator was haranguing a mob from a Casa Rosada balcony on the subject of inflation. Suddenly two bombs exploded, killing several persons, maiming many others. Perón reacted with threats of death to his enemies, and this was the signal for Peronista mobs to unleash a reign of terror in the capital.

As the police looked the other way, mobs burned and looted the buildings of the Radical, Socialist, and Conservative parties. Then the torch was set to the Jockey Club, and the proud old building, housing a famous collection of books and paintings, burned to the ground. Five weeks later the government dissolved the Club and took over its racing activities. This was Perón's final strike at the oligarchs of Argentina.

The Jockey Club affair was followed by wholesale arrests

of all those who, because of their background, past or present
activities, could be regarded as opponents of the dictatorship.
Perón's plain-clothes men concentrated on intellectuals and
professional men. Some of this repression was aimed at the
new Christian Democratic Party, which had the support of a
number of progressive Roman Catholic priests. In his rage at
the Christian Democrats, Perón collided head on with the
church, which, theretofore, had either backed him or remained conveniently neutral.

In a speech on November 10, 1954, Perón officially declared war on the church by charging that three provincial
bishops were plotting against him, while other priests were
infiltrating the trade-unions and other organizations. Many
priests were arrested throughout Argentina; Catholic profes-
sors were dismissed from universities, which some time ago
had lost their traditional autonomy and were run by Peronista
rectors.

To add fuel to the dispute, Perón's Congress legalized
divorce in Argentina and sanctioned official prostitution. A
pastoral letter signed by Cardinal Copello condemning these
measures was read from the pulpit of every Argentine church.
Perón countered on November 25 by calling a mass rally at
which the church was denounced. Catholics came back with
their own demonstrations, and blood was spilled again in the
city's streets. On December 2 the dictator signed the divorce
and prostitution laws, and also one ending compulsory religious education. In the opening days of 1955 the regime
abolished several traditional religious holidays.

By then Perón had turned against himself a vast segment
of the Argentine population. Many workers faced the conflict
between allegiance to their church and to Peronismo. The
armed forces were restless. Something of an armed truce prevailed until June 6, when the Catholics defied a police ban to
stage a huge Corpus Christi procession in Buenos Aires. The

following day Perón ordered the arrest of two Buenos Aires bishops and immediately exiled them from Argentina. The Holy See excommunicated "all those involved" in this action.

But now the church and other forces opposed to the dictator had found allies in the navy and the air force. At one o'clock on the afternoon of June 16, 1955, waves of low-flying navy and air force planes roared over Casa Rosada and downtown Buenos Aires in a bombing raid. Perón's luck still held—he had left his office a few minutes earlier—and he escaped death. But Casa Rosada was hit by a number of bombs, and over three hundred persons were killed. Marines jumped off to invade the capital from the navy ministry and the port area.

But the revolt failed. Thick fog in the estuary of River Plate prevented warships from coming into position to bombard the capital. The overcast interfered with precision air bombing. Ground forces refused to join their navy colleagues. By evening Perón had the situation in hand and was ready for reprisals. Peronista mobs, as usual protected by police, burned several churches.

In a few days, however, Perón cooled off. The navy revolt, unsuccessful though it was, had scared him. He reorganized his government, released all the detained priests, and tried the path of conciliation. It was too late.

14

For over two months following the June 16 revolt, a chastised Juan Perón experimented with every trick at his command to persuade the nation that he was not a dictator. He allowed opposition political parties to function again, let his opponents speak without the usual retaliation, and busied himself emptying his prisons.

In July he resigned from the chairmanship of the Peronista Party "in order to become President of all Argentines." On

August 31 he offered to step down from the presidency, but it soon developed that the entire production was a hoax. On the afternoon of the same day a huge Peronista rally in front of Casa Rosada demanded that he continue in office. A nation-wide strike was proclaimed by the labor leadership in support of that objective.

Intoxicated with the old feeling of power Perón now shed his disguise. He easily agreed to remain as president, demanded that his enemies be fought without mercy, and ordered that for every dead Peronista there be four dead "enemy agents." Simultaneously, the labor confederation announced that weapons would be distributed to workers, and the new police chief issued a list of punishable offenses that made earlier periods of repression seem like a picnic. Martial law was declared in the province of Buenos Aires.

To protect his flanks Perón swamped senior military officers with favors, gifts, and promotions. But that, too, was too late. The military conspiracy was too far advanced to be stopped by bribery. On September 4 the garrison at Río Cuarto, in the province of Córdoba, attempted a premature uprising that failed. Elsewhere, officers and civilians alike were plotting. At the old university in Córdoba a full-fledged anti-Peronista underground of students and teachers was in operation. Acts of defiance were gaining in frequency.

Perón faced trouble from other quarters as well. The nation, including thousands and thousands of his former admirers, were protesting the steady inroads of inflation, the mismanagement and dictatorial practices of the regime. The supreme council of the Peronista Party and the labor confederation struck a painful blow at Perón by refusing to endorse an exploration contract he had signed with a United States oil company. Many top Peronistas saw it as a betrayal of the old principles.

The nation was on a powder keg and it was just a question of time before the explosion came. But in Buenos Aires, the United States embassy, unbelievably, insisted in its reports to Washington that Perón was firmly in the saddle and worked on final details of the steel mill loan. Anti-Perón politicians complained openly of the United States continuing its support of the dictator and charged that it was helping to keep him in power.

Then, at dawn on Friday, September 16, three months to the day after the June revolt, the revolution erupted. And this time it was well planned. In Córdoba, General Eduardo Lonardi, chief of the revolution, struck at the head of troops from the air force noncommissioned officers' school. In town, students battled army tanks in the streets. Civilian commandos captured the radio stations and proclaimed the start of the revolution to the world. The next day the western armies joined the movement, and the whole western section of Argentina fell into rebel hands. Rebellions erupted in Entre Ríos and Corrientes.

The navy and the air force captured the bases of Rio Santiago, Puerto Belgrano, and Bahia Blanca. The navy, commanded by Rear Admiral Isaac F. Rojas, steamed toward Buenos Aires. In the capital the army troops remained loyal to Perón, and War Minister General Franklin Lucero assumed command of the "Forces of Repression."

By Monday, September 19, Córdoba was liberated and Lonardi established a provisional government. Warships stood off Buenos Aires and Admiral Rojas radioed an ultimatum that the city would be bombed if Perón did not resign. Perón made a feeble attempt at negotiations, but Lucero and the other generals had seen the handwriting on the wall and turned their backs. At noon on September 19, 1955, Lucero announced Perón's resignation. In the evening, in heavy rain,

Perón, carrying only a brief case, fled to the Paraguayan embassy and asked for asylum. A few hours later he was transferred to a Paraguayan gunboat in the harbor.

Just one month short of ten years since he had first grabbed power in Argentina, Juan Perón was expelled from the presidency, and his decade of dictatorship ended. He had a parting message couched in his classical, demagogic style:

> I, who deeply love the people, have suffered profoundly. I would not wish to die without making a last attempt to secure their peace, tranquility, and happiness. While my fighting spirit moves me to struggle, my patriotism and love for the people impel me to make every personal renunciation.

15

While Argentina celebrated his overthrow and joyously destroyed all external signs of his rule, Perón suffered the added humiliation of spending almost a week as a virtual prisoner aboard the gunboat in Buenos Aires harbor while the two governments negotiated the terms of his exile. He whiled away his time smuggling love letters to Nelly.

On October 7, 1955, a day before his sixtieth birthday, Perón landed in Asunción, Paraguay, after a flight from Buenos Aires. His friend, President Stroessner, Paraguay's dictator, greeted him at the airport and offered him all the courtesies of the house. This included freedom for Perón to make statements about his return to power, as a consequence of which the Argentine government put pressure on Paraguay to get rid of him.

The ex-dictator flew to Panama, where he established himself in a hotel in Colón owned by the United States government. Congressional pressure in Washington made him unwelcome there, too, and Perón moved to Panama City and a modest apartment in the Lincoln Building. There he acquired a blond secretary-mistress—an Argentine dancer in a Panama night club—and two poodles. He also wrote a book, *Might Is the Right of Beasts*, a defense of his regime. No United States publisher would touch it, and finally Perón put it out at his own expense.

In July, 1956, Perón had to leave Panama because of the approaching conference of American presidents, which was to include Argentina's new provisional president, General Aramburu. This time he went to Nicaragua, the scene of the dictatorship of President Anastasio Somoza.

In September of the same year Perón moved voluntarily to Caracas, at the invitation of Venezuela's dictator Marcos Pérez Jiménez. He thought he had settled for good: he invested money in local enterprises and set up headquarters for the Peronista movement in exile. Day after day, instructions, money, and agents flowed from Caracas to Buenos Aires to keep alive the Peronista commandos in Argentina and influence his followers. Because of these activities, which Venezuela refused to curb, Argentina broke off diplomatic relations with Pérez Jiménez in July, 1957.

Perón was all affability in Caracas, granting interviews, issuing statements. He gathered around himself a staff of advisers and aides, mostly former cabinet ministers. Soon Peronista branch outfits were formed in Brazil, Paraguay, Uruguay, and Chile. Perón, with a home and an office, was behaving as a president temporarily away from his capital rather than as the deposed dictator that he was. To show gratitude to their host, Perón and Guillermo Patrick Kelly, the chief Peronista gangster who had escaped from an Argentine prison in Patagonia, drew up a detailed plan for Pérez Jiménez on how to repress the revolution that was threatening his dictatorship. But Perón's advice to Pérez Jiménez was as poor as that he had given to himself in 1955 in Buenos Aires: on January 23, 1959, the pudgy Venezuelan dictator was ousted and Perón fled for asylum to the Dominican embassy in Caracas.

Still he kept his aplomb. His acne was more pronounced than ever before—a sign of nerves—and he could no longer control the disturbing facial tic that made him wink his left eye every minute or so. He spoke of his certainty of staging a return to power in Argentina, but, in the meantime, he had to make the dash to the Dominican Republic and another place of exile.

There, under the wing of Generalissimo Trujillo, Perón joined the growing "Dictators' Club," which in January, 1959, was expanded to include Cuba's Fulgencio Batista. From Ciudad Trujillo Perón continued his meddling in Argentine politics. He ordered his two million followers to cast their votes for Arturo Frondizi in the expectation, that soon proved to have been erroneous, that he would be allowed to go back to Argentina. In mid-1959, as Trujillo's own regime experienced its first subterranean rumbles and felt new, powerful external pressures threatening its survival, Juan Perón may well have been wondering where next he could go in the vanishing world of dictators.

Chapter Five

MANUEL ODRÍA
OF PERU

1

For seven years and nine months, beginning in October, 1948, Peru prospered economically but starved politically under the dictatorship of General of Division Manuel Amoretti Odría, a retiring, middle-aged war hero, chess player, and opera lover.

Of all the modern South American dictatorships Odría's unspectacular rule was the most positive in its immediate achievements, which were to bring order out of chaos and to promote wisely the economic development of the country. While Odría was not oblivious to the social pressures at work in Peru reflecting basic Latin-American trends and of the growing importance of the industrial proletariat, he refused to engage in demagoguery of the Perón type. Instead, he quietly went ahead with promulgating workable labor legislation, building hospitals and schools, and making a modest effort to solve the awesome problem of the destitute and restless Peruvian Indian populations spilling down from the inhospitable Andean slopes.

Capturing power through a military coup d'état at the height of political and social convulsions that threatened to submerge Peru in a civil war, General Odría was the antithesis of a social revolution. Believing in the slow, gradual approach to the explosive problems of a rapidly changing society, he unquestionably accomplished more for the working man during his political, dictatorial rule than APRA's crowd-haranguing prophets of social justice who virtually controlled Peru for the three years preceding his "restoration" revolt of 1948.

It was APRA (its Spanish initials stand for Popular American Revolutionary Association) and its own thirst for absolute power that generated most of the turmoil in the country and created the climate for Odría's emergence as a dictator. A leftist but anticommunist organization, APRA was the oldest of Latin America's "populist" parties, beating the drums for social justice, playing up the Indian problem, and concentrating much of its propaganda against "imperialisms." It once entertained dreams of spreading throughout Latin America, and in wartime one of its aims was the internationalization of the Panama Canal.

Exercising an immense appeal to Peru's poor masses, including millions of Indians and half-breeds, APRA had been the greatest political influence in the country for the past two decades. But, invariably, conservative interests—including the army and the powerful Peruvian aristocracy that traced its lineage to Spanish viceregal days and in twentieth-century Peru still held most of the nation's wealth in what was one of South America's tightest feudal systems—prevented APRA's radicals from taking over the government. In 1945 the election of President José Luis Bustamante Rivero, a liberal but weak man, gave APRA its long-awaited opportunity. Infiltrating the government on all levels, as well as labor unions and universities, Apristas reached for ultimate domination of Peru much in the way Perón fought for power in Argentina. And APRA's tactics in those days hinted that if the party had ever achieved its objectives Peru would have been turned into something akin to a Justicialista state, with all its fascistoid and mob-rule characteristics. Of course, the shortsighted policies of the rich right-wing groups were fuel for its demagoguery.

Before and during President Bustamante's administration APRA often used political terrorism to win its goals. It was blamed for a series of political murders, including those of two top Lima newspaper publishers, and the army, which hated Apristas more than Communists, claimed that scores of officers and soldiers had been killed by APRA triggermen on different occasions. Early in October, 1948, APRA staged a full-dress rebellion in the port city of Callao, hoping, Kronberg-style, for the support of the navy's sailors. It was beaten down and Dr. Bustamante finally declared the party illegal. But Odría, former army chief of staff and Bustamante's interior minister, concluded that tough military rule was the only solution in a situation of deepening chaos that was pushing Peru to the brink of economic and political catastrophe.

Frightened by APRA's objectives, which threatened its very existence, the moneyed aristocracy turned to Odría as if he were a savior. They assumed that he would put an end to all the liberal and Aprista outcry about social justice. Many of these gentlemen expected that this General, whom they took to be politically unsophisticated, would be a tool in their hands. But Odría surprised them on both scores. Although he let some of the oligarchs help finance his revolution he accepted no commitments and doggedly pursued an independent course between the left and the extreme right that, in time, an-

tagonized the aristocracy. The new middle class, which flour-
ished under the economic prosperity of his regime, provided
most of his support.

While APRA had made a fetish of social gains for the
downtrodden masses, it was Odría who unostentatiously introduced such fundamental measures as the promulgation of
social security in Peru. It was his government that created a
Ministry of Labor and Indian Affairs, wrote progressive labor
laws and, not forgetting the Indians, began to organize bilingual schools where Quechua-speaking highlanders could
learn Spanish as a first step toward integration into the country's modern society.

In the political sense Odría's regime was a cooling-off period
in Peru. With the outlawing of APRA the country was left
without a strong, traditional party. The other parties were
largely of a fly-by-night variety, and with his hated APRA
out of the way General Odría did not have too much trouble
imposing a political moratorium on the nation. The six parties that nominated him as a candidate for constitutional president in 1950 meant very little ideologically or politically and
left practically no trace on the nation's political consciousness.
At that time Odría, fearing that his lack of popular appeal
would defeat him, prevented his opponent from running for
office and was "elected" in a one-candidate election. This,
incidentally, was the worst dictatorial offense during his years
in power. But when democracy was restored in 1956, the
country still suffered from a Franciscan poverty in meaningful
political parties, and the situation has not changed perceptibly
in the ensuing years despite the full liberty now prevailing
in Peru.

Like all dictators, Odría made his grab for power with the
excuse of restoring order and progress. Like all dictators, he
promised to step down and allow the resumption of democratic practices when he would arbitrarily determine that the

time for it had come. But, unlike all dictators, he kept his word. In contrast with Trujillo, Vargas, Perón, and dictatorial rulers who later came on the scene, General Odría refused to alter the constitution which in Peru, as almost everywhere else in Latin America, barred a second presidential term. He stood aside while three candidates disputed the presidency in 1956, silently left the country a few days before the elections, and watched from afar his hand-picked candidate being soundly trounced. Skeptics say that Odría would have tried to upset the results of the elections if he had not broken a hip a week before balloting day. A military conspiracy along these lines was actually hatched, but it came to naught and there is not a shred of evidence to indicate that Odría had a hand in it. Since a man should be judged by his acts and not on unproved suspicions, General Odría deserves credit for unprecedented behavior in the annals of Latin-American military dictatorships, that of voluntarily yielding his power.

In his own way Odría did prepare Peru for the resumption of democracy, and since 1956 it has functioned with reasonable smoothness. Politically, socially, and economically, his regime thus was a useful transition and an important milestone in Peruvian history. It may well have supplied the essential conditions for the present and future success of democracy, which, in common with all other systems, must repose on solid foundations. Although he proved the sincerity of his oft-expressed desire to withdraw from public life, it is conceivable that this reluctant dictator would like to be called back to power as a freely elected president in the 1962 elections. And it is conceivable that Peruvians, who are appreciating him more now that he is gone, may do just that. Since the end of his term Odría has lived quietly in Washington, D.C., following a brief stay in Spain.

Odría's notion of good government was to calm down political passions and advance Peru economically. He was successful in both endeavors, though he often had recourse to arbitrary strong-arm methods to have his way. This, unfortunately, was a serious blemish on what otherwise would have been a first-rate administration. Odría had no mercy for the Apristas, whom he jailed and exiled, but early in 1956 his political cunning led him to seek a truce with them for the support of his candidate, a colorless lawyer named Hernándo de Lavalle. There was a congress after the 1950 elections, but, with the exception of a handful of independent members, it was a rubber stamp for the government. An internal security law gave Odría ample dictatorial and police powers, and he used them at his discretion. The press was gagged, but the Odría era was not studded with brutal police excesses on the Peronista, or even the Vargas, model. There was the unavoidable graft that characterizes all Latin-American dictatorships, but it never assumed the astronomic proportions of Argentina, Colombia, Venezuela, or Cuba. There is no reason to think that Odría became a millionaire in office, though he is certainly well off.

With its sacrifice of liberty Peru won a prosperous economy. Unlike most of the other dictators, Odría was not a rabid nationalist, and legislation passed under his rule attracted hundreds of millions of dollars of foreign investments. This, in turn, created new employment, raised living standards, and vastly increased Peru's export earnings, vital for its survival. A completely free economy was inaugurated in Peru under Odría, and the nation has greatly profited from it. Important irrigation projects, essential for a country of deserts like Peru, were built. New roads were opened, somewhat breaking the isolation of the high mountains and deep jungles that, along with the coastal deserts, form the geography of Peru. A steel industry was established.

If a comparison is needed, Odría's greatest intellectual affinity in the dictatorial family was with Venezuela's Marcos

Pérez Jiménez, a graduate of Peruvian military schools where Odría studied and taught. Both men subscribed to the thesis of no politics and of stressing economic development. Both eschewed public demagoguery. But where Odría was a balanced and responsible ruler, Pérez Jiménez imposed one of the hemisphere's worst reigns of terror, clung to power desperately until a bloody revolution threw him out of office, and distorted his country's economy through fantastic public works schemes and graft and corruption on a heroic scale.

2

As a dictatorial personality Manuel Odría was not particularly impressive. A short, stocky man with slightly bulging blue eyes, large ears, sandy hair streaked with gray, and a big irregular nose, he always seemed a little out of character in the ornate presidential palace on Lima's Plaza de Armas. He also was a quiet, almost timid person, who often appeared to be ill at ease with strangers. The palace has balconies and big windows, but Odría was never known to have used them for speechmaking to massed crowds below. In fact, the last thing he ever wanted to do was to gather multitudes and excite them for or against anything.

When he addressed the nation, which he did a few times a year, and usually when he had something important to say, Odría preferred to speak over the radio. He did it in calm, measured tones. Once a year, on the national holiday of July 28, he personally read a message to Congress, a State of the Union report, serving as the introduction to a fat volume distributed to congressmen and containing an exhaustive and detailed account, studded with statistics, of his stewardship during the past year. In the messages Odría discussed politics and economics, announced new policies, and expressed his opinions on national affairs. Allowing for a natural partiality and bias in them, these reports constitute a remarkably comprehensive history of his regime.

In his first annual report to the nation, nine months after assuming power, Odría declared that when the military moved to overthrow President Bustamante, "the country was on the verge of the most grave moral and political chaos of our history and the republican institutions were passing through a period of painful and anxious crisis, whose only solution was a complete change of methods and men in the direction of the State." He said that "our economy was virtually on the verge of collapse."

Six years later, in 1955, Odría rose in Congress to announce that within exactly one year he would "comply with my constitutional duty of delivering the Supreme Power to the citizen who has been elected, democratically, by the Peruvian people as President of the Republic." He reported that "order and tranquility have been maintained unaltered in the territory of the republic" and that "surpassing all expectations, the accelerated economic and financial development of Peru has continued." In a special message in September, 1955, on the theme of forthcoming elections Odría complained in hurt tones that his regime was being described as arbitrary, dictatorial, and as having "converted the country into a police state." He denied all these charges, and it is likely that it had never occurred to him to think of himself as a dictator. Odría had hoped to deliver his final message to the nation while handing the presidential office over to his successor, but the accident in which he broke his hip deprived him of the glory of such a farewell gesture.

While he was in power Odría led a personal life that was as unostentatious as his public performance. He made all the usual presidential appearances at ceremonies and inaugurations of different public works projects, but he did not force himself upon the people in the manner of a Perón. He was extremely proud of his generalship, which he had reached at the age of forty-nine, one of the youngest generals in Peruvian history. His main point of vanity, in fact, was his insistence that his full title of General of Division, and in capital letters, be always mentioned along with his name. In time it became a mild political joke in Peru, one of the very few anecdotes told about Odría. Peruvians are well endowed with political humor, but the General of Division just did not provide much inspiration for jokesmiths and caricaturists.

Despite his pride in his gold braid Odría had a penchant for civilian attire. He wore perfectly tailored, conservative suits, and had a marked predilection for waistcoats that, with the glasses he sometimes put on, made him look more like a prosperous businessman than a dictator. His pleasures were those of a cultured Peruvian bourgeois: he enjoyed bullfights, which are occasionally good in Peru; was a good chess player; and something of a music lover. He was an accomplished amateur pianist and liked the opera and Peruvian folk music, its slow waltzes and jumpy *marineras*. He was a pleasant conversationalist but preferred to listen rather than to talk.

Odría was married at the age of thirty, when he was a captain attending the Superior War College in Lima. His wife, Señora María Delgado de Odría, bore him two sons. While he doubtless engaged in extramarital affairs, as Latin-American males are wont to do, it was always done without ostentation or scandal. As personal weaknesses go, a liking for tippling, favoring the native Peruvian *pisco* or Scotch whisky, was Odría's only known vice. After he broke his hip in 1956, in fairly mysterious circumstances, the story was told in Lima that he had stumbled and fallen during an all-night drinking party at the palace. An American friend ran into Odría one night in 1956 at the deserted bar of a provincial hotel he had inaugurated a few hours earlier. The President was well in his cups, and he tearfully confided to the friend that he was tired of running the country, that all he wanted was to get out of the palace and retire as a private citizen.

As a dictator and as a human being Odría was a man of principles, although some of his former political associates have said he thought nothing of being disloyal when the occasion called for it. But, after all, he was in a power game for big stakes. All indications are that Odría had less craving for power for power's sake than any of his fellow dictators of that era. But he knew what he wanted and he knew how to get it. In a sense he was uncompromising in his beliefs: when President Bustamante refused to follow his advice on getting tough with APRA in June, 1948, Odría resigned his post as Minister of Government and Police, and as a private citizen began to plan his revolt. As dictator, Odría was not particularly vindictive. In 1955 he let his war minister be taken aboard a warship to California and exiled after the latter had tried to overthrow him. Reporting on it to Congress, Odría remarked rather sadly that the Minister had been "one of my closest collaborators" and dropped the subject by calling the conspiracy a "witless action." Four months before the 1956 elections, another general, who had also served in one of Odría's cabinets, staged an abortive revolution in the jungle town of Iquitos. Odría had him arrested along with a number of distinguished citizens, let most of them go in a short time, but it took President Prado to release the rebel general.

Odría had a streak of stubbornness and a good deal of cunning in dealing with men and situations. This may have been the heritage of the few drops of Indian blood he was said to have, not an uncommon occurrence in Peru, since these characteristics are frequently associated with people from the high Andes.

3

Actually, Odría was not born in the forbidding mountains that once were the realm of the Incas, but in the town of Tarma in the department of Junín atop a pleasant plateau in central Peru. There is enough provincialism still left in Peru for men to go through life identifying themselves with their place of birth, and Odría was no exception. During his dictatorship charges were made that he favored Junín in his program of public works, but if he did so it was not in a very massive way.

He came into the world on November 26, 1897, the son of a moderately prosperous family. His grandfather, Colonel Manuel Odría, has a niche in Peruvian history for his bravery in repulsing the attack of a Spanish naval force on Callao in 1886. With this family tradition behind him, Odría did what many Peruvian youths of similar background but no great wealth were likely to do in the years that coincided with World War I: he entered the Chorrillos Military School as the first step in an army career.

His father had died when Odría was a child and the task of bringing up the family fell upon his mother. Young Manuel's enrollment as cadet at Chorrillos in 1915 shortly before his eighteenth birthday somewhat lessened his mother's responsibilities, but she always remained close to him. Before her death at the age of eighty-three, she had the satisfaction of seeing her son ruler of his country.

Chorrillos Military School was, and is, one of the best institutions of its kind in Latin America. Heavily influenced in those days by French army instructors and imbued with the spirit of St. Cyr, it had always attracted students from the rest of the continent. In 1919 Odría was graduated at the head of his class and received the commission of an infantry second lieutenant. His distinguished student record and his scholarly turn of mind led the school to obtain his assignment there first as instructor, then as full professor.

Odría remained at Chorrillos until 1927, when he was promoted to captain and sent to the Superior War College in Lima. He graduated in 1930 with a diploma of staff officer, and went on to the Naval War College for further studies. Considered one of the most promising young officers in the Peruvian army, Odría was given the rank of major in 1930, and named commander of an infantry battalion at Chorrillos, where he served until 1936.

These were years of great political turmoil in Peru. APRA and other radical forces were making their influence felt, there was chaos in the country, and a succession of provisional governments. A military-civilian junta took power in 1930, was succeeded by a military junta of Colonel Sánchez Cerro, who became general and president in 1931 and was assassinated in 1933. He was followed by another general, Oscar Benavides, who managed to remain in power until the end of his term. At Peru's military schools and in garrisons throughout the country young officers began to develop ideas about the role of the armed forces in national life, which they saw as an essential stabilizing element in the midst of the civilian political upheavals. It is probable that Odría's own views about authoritarian regimes began to be formed in those days.

In 1936 Odría was promoted to lieutenant colonel and assigned as chief of staff of the Fourth Army Division in Cuzco, the old capital of the Inca empire. There he came in touch with the past greatness of his land under the Emperors of the Sun and with the misery-steeped present of their descendants. It may have given him an understanding of the depth of Peru's Indian problem. While Odría served in Cuzco, APRA's strong-arm tactics were shaking the country. In Lima, Antonio Miró Quesada, publisher of the newspaper *El Comércio*, and his wife were murdered by men described as Aprista gunmen. There was an APRA uprising in the town of Huancavelica, and a number of officers and soldiers of the Civil Guard were killed. Later Odría often cited these occurrences, which must have profoundly impressed him, as two of the reasons for his unforgiving hatred of APRA.

From Cuzco, Odría went to Lima to become chief of the Third Section of the Army's General Staff. His next assignment was as chief of staff of the First Light Division, with headquarters in Piura in northern Peru. He rose from this job to the glory of a war hero.

Since the nineteenth century Peru and Ecuador, its small northern neighbor, had been embroiled in a succession of border disputes which often erupted into armed conflicts. The latest one came on July 5, 1941. It is not very clear what started the war; in an argument reminiscent of the controversy over who fired first on Fort Sumter, the Ecuadoreans claim they were attacked and the Peruvians insist that all they did was to mount a counteroffensive after throwing back an Ecuadorean assault. Whatever the truth in these contradictory allegations, the fact remains that after their victorious breakthrough in the battle of Zarumilla River, the Peruvians kept going until they occupied a vast section of Ecuador's jungle provinces and deprived that country of access to the Amazon. Peru's conquests were subsequently legalized by a Brazilian commission acting as mediator on behalf of foreign ministers of the hemisphere.

Odría was credited with masterminding the Peruvian victory at Zarumilla on July 24 when all seemed lost and, in the words of a Peruvian military historian, "we were on the brink of military disaster." The First Light Division was part of the Northern Group of Armies under Brigadier General Eloy G. Ureta, and, when the Ecuadorean attack got under way, its headquarters were moved from Piura to Tumbes, near the frontier. An earlier Peruvian offensive on a twenty-five-mile jungle front had collapsed, and six crack Ecuadorean battalions were pressing the Peruvians hard. As the situation was deteriorating from hour to hour, Odría left his Tumbes headquarters and rushed to the front lines. There he gathered his regimental and battalion commanders and ordered the regrouping of Peruvian forces. A small unit, acting as a decoy, began withdrawing rapidly with a large Ecuadorean force in hot pursuit. It was caught in the crossfire of Peruvian detachments lying in wait and promptly destroyed. Jumping off immediately, Peruvian troops threw the enemy off balance and captured the town of Chacras, a key position; this surprise strike disorganized the Ecuadorean army and forced it into retreat. The Zarumilla-Chacras battle was decisive in the war, and soon thereafter the Ecuadoreans laid down their arms.

Odría returned to Lima as a hero, although nothing was said of Colonel Luis Vinatea, who commanded the First Light Division. He must have left everything in Odría's hands. A grateful government promoted Odría to full colonel and General Ureta to marshal. This wartime association proved useful to Odría seven years later when he staged his revolution: Marshal Ureta threw the Lima garrison behind the Odría movement. Some of his jungle campaign companions became his collaborators in the military regime, such as Lieutenant Colonel Carlos Miñano, commander of an infantry battalion of the First Light Division, who served later as an Odría cabinet minister.

As peace returned to Peru Colonel Odría was appointed first assistant director then director of the Superior War College in Lima. He held these positions for five years and during that time twice visited the United States. Under his stewardship, the Peruvian War College had become a center of military and political thinking that was to influence not only the future of Peru but also that of other Latin-American republics.

With the approach of the Axis defeat in World War II, the winds of liberalism were spreading throughout the world, and Latin America could not escape them. Social pressures were rising to combine with leftist political trends. Dictatorships were being shaken. In Argentina Juan Perón was rising to power at the crest of a wave of social demagoguery. In Peru, as the term of conservative President Manuel Prado was coming to an end, APRA was again agitating the country. The officers at the War College in Lima were watching these developments with concern: they feared that the rising political and social struggles would plunge the nation into another cycle of turmoil. Cliques of officers dedicated to the concept of strong military governments as deterrents to chaos were being quietly formed. Colonel Odría definitely leaned toward this thinking in assessing the Peruvian situation, though time for action was still far in the future. And one of his Venezuelan students, Captain Marcos Pérez Jiménez, was entertaining similar thoughts in relation to his country.

4

In July, 1945, Dr. Bustamante was elected for the presidential term that was to run until 1951, defeating Marshal Ureta. He was the candidate of the Democratic Front, a coalition of leftist and liberal groups among which APRA was the prime influence. A native of Arequipa, the southern "White City" and one of Peru's most politically conscious centers, Dr. Bustamante represented an enlightened middle-of-the-road liberalism. He was wary of the extreme left, and of APRA, which he legalized, but in the end he proved too weak to resist its domination. On the other side of the spectrum were the entrenched right-wing business and industrial interests, and the patricians of what was known derisively as La Llamada, the shortened designation of Llamada Aristocracia, or So-called Aristocracy.

From the day of Bustamante's inauguration on July 28, 1945, it was evident that the new government was in for terrible difficulties. A boycott by conservative senators prevented the organization of Congress. The armed forces were unhappy over the defeat of Marshal Ureta but, respecting the constitution, they were willing to support the elected regime as long as possible. And looming as the key man among the military was Manuel Odría. In 1946 Bustamante promoted him to brigadier general and named him chief of staff of the army. Now Odría held decisive power in his hands, but for the next two years he exercised it for Bustamante's benefit.

By the time the year 1947 began Peru had fallen into a state of uproar seldom witnessed in its entire agitated history. There was an uninterrupted succession of strikes, productivity declined instead of rising, exports dropped, the country's dollar reserve dwindled, vital foreign investments began drying up, the cost of living skyrocketed, and inflation swamped the country.

Politically, APRA was deeply infiltrated into the government, universities, schools, and labor unions. The party had representatives in the cabinet and a majority in Congress, it controlled most of Peru's provincial departments and many of its municipalities. The rector of San Marcos University in Lima was an Aprista and so were many of the faculty. In the mountain villages of Peru's backlands Aprista teachers led children under the flags of Peru and APRA. In Lima and other towns of the republic APRA organized mass rallies to back its policies, and the streets and plazas frequently turned into a white sea of waving handkerchiefs, the party's salute.

Organized in cells with national, departmental, and municipal directorates, APRA also had its strong-arm squads of thugs. Known as "the Buffaloes," they could be seen around party headquarters wearing armbands with the five-point star insignia. Outside, they administered beatings to opponents of Aprismo, and this activity reached such proportions that many Peruvians began to attribute every act of violence to APRA, whether it was responsible for it or not.

These tactics were nothing new to APRA; they had been in use in varying degrees since the early 1930's, and many political murders were laid at its door—again, rightly or wrongly. Every few years a general amnesty would be declared in Peru and APRA's offenders would be released. The last amnesty had been granted by Bustamante when he took office in 1945. And during his administration, APRA spokesmen in Congress repeatedly warned that they would vote new amnesties should the government crack down on the party and begin arresting its "activists."

Tensions in Peru reached a climax on January 7, 1947, when gunmen shot and killed Francisco Graña Garland, publisher of the Lima daily *La Prensa*, in front of a downtown office building in full daylight. Subsequent investigations by the Bustamante government concluded that the triggermen were APRA members. *La Prensa* had been violently critical of the party's methods and it also opposed the plans of the Bustamante government to sign a contract with several United States oil companies for explorations in the Sechura desert region of the north. In the curious pattern of Peruvian politics of those days, the anticapitalist APRA supported the contract while the conservative groups were against it. But this opposition stemmed mainly from the fact that, as a rule, conservatives opposed everything APRA favored.

The Graña assassination shook the nation, and the next day Bustamante's cabinet resigned. For the first time Bustamante decided to react, and named a predominantly military cabinet headed by Admiral José R. Alzamorra. General Manuel Odría, army chief of staff, was appointed Minister of Government and Police, the key cabinet job.

But neither the new cabinet nor the new minister could bring peace to the country. The problems were too deep, the difficulties too acute, the resentments too searing. Odría advocated from the outset the outlawing of APRA, but President Bustamante was reluctant to do it. A sincere liberal, he felt that such an act would be undemocratic. And so Peru lived from crisis to crisis. In October, 1947, a new series of strikes and labor pressures forced the resignation of the Alzamorra cabinet. Admiral Roque Saldia was named premier and retained Odría as Minister of Government and Police. This was the beginning of a collaboration that was to last for almost nine years. When Odría became president, Admiral Saldia served as premier throughout most of his regime.

As the year 1948 dawned over Peru the situation was deteriorating at an ever-increasing pace. In January APRA sought to organize an international labor conference in Lima, apparently to spread its influence to other Latin-American labor movements and to increase its international prestige. A strange combination of right-wing interests and Communists, numerically few but extremely loud, set out to torpedo the conference. They received an assist from Odría, already universally recognized as the strong man of the Bustamante regime, who sent out his policemen and Civil Guardsmen to break up with clubs and rifle butts Aprista protest demonstrations in wide Plaza San Martín in Lima.

The open clash between Communists and Apristas over the issue of the labor conference served to expose as nonsensical the efforts of Odría and his military colleagues to equate communism with APRA. He realized that a coup against the government—and he evidently was already thinking about it —would gain more sympathy abroad, and particularly in the

United States, if it could be presented as an anticommunist move. After the revolution Odría went on insisting that Apristas were Communists in disguise and that by outlawing the two parties Peru acted to "eliminate any Soviet or totalitarian influences capable of creating danger for the democratic organizations of America. . . ." Actually, Communists and Apristas were, and are, sworn enemies and it was the appeal of APRA to the masses that has kept down the growth of communism in Peru. But later, like all dictators who made anticommunism their profession of faith, Odría did quietly co-operate with the Communists.

In February the crisis reached a new peak with the assassination of Francisco Tovar Belmont, governor of Pasco department. Again APRA was blamed for the murder. Twelve days later, on February 28, Bustamante received another cabinet resignation. He reappointed Admiral Saldia as premier, and this time an all-military government was named, with General Odría returning as Minister of Government and Police. Now Saldia and Odría openly pressed Bustamante to outlaw APRA or face the consequences. Again, the President refused to heed this advice. The military were in full control of the government but they still hesitated to take the final step, although it was amply clear that a revolution by the armed forces was just a question of time.

In June Odría took the first step in that direction. Unable to persuade Bustamante to act with energy against APRA, he resigned from the cabinet along with Admiral Saldia. He applied for retirement from active duty in the army and, remaining in Lima, set about preparing the revolution. His resignation was what Peruvians call "to go down to the plains," which means to give up power voluntarily in order to have a free hand for action.

While Odría thus removed himself from the government, the military throughout Peru were growing in restlessness.

If anything, it was Odría who was a moderating influence on his colleagues. On July 4 Lieutenant Colonel Alfonso Llosa led several regiments of the Fourth Light Division in Juliaca, in Puno Department, in an abortive revolt. It failed largely because other garrisons refused to join the movement. The time was not yet ripe for a successful uprising, since Bustamante still retained the loyalty of many army commanders. Odría knew in advance of Llosa's plans, but made no move to use his influence to help him. In fact, he was quoted as saying, "I do not support revolutions; I start them. Llosa moved prematurely."

The truth was that the armed forces were deeply split: some commanders advocated an immediate revolution, others were hesitant to risk it. Odría's self-appointed job as the officer with the greatest prestige in Peru was to co-ordinate the revolutionary sentiments in the armed forces and place himself at the head of the conspiracy. He personally took charge of winning the support of the garrisons in Lima and in northern Peru while, at the same time, seeking the political backing of landowners and industrial and commercial interests. These helped him to finance the movement.

Meanwhile Colonel Llosa established a secret "revolutionary command in exile" at La Paz, Bolivia, and made contact with younger officers of the Third Light Division in Arequipa. The plotting in Arequipa thus began shortly after the frustrated Juliaca attempt and, without Odría's direct participation at the outset, became the nucleus of his victorious revolution three months later.

But it was APRA that took it upon itself to crystallize all this rebel planning and force a showdown. In a desperate bid for power it mounted on October 3, 1948, a revolt against Bustamante in a movement that erupted in the port of Callao but failed to spread to the rest of the country. Some naval cadets and a few navy units joined the rebellion, but it was crushed virtually the same day. It cost fifty lives.

As far as the military were concerned, Callao tipped the balance. Bustamante now stood alone: the armed forces and the conservatives had been in opposition to him for some time, and APRA, which he had protected for so long, had now also turned on him. Peru was under a state of siege and the military were demanding stern measures to pacify the country and punish APRA. Finally, the well-meaning but weak President made up his mind to take a stand. Completely disillusioned with APRA he declared it illegal. But he had waited nearly three weeks after the Callao uprising to outlaw the trouble-making party and, in the eyes of the military, he fell short of meting out the kind of punishment they thought APRA deserved. From then on, in the words of one of the military rebel leaders, it was "the Army against APRA, a war to death by Peru against the anti-patriots."

In those October weeks Peru faced a complete breakdown of authority. The nation had lost what was left of its confidence in the government. Economic activity was practically at a standstill, the Peruvian Sol was rapidly losing its value in relation to foreign currencies, prices were soaring, and the government had to keep the printing presses going furiously to meet its most urgent bills.

The time had come for the revolution which in the opinion of the military was the only alternative for saving the republic from chaos and civil war. Manuel Odría stood ready to lead the rebellion.

5

But, inevitable as was the revolution, Odría still had to overcome last-minute hesitations and uncertainties before the word could be given. Arriving in Arequipa Sunday night, October 24, after a secret drive from Lima, he found that some of the key troop commanders there had suddenly become reluctant to act. They told Odría that if, indeed, he controlled the garrisons of Lima and the north of Peru, the revolution should start in any of those points instead of Arequipa. In a dramatic all-night session at the home of one of the colonels, Odría and his supporters argued that the rebellion should get under way immediately and that Arequipa was the place for it. At one point in the dispute officers on both sides drew their guns. But in the end Odría conquered the resistance of troop chiefs and the decision was made.

For the next three days Odría and his aides feverishly prepared the details of the move. In Lima, meanwhile, the army, on Bustamante's orders, used tanks to dislodge from San Marcos University the students who rioted against the dismissal of Aprista teachers. At that stage—it was Tuesday, October 26—the army commanders in the capital were still willing to obey the President, especially because the university affray was in accordance with their wishes.

The following day, October 27, at seven o'clock in the evening, Odría launched his revolution. Meeting no opposition, his officers deposed the garrison commander and the departmental governor. Addressing the nation over the radio, the rebels claimed control of all southern Peru. Odría was proclaimed head of the provisional government, and it was announced that the aim of the Revolution of Restoration was "to save the country from Aprista plots" and "political poisoning by the Leftists."

The rebels were in control of Arequipa but until late the next day none of the other garrisons in Peru stirred, despite Odría's radio appeals. In Juliaca, in Puno Department, the commander of the Fourth Light Division not only refused to join the revolution but threatened Odría by telephone that he would march against him. Odría countered with his own threat of attack, and by evening he was informed by junior officers in Juliaca that they had taken control of the division and declared themselves in rebellion.

But in Lima, General Zenón Noriega, garrison commander, was still loyal to Bustamante. All was quiet in the north, and it looked for a time as if the Arequipa revolution might fizzle out. Odría's victory came, however, on Friday, October 29, the third day of the rebellion. As news reached the capital of the defection of the Puno forces and of a successful uprising in Huancayo, Noriega and other generals met at noon with Marshal Ureta, Peru's military elder statesman.

Ureta, who had lost the election to Bustamante in 1945, advised the generals to oust the President. A few hours later a delegation of twenty-five army officers called on Bustamante at the palace and demanded his resignation. Word was being received simultaneously from Cuzco that the division there had also joined the revolution. Bustamante twice turned down demands for his resignation, suggesting at one point that the supreme court be called to settle the crisis. Late in the afternoon army troops replaced the presidential guard at the palace and Bustamante was informed that he was no longer president. He left the country that same evening but refused to sign a document of resignation.

General Noriega assumed the presidency pending Odría's arrival in Lima. The victorious leader flew into town on October 30, the day after Bustamante's fall, and in the afternoon was formally sworn in as provisional president of Peru. Not a single shot had been fired and not a drop of blood was spilled during the three-day revolution which elevated Odría to power a few weeks before his fifty-first birthday.

Odría immediately organized a military junta of government. Admiral Roque Saldia, General Noriega, and Colonel Llosa, the unsuccessful rebellion leader of Juliaca, were

among the members of this new government. The day he
took office Odría spelled out his political beliefs and his government program.

"Peru," he said, "will be reconstructed on a new basis." He
told the nation that he would remain in power long enough
to call free elections and install a truly democratic government, not a very original statement for a general taking over
a nation by revolution. As it turned out, this "long enough"
was to last almost eight years, but, unlike other countries beset
with dictatorships, the promised day did eventually come to
Peru without the need of a new revolution.

Meanwhile, Odría made it clear that his regime had no
desire to see the political game go on in the country. "Up to
now," he declared, "outrages have been perpetrated in the
name of freedom and democracy." And, Odría added,
"Party politics poison the hearts of people and sicken their
minds."

The military revolution was designed to end the chaos that
was brought to Peru through the mishandling of urgent social
problems, and Odría was fully aware that his "change of
methods and men" had to take the social problem into con-
sideration.

Consequently, he made a point of declaring in his first
speech as president that "the Government will attend to the
needs of the working class and it will call a national labor
congress to approve labor legislation." Addressing himself to
his conservative allies of the moment, he said he was neither
a leftist nor a rightist, and emphasized that his chief goal was
to "adopt a plan of effective social justice."

Since he had to rely on the armed forces as the mainstay
of his regime, he immediately promised that "military construction and the acquisition of matériel will be carried out
as to assure the Army's efficiency."

Touching upon another vital Peruvian problem, that of

food shortages, he announced that "agriculture will receive facilities to increase production."

In the political field the Revolution of Restoration was committed to "re-establish order, call elections, and eliminate the regime which spawned robbery and crime." To carry out these aims Odría issued decrees on November 2 confirming the outlawing of APRA as a political party and, additionally, banning the Communist Party. On November 4 Odría extended for thirty more days the state of siege that had prevailed in Peru since the Callao uprising early in October.

Next, the military regime, in its obsession with APRA, ordered wholesale arrests of persons identified with the party. By November 14 Odría was able to announce that at least one thousand Apristas were in prison. The previous day his policemen had arrested Ramón Prialé, APRA's secretary-general, and charged him with possession of documents proving that the party had planned a campaign of terrorism. Hundreds of other Apristas fled the country while helmeted soldiers occupied the Casas de Pueblo (the Houses of People) the name given to APRA headquarters. But the biggest fish of all, APRA's founder, Víctor Raúl Haya de la Torre, was still at large. Odría never had the satisfaction of catching him and, instead, Haya's fate was to become one of Latin America's great causes célèbres.

Alongside arrests of APRA leaders and activists, the Military Junta ordered a purge of Apristas from government jobs no matter how high or low, from schools, universities, and labor unions. But Odría's repression failed to smash APRA: it went underground for the duration of his dictatorship to emerge again in full force in 1956 and become the decisive factor in electing Peru's next president.

Meanwhile, Peru was facing a long period of authoritarian rule. Valid as may have been the excuses for the Arequipa revolution, the fact remained that democratic practices in the

nation had been interrupted. But in four weeks' time, bowing
to the realities of the situation, the United States recognized
the Odría regime. The recognition was based on a principle
embodied in Resolution Thirty-Five of the Act of Bogotá,
signed eight months earlier, establishing that ". . . diplomatic
relations with a government do not imply any judgment upon
the domestic policy of that government." To many Latin-
American liberals this principle loomed as the green light for
power-hungry generals. And two more South American military strong men were to benefit from it before long.

6

The first phase of Odría's dictatorship lasted for nineteen
months, until his "election" as constitutional president in July,
1950. It was a busy period of solidifying his power politically
and carrying out basic economic, social, and administrative
reforms.

In his first State of the Union message on July 27, 1949, he
could declare in all truth that "public order has been maintained without alteration throughout the country." He blamed
"the repeated subversive attempts of the extremist factions of
APRA" for the continued suspension of civil liberties in
Peru, although there is little evidence that the now illegal
party was actually engaged in any serious conspiring. But it
was a handy excuse for keeping tight controls over the nation
and for implanting his Internal Security Law of the Republic.
This law was a typical dictatorial catchall measure. But, at the
outset, Odría did not abuse it.

To keep alive the ghost of APRA's menace Odría went out
of his way to stress in his message that "the fundamental reason for the existence of the Revolutionary Government . . .
is the elimination of the sectarian menace which for more
than twenty years and through four political regimes has done

nothing but violate the law in every way to the detriment of all persons and institutions." Simultaneously, the government began issuing booklets and pamphlets, such as one titled *The Crimes of APRA* and another, *Truth About APRA—Aprism is Communism*. For years to come APRA was to be a convenient bogeyman for the regime and one that was good for plenty of political mileage.

On January 3, 1949, Haya de la Torre, the long-sought father of APRA, made his way to the Colombian embassy and the protection of political asylum. Faithful to Latin-American tradition, Colombia refused to turn him over to Peruvian police. With equal obstinacy Odría declined to issue a safe-conduct for Haya to leave the country for exile. The controversy, into which the International Court of Justice was dragged repeatedly, was to last for more than five years, while Haya lived in the embassy building, surrounded by trenches, troops, and armored cars. In August Peru broke relations with Cuba after two Aprista refugees fled from the Cuban embassy in Lima.

The Military Junta formalized its dictatorial rule on January 8, 1949, when it issued a decree vesting in itself all of the republic's executive and legislative powers. Odría had twelve military ministers who, with him, formed the Junta. On June 1 he accepted the resignation of the whole Junta but re-appointed most of his trusted friends. The principal victim of this move was Colonel Llosa, then Minister of Public Works, who was dropped from the regime while undergoing medical treatment in Washington. Llosa charged Odría with betrayal of the Arequipa principles, and while it is not entirely clear what had motivated his dismissal there are some indications that the President was suspicious of his minister's ambitions. Subsequently, Odría had to cope with two revolutionary attempts by his trusted cabinet friends.

On September 2, 1949, less than a year after he captured

power, Odría felt sufficiently secure of his position to order nationwide registration of voters and promised to announce the date of general elections within thirty days. But to combine the requirements of democracy with his desire for remaining in office—he felt he was doing a fine administrative job, which he actually was, and believed that he should be allowed to continue it—took much more time. Thus it was not until January 5, 1950, that he issued the decree calling elections for president, two vice-presidents, and a congress for July 2 of that year.

The following day a coalition of six suddenly-formed parties proclaimed Odría as their candidate. Politicians were falling all over one another in their haste to be the first to nominate the General of Division. He had the backing of powerful landowning and business and industrial interests; of middle-of-the-road groups; of most of the press including even the daily *La Prensa*, now owned by Pedro Beltrán, a wealthy landowner of extremely liberal views. Beltrán and Odría quarreled later over the General's dictatorial tendencies and in 1956 the publisher was imprisoned by his onetime friend. Odría's efficient and businesslike administration, plus his social welfare policies, earned him widespread support, and within days of his nomination Lima's weekly magazine *1950* predicted a "walk-over" victory for the General. No new impressive political figures or parties had appeared on the scene and, with APRA in the underground, Odría faced no serious opposition.

The regime tolerated reasonable freedom of the press, and *1950* was able to declare in the same issue that the Internal Security Law must be abrogated at once if there was to be a "clean electoral process." But this was one concession that Odría was not prepared to make and thus the country readied itself for elections in a climate that was far from free.

In the middle of May a movement calling itself the Democratic National League chose a little-known sixty-five-year-old general named Ernesto A. Montagne as its candidate to oppose Odría. His running mate was a seventy-five-year-old Arequipa physician, Dr. Juan Francisco Mostajo. The Socialist Party nominated one Luciano Castillo.

Montagne and Mostajo were complete political nonentities and it was unlikely they could defeat Odría. But the President apparently lost his nerve and decided that the two elderly gentlemen were Aprista figureheads. Rather than risk a possible electoral contest with APRA, and evidently not trusting his own popularity, Odría resolved to eliminate them from the race. Consequently, the Supreme Council of Elections, a body appointed by Odría and including two of his relatives, refused to register Montagne's candidacy on the transparent ground that he had been nominated in a fraudulent manner.

For the balance of the electoral campaign, if it could be called that, Odría borrowed freely from the tactics of his fellow dictators. On May 31 he left the presidency so that he could run for office as a private citizen. General Noriega, Peru's vice-president and war minister, became acting president in what was evidently a game of musical chairs. When protests arose over the liquidation of the Montagne ticket, Odría answered primly that he was a private citizen and that, anyway, the Council of Elections was an independent body. There could be no question of Dr. Bustamante being right in charging from exile that Odría was using all the tools of government in his campaign for election. Late in May, a week before Odría "resigned," a severe earthquake had shaken the Andean city of Cuzco. Without wasting any time the President had rushed uphill to take charge personally of relief operations, in a gesture somewhat reminiscent of Perón and the San Juan earthquake. The only difference was that Odría concentrated only on political and not financial profits.

The Cuzco expedition, by the way, was probably the only act on Odría's part that could be described as electoral demagoguery. As far back as November, 1949, when he abolished the remaining government subsidies on food and other essential imports and inaugurated a system of free economy in Peru, Odría roundly condemned the previous regime's policies of artificially keeping down the cost of living in order to win "popularity" for the government. A man like Perón would not have missed a chance to restore subsidies on the eve of elections, without regard for the nation's economic health, if it could have brought him votes. There is no reason to think that Odría's social and labor policies were primarily motivated by electoral considerations.

On June 14 as the one-sided election campaign progressed in a desultory fashion, a bloody revolt against Odría broke out in Arequipa, the traditional breeding ground of Peruvian revolutions. It was led by the septagenarian, Dr. Mostajo, the frustrated vice-presidential candidate and one of Arequipa's most respected citizens. Armed mobs beat down the police and for a day Dr. Mostajo ruled the city as president of the Civilian Revolutionary Government organized by him to end "the tyranny of the Lima Military Junta." But the following day the army reconquered Arequipa and arrested Dr. Mostajo at the city hall. The death toll neared fifty.

The government accused Apristas and Communists of staging the rebellion. It also charged General Montagne with actual leadership of the conspiracy and arrested him at his Lima home. Hundreds of other arrests were made in the wake of the Arequipa movement including, surprisingly, Luis A. Flores, head of the fascistoid Revolutionary Union Party, which was said to have been implicated in the uprising.

Five days before the elections Montagne was released from prison to watch Odría calmly go through the motions of the voting farce. The regime said that eighty per cent of the voters—considerably less than ten per cent of the population were eligible to go to the polls—cast ballots for Odría. Those who opposed him abstained from voting for president and voted only for congressional candidates.

The one surprise in these lethargic elections was the victory, in a Lima Senate race, of an independent candidate who opposed the regime's hand-picked man. In voting for him the people had their only chance of expressing disapproval of Odría's dictatorial tactics.

On July 24 the National Electoral Board duly proclaimed Odría elected, and four days later he was sworn in for a six-year term as Peru's constitutional president. Having thus created an illusion of democracy, Odría named a cabinet of six military and six civilians—his friends General Noriega and Admiral Saldia retained their old jobs—and went back to his administrative endeavors. This was what interested him most.

7

If Odría's political behavior may have left much to be desired, his administrative record was impressive. In the relatively short span of time between his revolution in October, 1949, and his election in July, 1950, he put Peru back on its feet economically and launched far-reaching programs in most fields of government.

His approach to economic problems was many-pronged. Convinced that the tight price and foreign exchange controls imposed by preceding regimes were "strangling the vital forces of national economy," Odría's first concern was to free it. He went gradually about relaxing these controls, eliminating price subsidies one by one, and exempting exporters from the obligation of selling a portion of their foreign earnings to the government at a fixed low rate. That obligation had kept artificially high the price of Peruvian export commodities and prevented them from competing advantageously in the world market. It had been, however, a necessary tem-

porary measure, because upon assuming power in 1948 Odría
found only 270,000 dollars and 880,000 pounds sterling in the
nation's treasury while Peru's outstanding commitments stood
at $32,000,000.

An artificially low exchange rate discouraged foreign investments, and Odría believed that they were essential for the
country's development. The fact that the dollar cost almost
four times as many sols on the free market as in the official
bank encouraged favoritism in the granting of foreign exchange to importers and promoted graft and corruption in
government circles. In fact, manipulations of exchange rates
had been for years an instrument of patronage for many
Latin-American governments and it took considerable political courage for Odría to abolish them in Peru. The success
of this measure subsequently led Chile, Colombia, and Argentina to imitate Peru.

Odría ordered the complete freeing of the Peruvian economy through the elimination of all forms of control on
November 11, 1949, acting on advice of a mission of American economic consultants contracted by Odría and the International Monetary Fund. It was the cornerstone of all his ensuing economic policies, and, in characteristic fashion, Odría
took the trouble to explain it in painstaking detail in a lengthy
radio address to the nation.

Efficient methods of administration and "financial honesty"
inaugurated by the Military Junta allowed Odría to cut down
by twenty-five per cent the anticipated large budget deficit
for 1948. In 1949 the budget showed a surplus, even though
the government launched extensive public works. It concentrated on irrigation schemes designed to provide more arable
land in the parched desert and mountain regions and thus
began to alleviate the prevailing hunger in Peru's hinterland.
At the same time increased agricultural production cut down
the import requirements of foodstuffs. Roads across the

wilderness of jungles, mountains, and deserts also ranked high on the government's agenda, as did low-cost housing. A fund for education was established to begin combatting general illiteracy and the cultural isolation of the Indians who constitute the majority of Peru's population.

The balancing of the budget allowed Odría, late in 1949, to raise salaries of government employees by twenty per cent and to authorize private employers to do the same. Coming as it did a year after his conquest of power and almost a year before the elections, this wage rise move could hardly be regarded as a demagogic political act. A bid for labor support could be detected, however, in Odría's haste in creating a system of social security for workers nineteen days after the 1948 revolution. It was the first in a long series of social welfare steps undertaken by Odría and highlighted on May 1, 1950, with his promulgation of "Fundamental Rights of the Peruvian Worker." But, after all, he had to appear to be delivering plenty in the social field if he was to steal APRA's thunder of social justice.

On April 30, 1949, Odría established a new Ministry of Labor and Indian Affairs. The decrees on the subject of this ministry declared that one of the principles of his revolution was to "promote true people's welfare, restoring the natural rights of the vast working masses, and especially in the peasant sector that is the most numerous in the Republic." Odría then ordered the erection of a showy twelve-story building in Lima to house the Ministry of Labor, opening himself to charges that he was overdoing his dedication to labor problems.

By the end of 1949 Odría was in a position to report a "slow, stable advance toward increased prosperity through special benefits and increased production." Exports that had fallen alarmingly in past years were picking up rapidly, more food was being produced and more exportable cotton grown, new foreign investments attracted by political stability and Odría's policies of enticing capital to come to Peru were creating new employment, confidence in the national economy was being restored, the rhythm of inflation was slowing down. The government settled accounts with holders of old, defaulted Peruvian bonds and thus made Peru eligible for loans from the Export-Import Bank and the World Bank. The nation was moving toward recovery along a sound path.

8

In the six years of Odría's constitutional regime, between 1950 and 1956, Peru continued to prosper economically despite periodic ups and downs, but it also witnessed a toughening of his dictatorial rule. Odría did not relax it until the opening of the electoral campaign that was to produce his successor.

This tightening of the screws on the nation was Odría's way of reacting to a perceptibly growing political opposition. His cavalier treatment of General Montagne in the 1950 elections alienated many liberal groups that had earlier been willing to go along with the regime because they approved of its economic policies and because they had trusted Odría's promises of restoring a modicum of democratic rule following the Military Junta phase. The falling-out between Odría and Pedro Beltrán was a case in point, and shortly after the elections *La Prensa* had become as much of an opposition organ as the censorship would permit.

The ultraconservative moneyed people turned on Odría in resentment to his no-nonsense handling of economic and financial affairs, which was often to their detriment. And they did not look kindly upon his quiet but persistent efforts in the field of social welfare. Emphasizing his middle-of-the-road position—and his dislike of extremes of either left or right—Odría had said upon assuming power that he was "free of all commitments with persons or political parties." In 1955, when disillusioned politicians loudly criticized him, he made a point of repeating that statement and adding that "no one can call on me for compliance with any pact or agreement, for I have made none."

And specific individuals and groups had specific complaints. Thus the powerful industrial and business Miró Quesada family, owners of Lima's newspaper *El Comércio*, could not forgive Odría for allowing Haya de la Torre to leave Peru on a safe conduct in April, 1954, after more than five years in the Colombian embassy. Under pressure from the World Court and the Organization of American States, Odría had accepted in January, 1954, a recommendation from the Inter-American Peace Commission to negotiate Haya's fate with Colombia, and three months later APRA's founder regained his freedom. But the Miró Quesadas had not forgotten the 1935 murder by the Apristas of *El Comércio* publisher Antonio Miró Quesada, and from the moment of Haya's departure for Mexico this old Lima clan declared war on Odría.

Nationalistic groups, in many instances supported by business interests, fought Odría's plans for liberal mining and petroleum legislation designed to attract new foreign investments to Peru. Even the dictator's rubber-stamping Congress resisted for a time the passage of a new petroleum law which stipulated a fifty-fifty split of profits between the government and the foreign oil companies. There was much sentiment in Congress in favor of nationalizing the country's oil resources —the emotional feeling about oil that has always prevailed throughout Latin America also exists in Peru—and specific opposition to the signing of a contract for explorations in the vast Sechura desert in the north. This was that same contract that President Bustamante and APRA had unsuccessfully tried to push through before the 1948 revolution. Odría be-

came convinced that to open Sechura to intensive exploration
by foreign companies was essential if Peru was to remain self-
sufficient in petroleum, as the old fields around Talara were
fast drying up.

Calling a special session of Congress in November, 1951,
Odría finally forced approval of the Sechura contract and the
new petroleum law, and was able to sign them in March,
1952. However, the irony of fate made all this useless: after
spending over $30,000,000 in Sechura, the foreign oil com-
panies abandoned the project, unable to strike petroleum.

While the President thus faced opposition and criticism on
such clearly defined issues, human nature simultaneously intervened to encourage resistance to him. As the grave national
emergency of the post-revolutionary days vanished in the
flush of prosperity that Odría helped bring to Peru, politicians
and people at large began to find more and more fault with
his regime. The natural political restlessness of Latin Americans was reasserting itself.

By mid-1952 the nation was free of the old scourge of unemployment. Agricultural production had risen by twenty-
five per cent and mineral output by twenty. Exports to the
United States ran fifty per cent higher in 1951 than the year
before. The Peruvian sol had stabilized itself at a level twenty-
five per cent higher than the collapsing 1948 rate. The Export-
Import Bank and the World Bank had just approved $60,000,-
000 in loans to Peru for irrigation schemes, agriculture, and
modernization of ports. Two ambitious Five-Year Plans, one
for irrigation and one for an inland highway system, were
launched by the government.

Lima, ancient capital of Spanish viceroys, was a mirror of
the new prosperity. Two new banks were organized to participate in the increasing economic activity. Lovely residential
suburbs spread toward the Pacific Ocean with comfortable
modern homes of the nouveau riche and middle-class bread-

winners alike. Of course, age-old misery had not been eradicated, low-cost housing was slow in coming, and in the dark sands of the desert surrounding Lima the poor still lived in squatterlike *bidonvilles*. In October, 1952, Odría further liberalized his labor policies, authorizing strikes.

Late in 1953 Odría inaugurated his first major irrigation and reclamation project on Quiroz River. Irrigating 230,000 arid acres in Piura Department, the project cost $10,000,000 and was completed in thirty months. When the end of the Korean War had forced a dangerous slump in world prices of commodities, Odría reacted wisely by cutting the government budget, halting nonessential public works, and raising taxes. Thus the country weathered the economic difficulties of that period without serious injury to continued prosperity. All in all, Peruvians were doing so well that they could afford to become tired of the political dictatorship.

In August, 1952, Odría had his first cabinet crisis. Reorganizing the government he made General Noriega premier and the strong man of the regime. Faithful Admiral Saldia remained in the cabinet. Political peace prevailed throughout 1953, but the following year brought complications to Odría. Haya de la Torre's release set off a storm of protest, and the dictator reached for the Communist Party as a convenient means of distracting attention. Although he had quietly played with the Communists since 1950 and allowed them to win a certain amount of control in the labor unions, he now struck at them. At the end of April, 1954, a military court sentenced to prison terms, ranging up to seven years, thirty-nine labor leaders, mostly Communists, for directing strikes the year before. Two top Communist Party leaders went to prison.

Less than four months later the political crisis was in full swing. General Noriega had pressed for a cabinet reshuffle, and taking advantage of it attempted a coup d'état to oust Odría. The President had no trouble quelling the rebellion, and his old friend Noriega was packed off aboard the frigate *Castilla* and taken to exile in San Francisco, California. In December a new conspiracy was unveiled by the government. Carlos Miró Quesada Laos, a member of the great Lima family that was now fighting Odría with all the means at its disposal, was arrested on Christmas Day on charges of plotting, and exiled to Chile. Edmundo Noriega, a congressman and a brother of General Noriega, was exiled to Argentina.

The year 1955 dawned with more political troubles. Another antiregime plot was said to have been crushed in January and still another one in March. Faced with so many forms of opposition, Odría let his police act sternly against one and all. Alejandro Esparza, civilian Minister of Government and Police, invoked repeatedly the Internal Security Law for mass arrests and other acts of repression. Public demonstrations were broken up with violence. The use of police tank trucks to throw jets of pink-dyed water on demonstrators became commonplace. And the harder Odría fought against the spreading opposition, the deeper ran sentiment against him.

9

During his entire period as dictator and president General Odría enjoyed the full support of the United States. There could be no valid criticism of Washington's economic aid to his regime; it was one of the few governments in Latin America practicing sound economic and development policies and it deserved help, for the sake of the people and the country as a whole rather than for the aggrandizement of its dictator. Odría's friendly attitude toward United States investors made him especially popular in Washington, which, under the Eisenhower administration, based its Latin-American policies on the premise that private capital should play the principal role in the development of backward countries. But Peru, its credit vastly improved by Odría, received several important project loans from the Export-Import Bank; and sizable grants of foodstuffs to cope with the disastrous droughts in the Andes and the south of Peru were made regularly. To help Peru to solve its basic agricultural and social problems, Point Four established one of its largest Latin-American programs in that country.

But there was much less justification for Washington's other policies in Peru. In fact, it was the old story of cordiality with dictators as a questionable political expediency. Thus on June 26, 1953, Ambassador Harold Tittman, acting on President Eisenhower's instructions, decorated Odría with the United States Legion of Merit in the rank of commander. Two weeks later Dr. Milton Eisenhower, touring South America on a good-will trip that turned out to be a bid for friendship with dictators, was lavishly entertained by Odría in Lima. It was on that same tour that Dr. Eisenhower stopped in Buenos Aires for his whirlwind courtship of Perón.

Odría may have been a good president and a reasonably benevolent dictator, but he was in office as a result of a farcical election in which his opponents were intimidated or jailed. Despite his denials that a formal censorship existed in Peru the press was far from being free. Arbitrary arrests were frequent occurrences. It was not surprising, therefore, that liberal Peruvians were shocked to see the United States thus reward their dictator.

The Odría regime also received important military aid from Washington. Three destroyers were turned over to Peru in May, 1952, and, later, the Export-Import Bank in an unprecedented move lent Odría money to order the building of two submarines in the United States. Peru is still paying this debt, and Odría's successor inherited also huge bills for jet aircraft purchased in Britain. The General of Division argued that he needed modern armament because of the unresolved border dispute with Ecuador arising from the 1941 war, but the result was a baby armaments race in that part of South America. Ecuador ordered British jets right after Peru. Chile, which had defeated Peru in a war in 1871, now worried by the arming of its northern neighbor, also continued to spend money for arms. The truth was, of course, that none of these republics could afford heavy purchases of armaments.

A dictator must keep his army happy in order to stay in power—or, at least, this had been the tradition up to then— and Odría did not skimp on Peru's armed forces. Shortly before the end of his government he ordered the erection of a radar fence near the Ecuadorean border. It was never built, but it was politically convenient to keep alive the threat of an Ecuadorean attack. For their part, succeeding Ecuadorean governments never tired of speaking of the Peruvian threat. Thus, for reasons of domestic politics in both countries as much as anything else, no serious progress had been made in all those years to settle their frontier controversy. It had gone on unresolved for fifteen years and was still not decided when Odría departed in 1956.

One possible reason for the United States to court Odría was his determined opposition to Perón's efforts to spread his influence throughout the continent. Although Washington did seek to maintain good relations with Perón, it took a dim view of his political expansion plans and quietly encouraged countermeasures. After all, Perón's ideas of continental hegemony were directed against United States leadership in the Americas. It may have been a coincidence that Odría was decorated with the Legion of Merit less than two months before his trip to Brazil in 1953, a trip widely advertised as Peru's answer to the Economic Union pact Perón had signed with Chile earlier that year. In Rio de Janeiro the two governments declared they opposed the formation of any continental blocs, and press commentaries spoke of the creation of an anti-Perón

Rio-Lima axis. Later, in 1955, Odría and Venezuela's Pérez Jiménez exchanged state visits, setting off talk of a Lima-Caracas alliance of military dictators. But it was never seriously followed up. In the end all these dictatorial ambitions for regional power vanished in mere conversations.

10

Early in 1955, when his dictatorship was at its toughest stage, General Odría began hinting that he intended to step down at the end of his constitutional term in July, 1956. These vague promises met with considerable skepticism, because Latin-American dictators do not customarily give up when they do not have to, and because Odría's performance in the 1950 elections suggested that the General had been infected by the virus of power. In mid-April, however, Odría put his commitment on public record by declaring in a New York *Times* interview that, indeed, he would not seek re-election in 1956. He said that he was tired of being president and, besides, he pointed out, the constitution banned a second term.

On July 28 Odría went before Congress to announce in his annual message that within a year he would be turning the presidential office over to his elected successor. He was visibly annoyed by widespread doubts "as to the honesty of my intentions" and said there was no justification for them, "because I have not encouraged at any time a proposal for re-election or the prolongation of my mandate." This statement was fully accurate and, just to make sure that he was well understood, Odría added: "My greatest satisfaction, I declare emphatically, will be to deliver the Executive Power to my successor on the twenty-eighth of July, 1956, and this I will do."

He told Congress that the work of his regime was "virtually completed in its totality with rewarding achievements that

justify a precept of my Government: 'Deeds, not words.' "
With it Odría unrolled the long record of his accomplishments and remarked that "Peru only needs ten or fifteen years
of internal peace and of the maintenance of this same rate of
labor, of order and progress, to arrive at its objectives and
stand in a position of equality with any of the most advanced
countries of America."

Rare is the dictator who will admit that his work is all done,
that he is no longer needed, and that his country is ready for
the restoration of democracy. Odría did achieve this unique
distinction, and his administrative accomplishments were indeed impressive.

In the political field he had brought internal peace, although
the price was a measure of denial of liberty. Now he stood
ready to return it to his nation. Elections were to be free and
untrammeled and, for the first time in Peruvian history,
women were given the right to vote.

According to his figures—and they were not seriously disputed—the national income had risen from about 7,120,000,-
000 sols in 1948 to 18,900,000,000 sols in 1954, almost tripling
in six years. Exports rose from $162,000,000 in 1948 to $248,-
000,000 in 1954. Mineral production, the mainstay of Peru's
economy, more than doubled, largely in the wake of substantial new foreign investments in copper mines. Government
revenues tripled.

In his endeavor to develop the country, Odría had built
about three thousand miles of new roads, many of them
through jungles, and improved three thousand miles of old
roads. Seventeen tunnels and eighty-nine large bridges had
been added to the highway network. Irrigation projects had
placed thirty-one thousand hectares of desert land under cul-
tivation, and projects under way when Odría retired from
government covered 130,000 hectares. The big San Lorenzo

dam in Piura Department provided a water reserve of 250,-000,000 cubic meters.

In six years the Odría regime had constructed twenty-seven large Central School Units, five teachers' schools, and two military colleges. Primary-school enrollment had jumped from 874,753 children in 1948 to 1,318,000 in 1955. In the neglected Indian-inhabited jungle and highland areas the government had built forty-four Peasant School Centers, thirty-two bilingual schools for Quechua-speaking children, and seventy-one prevocational rural schools. It was an important step toward the still-faraway goal of Indian integration in modern Peru. In the field of health Peru had gained forty new hospitals and made a major advance in the war against malaria.

To stimulate private industry the government had established a steel mill in Chimbote on the desert shores of the Pacific. It had built a deep-sea terminal, an industrial town, and a railroad to the iron mines of Marcona. Subsequently, United States companies invested more than $200,000,000 to develop Marcona iron.

But Odría's assurances that his government record was making it possible for him to withdraw from politics and that he really meant to keep his word were still doubted by cynics. On September 9, 1955, he felt it necessary to address another long message to the nation, declaring that "I have sufficiently demonstrated my sincerity . . . I, therefore, have the right to expect to be believed."

He reminded his listeners that the constitution prevented his re-election and that in seeking it he would be betraying the principles of the 1948 revolution. The rebellion, he said, had been designed to "re-establish . . . our democracy." But, Odría said, the programs of the revolutionary governments should be maintained to continue Peru's progress. Then he recommended that political parties be formed and that they select a joint presidential candidate, "an honest man capable of directing the destinies of the nation."

But this was too much to ask of a nation that had been promised the end of a long dictatorship and was anxious to practice democracy again without restrictions or impositions. It soon became clear that the emerging political parties would never agree on a "unity" candidate and that the election would be a hard-fought contest. By the end of 1955 Odría began relaxing his dictatorial controls. Freedom of speech was slowly returning, newspapers could say almost anything they wanted. But the President refused to abrogate his Internal Security Law or declare a full amnesty. His concession, instead, was to fire early in 1956 his Minister of Government and Police, one of Peru's most hated men. Esparza at once left Peru.

In February, 1956, as the nation was moving toward the elections, General Marcial Merinos, who once held a cabinet post in Odría's government, rose in rebellion in the jungle port of Iquitos on the Amazon River. The motives of this uprising were obscure, but in Lima many persons hailed it as a symbol of Peru's liberation. Odría allowed himself to lose his head to the point of declaring a state of siege and re-imposing all the trappings of dictatorship. Many arrests were made, including the detention of Pedro Beltrán, publisher of *La Prensa*, who was kept for nearly three weeks at the island prison of El Frontón.

The Iquitos revolt collapsed in a few days, largely because it made so little sense. Most of the political prisoners were released and Peru, somewhat shaken, returned to its electoral preparations. But it sighed with relief; the skeptics had been certain that the Merinos rebellion would be used by Odría as an excuse for calling off the elections and postponing indefinitely the return to democracy.

After a few desultory attempts to produce a "unity" candidate politicians turned to the serious task of nominating presidential contenders. A young architect, Fernando Belaunde Terry, was the first to jump into the ring, with the support of liberal and leftist forces, students, and young professional people. Odría sponsored Hernándo de Lavalle, a corporation lawyer and director of many companies. Manuel Prado y Ugarteche, who was Peru's president between 1939 and 1945, came out of retirement in Paris to announce his candidacy.

It did not take long for all the politicians, including Odría, to realize that it was the long-proscribed APRA that held the balance of power in Peru. At once the candidates and their managers began to court the Apristas. Although Odría would not proclaim an amnesty he quietly released hundreds of Apristas from prison and allowed others to return from exile in a bid for votes for Lavalle. Simultaneously, Prado's emissaries went into conferences with Ramón Prialé, APRA's secretary-general, who in a few days was transformed from a political prisoner into one of Peru's key political figures. Belaunde never seriously sought APRA's support, knowing that as a leftist candidate he was not eligible for backing by a rival group.

In the end APRA threw its votes behind Prado in a dramatic, last-minute decision following a secret conference between him and Prialé. On June 17, 1956, Prado and APRA defeated Belaunde. Lavalle never had a chance despite all the campaign assistance he had received from the Odría regime.

General Odría was not in Peru to see the election and with it the culmination of his revolutionary regime. Thirty-six hours before Peruvians went to the polls he flew into the night on a stretcher aboard a chartered airliner to Washington where his broken hip was to be treated. Only a few friends gathered at the darkened Limatambo airport to bid him farewell. And on July 28, 1956, General Juan Mendoza, Odría's premier, handed the sash of presidential office to Manuel Prado.

Chapter Six

GUSTAVO ROJAS PINILLA
OF COLOMBIA

1

When Lieutenant General Gustavo Rojas Pinilla was thrown out of power on May 10, 1957, Colombia witnessed not only the end of his confused and inept four-year dictatorship but also of a decade of blood-drenched political folly. For this reason, the regime of this vain, pompous, and often irrational general must be seen as an almost accidental outgrowth of the events that preceded him on the Colombian scene rather than as an enterprise of his own creation. In a larger sense, Rojas was the victim of circumstances and later of ambitions uncontrollably arising amidst upheavals that dwarfed him as a personality in his own right.

Rojas' rule, particularly during his first two years, was incomparably less oppressive or harmful than the government of President Laureano Gómez, whom he ousted in a deliriously applauded coup d'état in 1953. It was Gómez, a man craving for a degree of power more absolute than anything ever known in Colombia, who plunged the country into a nightmarish dictatorship and a terrible civil war. The actions of Rojas' predecessor and other earlier happenings were a suitable prelude for the ultimate explosion.

Colombia was gasping for breath after years of civil war and General Rojas was greeted as a savior. The warring Conservative and Liberal parties joined in pledging him their support, and within two days Gómez' own legislature legalized his coup. Rojas was expected to bring peace, prosperity, and even remedies for Colombia's desperate social problems that still lurk—and perhaps more so in the present postdictatorial period than ever before—as the greatest danger to the nation's long-range stability. This obviously was a big order, even for a big man. But Rojas lost little time in demonstrating conclusively that he was a man of small moral, political, and even administrative stature.

A comparison between Rojas and Peru's General Odría is inevitable at this point. Odría took over Peru at the height of a conflict that, different as it was in scope and origins from Colombia's difficulties, was essentially as dangerous. As Rojas was to do five years later, Odría brought the prestige of the armed forces to the task of pacification. After accomplishing it, he succeeded in giving Peru an efficient, reasonably honest, and fairly progressive economic and social administration. He did rig an election to extend his time in office, but when the country was ripe for it he stepped down from the presidency. It was an act of a statesman and an act of faith in his own countrymen.

Rojas, on the other hand, was incapable of either act. He was a man who did not know when to quit, and in short order he downgraded himself from an exalted status of national savior to the pitiful status of a power-hungry narcissist enjoying the initial advantage that his "Government of the Armed

Forces" had not been tainted with political suspicions, unlike
Odría's regime in Peru. In Colombia, the army has been traditionally neutral in politics but Rojas thoughtlessly transformed the military into a political instrument. The Military
Junta that replaced him in 1957 restored the army to its normal role when, a year later, it officiated at the inauguration of
a civilian president.

When his first term expired a year or so after his rebellion
—he was legally serving out Gómez' unexpired term—Rojas
prevailed upon the legislators to violate the constitution for
the purpose of re-electing him for a full four-year period. The
continuing violence in Colombia's backlands was the excuse
for this step. Colombians blinked uncomfortably, but swal-
lowed the imposition for the hope of peace. They were still
convinced that Rojas was right in insisting that a return to
normal democratic practices would only encourage the bloody
rivalry between the Liberals and Conservatives.

For the next two years Rojas tightened his dictatorship—
though it never reached the extreme measures of the Gómez
rule or approached the excesses of other Latin-American dictatorships—and, invariably, the justification was his anxiety
for maintaining public peace. He never lifted the state of
siege in effect since 1949. By early 1955 it had become obvious to anyone who cared to look that Rojas fully intended
to stay in power even past the expiration of his second term
in 1958. He had established severe press censorship and created a propaganda office for the propagation of his personality cult. Opposition newspapers were closed or forced out
of business. Instead of pacifying the countryside his troops
often engaged in senseless acts of retaliation that fomented violence instead of curbing it.

Whereas the purpose of his 1953 anti-Gómez coup was to
force a moratorium on the murderous byplay of political
parties—and he did prevent both the Liberals and the Con-

servatives from functioning as party entities—Rojas eventually attempted to form a party of his own, an amorphous group known as the Third Force, with vague designs of fostering social justice. Much as Colombia needed, and needs, social justice Rojas' efforts were a pale imitation of Perón's Justicialismo, aided and abetted by Argentine embassy labor attachés. But the Roman Catholic Church, a great power in Colombia, killed the Third Force idea before it seriously got off the ground, and Rojas turned for political support to a splinter group of the Conservative Party.

The Rojas regime was studded with incidents of political brutality, aside from what was happening daily in the guerrilla wars of the hinterland, and there were arrests and killings. And, perhaps worst of all in the eyes of Colombians, who are less mindful of violence than of dishonesty in government, there was vast corruption and graft under Rojas. The General considerably enriched himself in office and the ugly details of his dealings were brought out during his trial before Congress in 1958 and 1959. His friends and immediate relatives did even better. The military had become a pampered and privileged class.

With all this Rojas did not even have the redeeming feature of administering the country well. He was rich in plans but poor in accomplishments. Although coffee prices, Colombia's main source of income, soared during the first three years of his regime, Rojas squandered these revenues and left the country deeply in debt.

As late as the summer of 1956 Colombians were universally opposed to him but they were still willing to let the president serve out his term, provided he would allow the holding of free elections in 1958. Despite everything Rojas' government still appeared to be preferable to a revolution and the dreaded return to chaos and recrudescence of civil war. But Rojas' blinding appetite for power defeated him. Early in

1957 he set the stage for his immediate re-election for the 1958-1960 term and for the refashioning of Colombia into a fascist-type corporativist state. Now he had gone too far, and the nation reacted. Liberals and Conservatives joined forces for the first time in Colombia's history, and a succession of fast developing events in May, 1957, resulted in the revolution that deposed him.

The most significant fact about Rojas' dictatorship was, therefore, that it forced the union of the two parties, something unthinkable two years earlier. Despite all the blood that had been shed between them, it finally seemed better to forgive and forget than to go on serving as an excuse for dictatorships. Gómez' domination had been much worse than Rojas' regime, but its downfall failed to restore democracy. This only came in the wake of Rojas' ouster, and, consequently, his period in office, with its aftermath, looms as a truly important historical milestone for Colombia. And in an extraordinary turn of events, one that makes the observer catch his breath, it was old Gómez who emerged as one of the pillars of Colombia's return to democracy. His own time of tyranny inexplicably forgotten, he was acclaimed as the leader of the majority faction of the Conservative Party, and from exile in Spain he bombarded Rojas with charges of "tyranny" and "usurpation" delivered with colossal political nerve. But Laureano Gómez is a story in itself, a paradoxical study in power instincts and power flexibility.

More than anything else, then, the rule of Rojas Pinilla was a period of great disappointment and great disillusion. Yet, in the mysterious ways of politics and of human nature, it became transformed into the bridge that led to a return to maturity, responsibility, and democracy. It proved that Rojas had been wrong all along: that democracy could function in Colombia without the spilling of blood. And it also proved that, despite the tremendous social problem dividing Colombians, they could unite, from millionaire landowners to semi-starved workers, to fight for freedom.

But the re-establishment of political democracy has not yet alleviated the awful distortions of Colombia's social life. Neither the Liberals nor the Conservatives have shown any inclination to deal seriously with the central national fact —that the have-nots outnumber the haves by almost one hundred to one in what is one of Latin America's most dramatic social situations. If Colombia's new democratic government does not rapidly awaken to this truth the forces that have acted so constructively to help bring back political democracy may turn tomorrow to the destructive path of social strife. The terrible human explosion of Black Friday in 1948 that shook Bogotá after the murder of Jorge Eliecer Gaitán, one of the few popular leaders Colombia ever had, and indirectly set off the Liberal-Conservative civil war, could happen again in one form or another. And it is not accidental that communism is currently on its greatest upswing in Colombian history.

2

While Colombia thus began to reconstruct her democracy, repair her economy, and perhaps even come to grips with her social ills, Rojas' only and abiding interest was to prove that the country had not heard the last of him when it got rid of his dictatorship in 1957. He returned to Bogotá from Spanish exile in October, 1958, with the stated purpose of "defending his honor" in the charges of abuse of power and enrichment in office that were being brought against him by the Senate. But, as it developed very soon, his real intent was to recapture power. Early in December, as Death Brigades of his few remaining supporters moved surreptitiously into Bogotá from the provinces, the government of President Alberto Lleras

Camargo discovered the conspiracy. The plot called for murdering Dr. Lleras and the key political leaders and reinstating Rojas' dictatorship. It was fully in character with his romantically macabre turn of mind—a Colombian psychiatrist described the ex-dictator as an extremely dangerous "criminal psychopath"—and in tune with his earlier threats that "my enemies will hang from Bogotá's lampposts." In May of the same year, Dr. Lleras and four members of the ruling military junta were briefly kidnaped by a military police unit which brought off an unsuccessful coup inspired by Rojas from abroad.

In practical terms neither the May nor the December plots amounted to much. After the December affair Rojas was arrested, held briefly aboard a navy frigate, and brought back to Bogotá to face the Senate trial and with it the latest of the many humiliations that had piled upon him since his ouster from government eighteen months earlier. But all these incidents—and his behavior before the Senate not being the least of them—shed light on his curiously twisted personality.

Without question vanity was the underlying trait of his character, vanity so immense as to ignore the most obvious reality. Rojas' thirst for power, as illustrated by his foolish, premature re-election scheme in 1957 and his conspiracies in 1958, was part of this vanity complex. After he seized power in 1953 Colombians greeted him as the Second Liberator and Rojas convinced himself that he was indeed the reincarnation of Simón Bolívar. His vanity, therefore, took the form of firmly believing that he was the only man capable of governing the nation. While such a belief is not a particularly novel thought among dictators of all ages and countries, it was based upon virtually nothing in Rojas' case. Both Perón and Vargas commanded the loyalty and the support of vast masses before and after their downfall, but Rojistas were a tiny minority in Colombia.

The shouts and cheers of forty thousand Bogotános who hailed his 1953 coup d'état had long since died down or turned into derisive slogans. But they still rang gloriously in Rojas' ears three years later as he sat in his office and proudly confided to this writer that a survey had revealed that "ninety-three per cent of Colombians love me." Outside San Carlos Palace that day the speculation was about the date of Rojas' ouster. And the current political joke told the story of Rojas, heavily disguised, asking a citizen what he thought of the president. The man, the anecdote went, bolted all doors and windows, looked under the beds, then whispered into Rojas' ear: "I like him."

His vanity, when hurt, could take on murderous aspects. Late in January, 1956, Rojas' daughter Maria Eugenia, head of SENDAS, the social welfare organization aping Eva Perón's Foundation, was booed at the Bogotá bull ring. Alberto Lleras, then the symbol of anti-Rojas resistance, was cheered and the crowd took up the chant of *"Este, no—Otro, sí!"* ("This one, no—The other one, yes!"). The following Sunday, February 5, Rojas packed the Santamaria ring with hundreds of police agents who proceeded to shout pro-Rojas slogans. Those persons who did not join them were beaten and several were hurled into the street from the ring's bleacher seats. Others were shot. Estimates of this Bull Ring Massacre vary between eight and twenty-five persons killed, and scores of injured.

In the middle of 1955 Rojas closed *El Tiempo,* Bogotá's principal Liberal newspaper, after its managing editor cabled a Quito colleague that the President had not spoken the truth during a state visit to Ecuador when he described as accidental the death of two liberal provincial newspaper editors. This, incidentally, was the opening shot in his campaign against the opposition press. And then there was the story, related earlier in this book, of Rojas' reprisals against United States Ambassador Philip Bonsal for attending a luncheon in honor of a Conservative Party newspaper editor.

Three days before his fall Rojas went on radio and television to claim the full support of the armed forces in what he promised to be a battle to death against the erupting revolution. Even as he spoke, generals two blocks away were readying the plans for the junta that was to replace him. It is beyond doubt that Rojas did not understand what hit him when at dawn of May 10, 1957, military leaders called on him to demand his resignation. He insisted on delivering a speech, duly rebroadcast later in the day, in which he announced that as president he was voluntarily naming the junta. It was an innocent piece of ego-gratification, and the generals let him get away with it. And the next day in Bermuda Rojas blandly declared that his overthrow was nothing but the work of "a few priests," a rather understated reference to the fact that the top hierarchy of the Roman Catholic Church had been in the forefront of the revolution.

Unbelievable as it may sound, this statement was not just a bit of face-saving bravado. It expressed Rojas' deep conviction that he still had enormous following in Colombia. His return from exile grew out of his misconception, skillfully nurtured by a clique of friends who had nothing to lose and everything to gain, that Rojas could indeed reconquer power. The first cold shower came when Bogotá virtually ignored his presence; instead of cheers and a grateful nation rising in his defense, only cruel silence. Several weeks later, after Rojas haughtily refused to recognize the authority of the Senate to judge him, came the second blow. Soldiers with drawn guns marched him to a Senate hearing as if he were a common delinquent instead of rallying to him. Still, Rojas' vanity prevented him from accepting reality; two months did not elapse before his plot was uncovered.

Standing before his Senate judges early in 1959 Rojas

seemed to have realized finally that he was finished politically. "I am alone, defending myself against the whole nation," he told an interviewer. But the vanity did not vanish; now he regarded himself as a martyr and felt that he was being made responsible for all of Colombia's past difficulties. His conscience, he said, was tranquil. But he did admit that his personal fortune had grown as a result of gifts while in office and that he never paid income taxes or kept books on a cattle company that he owned with his family.

It was Rojas' greed for cattle and land and other forms of material wealth that turned the nation against him as much as anything else. It was one of the specific charges on which the Senate indicted him—and not on any general accusations for what had gone so terribly wrong with Colombia in the past decade or so. Evidence before the Senate indicated, among other things, that between 1953 and 1957 the holdings of Rojas and his family skyrocketed from 200,000 to 8,000,000 pesos, exclusive of his cattle company assets. At the prevailing rate of exchange the latter figure is equivalent to more than a million dollars and there are indications that, actually, his fortune was much larger. The Senate also charged that during his tenure in office Rojas had forced banks to lend him, his friends, and relatives the equivalent of $700,000 without collateral. An interesting sidelight is the fact that Rojas' finance minister after 1956 was president of Banco Popular, one of Colombia's main banks.

Rojas acquired a number of cattle ranches throughout Colombia, some by purchase at very low prices from owners who could not turn down the President's bids. Others were political presents. A story told in those days related the gift of a bull to Rojas. The President thanked the rancher, then remarked: "But a bull is no good without a cow." The man took the hint and presented Rojas with a cow, whereupon he was informed that "a bull and a cow are no good unless they have grass to feed on." The story concluded with Rojas going home with the deed for the whole ranch. After stories about his acquisitive instinct gained wide circulation in Colombia in 1956, Rojas made a radio speech in which he angrily denied everything about it.

One of Rojas' favorite retreats was his country house at Melgar at the edge of an air force airfield where he installed a helicopter pilots' school. He often strolled to the field and took off at the controls of his personal 'copter. Actually, flying helicopters was Rojas' favorite hobby and he employed a civilian United States pilot to fly with him. Football, boxing, and tennis were his other outdoor interests.

Rojas' vanity found expression in what he developed into a full-fledged cult of personality, rivaling and even exceeding that of Perón. He insisted on being called Jefe Supremo (Supreme Chief) and on formal occasions appeared in gala uniforms of a general or an admiral, although he never had anything to do with the navy. His portraits in army or naval uniform decorated all the government offices in Colombia. In time Rojas supplemented the portraits with busts of himself that he had the army place in central plazas of towns and villages. He often gave friends wrist watches with his effigy in color on the face.

Rojas had a mercurial disposition. He alternately smiled and joked or fell into fits of depression or irrational anger. Tense and nervous, he had a habit of striking his leg with a ruler as he talked to visitors in his immense office, equipped with white telephones every few yards. He was so unpredictable and politically naïve that his aides feared leaving him alone with foreign newsmen lest he make an unfortunate remark.

A tall, fairly handsome man, Rojas had brown eyes and brown hair. In later years—he was fifty-seven when he was deposed—his hairline began to recede. And on his return from exile the following year his hair had gray streaks and a stoop had replaced his former erect posture.

He was married to Señora Carola Correa Londono de Rojas, and was the father of two sons and a daughter. The best known of the family were Maria Eugenia, the daughter, and her husband, Samuel Moreno Díaz, a newspaper publisher and one of the most disliked men in Colombia. Moreno also was one of the most influential members of the palace clique, which took it upon itself to isolate Rojas as much as possible from outside influences—and from reality—and to feed his stupendous vanity.

3

Gustavo Rojas Pinilla was born on March 12, 1900, in the small town of Tunja in the central department of Boyacá. His father, Julio Rojas, was a fairly prosperous rancher and cattle raiser who often doubled as a guerrilla soldier in the civil wars that, starting when Colombia won her independence in 1819, plagued the country until the opening years of the twentieth century. A tradition of violence, militarism, and attachment to land and cattle was Rojas' first inheritance.

Rojas graduated at the age of fifteen from the Tunja high school and went on to study philosophy and engineering at the small Boyacá College. His father died in 1919, and there was not enough money to finance the education of all six children. Gustavo Rojas, the youngest of them, did the only thing left to him if he wanted to further his studies: he enrolled in the military academy. The circumstances of his entry in the career of arms and the military family background curiously resemble that of Manuel Odría in Peru.

In 1920 Rojas left the academy as an artillery second lieutenant. After four years in the army, he resigned his commission—some people claim he was cashiered because of a situation involving him and the regimental funds—and went to the United States. Living in Angola, Indiana, Rojas received a degree in civil engineering from Tri-State College. According to his official biography he earned his keep and tuition by working nights on an automobile assembly line.

Back in Colombia Rojas spent several years as a highway engineer with the Ministry of Public Works. In 1932, however, he decided to re-enter the army—the money incident, if true, had evidently been forgotten—and Rojas was named technical adviser to the National Ammunition Factory. Nothing spectacular, only quiet advancement based on his engineering training, marked his military career for the following twelve years. But in 1936 a fitness report signed by his commanding officer said that Major Rojas Pinilla's "business instincts carry him to the point of sordidness." The report was produced by the prosecution at Rojas' Senate trial in 1959.

His business instincts that were to flower so profitably in subsequent years did not seem to interfere, however, with the progress of his career. Besides, it was not altogether unusual for officers to do a little business on the side to help out with the meager army pay. By 1944, as a colonel, Rojas was appointed assistant director of the Superior War College, and the road to success lay open to him. A year later he was named Colombia's Director of Aeronautics, an important job in a country so dependent on air transportation, and in 1946 was promoted to brigadier general and given command of the army's First Brigade. From there on, his rise was impressive; he was a competent officer and had good friends in the Conservative Party, which was then running the country.

In 1948 Rojas was elevated to the rank of lieutenant general, the highest in the army, and sent to Cali, Colombia's second city, to command the Third Army Brigade. This assignment, in a sense, marked his entrance into politics and at a crucial moment in Colombian history.

Since the elections in 1946, Colombia was governed by a Conservative president, Dr. Mariano Ospina Pérez, for the first time in sixteen years. His victory over two rival candidates of a hopelessly split Liberal Party loomed as the kiss of death for the on-and-off attempts of the Liberals to bring Colombia some form of social justice and make a dent in the armor of feudalism that the nation had been wearing throughout most of its history.

For all practical purposes the Liberals and the Conservatives stood largely for the same things: the preservation of the status quo under which five per cent of the population held ninety-five per cent of Colombia's wealth. Both parties were run by foreign-educated landowners and later, industrialists and businessmen, and on the top level the leaders jointly formed what Colombians call the Class of Oligarchs. The Liberals were somewhat anticlerical and the Conservatives stood closer to the Church. On leadership level the Liberals were probably more open to progressive ideas. But on lower rungs of party hierarchy, Liberal chieftains in the towns and villages were merely party hacks, just like their Conservative opposite numbers. Party allegiance and membership was a matter of family tradition; there were Liberal villages and Conservative villages, the houses of Liberals were usually painted red and the houses of the Conservatives were usually painted blue. The access to patronage by the party in power was one of the principal elements in partisan life and partisan strife.

In the late 1930's Colombia thus offered the paradox of being one of the few Latin-American republics without a left-of-center party of importance despite tremendous social pressures stemming from the distortion in the nation's economic structure. She had the reputation of being one of the

hemisphere's most stable democracies, but this democracy was
a bit of an illusion; it was practiced at top level and had
virtually no grass roots. And in the absence of strong leftist
parties catering to the rural masses and to the emerging urban
proletariat, the bottled-up pressures were building. With the
two parties adopting a fairly reactionary posture and monopolizing the political allegiances of the people, these pressures could not be drained off in Colombia as they were in
Peru through the activities of APRA, in Venezuela through
the Democratic Action, in Chile and Argentina through their
radical parties, or in Brazil through the social-welfare policies
of the Vargas dictatorship. When workers rioted, army and
police beat them or shot them.

A few Colombians understood the dangers inherent in this
situation and sought to remedy it. Alfonso López Pumarejo,
the country's Liberal president between 1934 and 1938, made
a serious attempt to legislate a social revolution in Colombia.
So did Jorge Eliecer Gaitán, leader of the left wing of the
Liberal Party. But they both came under furious attacks from
so-called "moderate" Liberals and the Conservative Party.
Under Eduardo Santos, a moderate Liberal who served as
president from 1938 to 1942, the López-instigated social program slowed down to a crawl. And when López returned
for a second term in 1942, the joint opposition of reactionary
Liberals and of Conservatives led by Laureano Gómez made
the furtherance of meaningful social reform impossible.
López was attacked not only for his domestic policies but also
for his support of the United States and the Allies in World
War II. A faction of the Conservative Party, inspired by
Gómez and Guillermo Léon Valencia (who in 1957 emerged
as the standard-bearer of Colombian democracy opposing
Rojas for reelection as the joint Liberal-Conservative candidate), went as far as to form a pro-Nazi organization known
as Acción Nacional.

By 1945 the combined assault of his enemies, who did not stop at personal slander, forced López to resign. The last year of his term was served out by Alberto Lleras Camargo who provided nothing but a stopgap administration. Lleras made the mistake of setting the precedent for press censorship to defend the government from Conservative assaults, a step he came to regret bitterly a few years later.

In 1946 the Conservatives put forth Ospina Pérez, more moderate than fire-eating Laureano Gómez but a weak man. Gaitán was one of the Liberal candidates and Gabriel Turbay was the other. Between them they garnered more votes than Ospina, but the party split led the Conservatives to victory. Gaitán's defeat almost brought about a revolution by embittered Liberals who rioted in support of their candidate. But Gaitán succeeded in calming the passions—at least for the time being.

Ospina named a few Liberals to his cabinet, but he governed in the shadow of Gómez. And Gómez had no use for the Liberal Party. Followers of the two parties began clashing throughout the country, tensions rose again, and Ospina countered by throwing the police against the Liberals. Wholesale killings and burnings of homes hit the backlands. The seed of a full-scale civil war was born. And while Ospina was thus launching political warfare, social pressures again mounted as the people watched Gaitán's repeated failures to persuade the Liberal-controlled Congress to turn its attention to social problems.

In this rapidly deteriorating atmosphere Lieutenant General Gustavo Rojas found himself in Cali, a Liberal stronghold, commanding a brigade of the army pledged to support a Conservative government. Making no secret of his Conservative sympathies Rojas struck hard at the Liberals. In his zeal he was even credited with organizing criminal elements in the department of Valle into Conservative guerrilla units. These groups later gained fame as Pájaros Azules (Blue Birds), bandits fighting for Rojas during his dictatorship. Meanwhile, in Bogotá, a terrible explosion was in the making, an explosion that changed the course of Colombia's life for nearly a decade, and in the process propelled Rojas to power.

4

On April 9, 1948, Gaitán was shot on a Bogotá street by an unknown man. His death a few hours later set off a wave of violence, killings, arson, and looting unequaled in Colombian history. Hundreds died, thousands were injured, buildings and churches burned brightly, and the presidential palace suffered severe damages as maddened mobs hysterically and senselessly sought to avenge the murder of their hero and leader.

It is not known how Gaitán's murder was engineered, but the suspicion immediately fell upon Laureano Gómez. Taking no chances, the old Conservative chief fled the country, exiling himself in Spain, as the plant of his newspaper, *El Siglo*, was dynamited. Responsibility for the crime was never established, but in testimony at his 1959 Senate trial Rojas, who may have had some information at the time, accused Gómez of planning the murder of Gaitán, his archfoe.

The Ninth Inter-American Conference of Foreign Ministers was being held in Bogotá when Gaitán was assassinated. The parley was interrupted by the riots, but on the insistence of General George C. Marshall, United States Secretary of State, work was resumed within a day or two. General Marshall believed that the Bogotázo, as the violence following Gaitán's death came to be known, was the work of Communists and he argued that they should not be given the satisfaction of breaking up the conference.

While the Communists undoubtedly took advantage of the riots and while there is evidence that they had planned some disruptive action of their own, there is nothing to prove that they were directly responsible for the events of Black Friday, unless one accepts the charge that they had murdered Gaitán. The grief of the population was legitimate and their sense of loss was magnified by the incipient civil war in the Colombian hinterland, by the smoldering hate of underdog Liberals for the Conservatives, and by the deteriorating economic situation that brought new hunger and misery to the destitute masses. Thousands of refugees from the provinces, symbolizing the ravages of the erupting civil war and their age-old misery, filled Bogotá at the time of the crime. They joined with the Bogotános in venting their wrath on everything and everybody that appeared in their way. All in all, the Bogotázo was a dreadful sample of what a social revolution can be in a country like Colombia.

To keep his regime together President Ospina had no choice but to bring back the Liberals into his cabinet. At the same time Ospina took some modest steps in the direction of social improvement, but they hardly made a dent in the problem and passed virtually unnoticed. But early in 1949 Ospina abandoned all pretense of conciliation. Now army troops and policemen were openly applying tactics of violent repression against the Liberals. As the latter countered with violence of their own the civil war spread and casualties began to be counted in the thousands.

In April, 1949, the Liberal ministers resigned and Ospina named a new cabinet. Lieutenant General Rojas Pinilla was appointed Minister of Communications, thus becoming directly identified with a regime of oppression and dictatorship. In this sense he shares the blame with the Conservatives for the partisan warfare into which they plunged Colombia and for the advent of the civil war. His subsequent statements about the guilt of the two parties—which, of course, is beyond dispute—thus sound rather hollow.

Presently Ospina dissolved Congress, established tight press censorship, and imposed the state of siege that was to last for over eight years. These measures set the stage adequately for the return from Spain of Laureano Gómez—he landed, raising his shaking arm in the Falangist salute—and the announcement of his candidacy for president. The Liberals nominated Darío Echandía, but government persecution prevented them from waging a campaign. Meanwhile, Gómez' campaign under the protective wing of Ospina was reminiscent of Perón's 1946 campaign under the stewardship of President Farrell: the Liberal opposition was not allowed to hold meetings, troops coerced Liberal peasants into signing Conservative registration lists, the press was gagged, and violence swept the land.

Under the circumstances the Liberals threw in the sponge and withdrew Echandía. On November 27, 1949, Gómez was elected without opposition. Taking office on August 7, 1950, he implanted a dictatorship so severe as to make the Ospina regime a pleasant interlude by comparison. Roberto Urdaneta Arbeláez, a mild-looking disciple of Spanish Falangists, was named Minister of War, with the mission of stamping out "banditry." In practice he established a reign of terror in Colombia's interior which only added fuel to the raging flames of the civil war. Now the war was being conducted by well-organized guerrillas of the two parties, and by the army and police, usually on the Conservative side.

In other fields Gómez put into effect his fascist policies with equal determination. Favoring the wealthy classes he struck savagely at what there was of independent organized labor. He replaced free trade-unionism with management-inspired and government-controlled unions, and to keep it under one roof, created the Unión de Trabajadores Colombianos. A few years later Rojas tried to use the UTC for his own purposes.

But for the time being the General was away from Colombia and completely detached from the mischief being wrought by Gómez. Shortly after the start of the Korean War Rojas, as army chief of staff, began organizing the Colombian forces for service with the United Nations in the Far East. Colombia, by the way, was the only Latin-American country to contribute troops. In 1951 Rojas went to Korea, remaining for several months in the war zone. In 1952 he was appointed Colombia's representative on the Inter-American Defense Board in Washington.

Late that year he returned to Bogotá to take up his new duties as commander in chief of the armed forces, the highest military post in the republic. He found Urdaneta, the former war minister, in the job of acting president, since Gómez had suffered a heart attack and had to pull the strings from his bedside.

Gómez' current project was a constitutional reform that would allow him to be re-elected or, at least, to appoint his successor. It also provided for the establishment of a corporativist Senate on the fascist model, curtailing extensively the attributes of the House and vesting dictatorial powers in the president. The proposal raised protests from Liberals and Conservatives alike. In the Conservative camp Ospina Pérez the man who paved the way for the Gómez government of inquisition and violence, turned on his erstwhile friend and announced for the 1954 presidential nomination.

Early in 1953, as opposition against the reform combined with generalized revulsion against the wholesale killings in the unabating civil war, Ospina found considerable support within the armed forces. By mid-April the crisis was in full bloom. The pro-Gómez Conservative directorate hinted that the old man would seek re-election, and on April 19 Gómez cut short his convalescence and went on the air to defend his policies.

At this juncture of events he developed a strong suspicion that Rojas was plotting against him. Consequently he ordered him to fly to Germany on a vague official mission so that he could fire him in his absence. Rojas was already aboard the aircraft and ready to leave, showing an amazing ignorance of the situation, when at the last moment he was warned of Gómez' designs and decided to remain in the capital. For the next seven weeks the crisis continued unresolved. Gómez, still unable to push through his constitutional reform, finally set June 15 as the date for the first meeting of his handpicked Constituent Assembly.

Early in June the army received evidence that a Conservative leader was plotting the assassination of Rojas and several other officers. Rojas ordered the man's arrest, and despite pressure from Gómez refused to release him. On June 12 Gómez resumed the presidency of Colombia and demanded from the cabinet that Rojas be arrested. The ministers refused, resigned in a body, and Gómez himself issued the arrest order.

Unbelievably, Rojas was again aboard a plane, this time preparing to go to the United States. Again he was warned by friends that Gómez was out to fire him. Again he returned to his quarters to await developments. When the new war minister came to put him under arrest Rojas took matters in his own hands and, instead, arrested the minister. In the evening he sent tanks and troops into Bogotá's streets, placed Gómez under house arrest, and thus put an end to the Conservative dictatorship. Still hesitant and uncertain Rojas thereupon offered the presidency to Ospina, then to Urdaneta. When both men refused the perplexed General proclaimed himself Colombia's provisional president.

Chances are that Rojas was vastly surprised to find himself in the presidential chair on the morning of June 13, 1953. He had not actively planned or plotted Gómez' ouster and, in fact, had been pushed into it by the old man's behavior. But he was about to hear the excited cheers of Bogotá's crowds, and this was to change his entire outlook on life.

5

On this joyful thirteenth of June General Rojas stood on the balcony of San Carlos Palace, which still bore deep scars of the *Bogotázo,* and promised peace to the crowds below. "Let there be no more blood, no more depredations, no more fighting between the sons of Colombia," he said.

Flushed with happiness and excitement over the end of the Gómez dictatorship Colombians put their faith in Rojas, looking to him to restore peace to the country and return the lost freedom. Liberals and Conservatives alike closed their ranks behind him, and few rulers anywhere enjoyed the almost universal national support that Rojas Pinilla commanded in these first days of his government. To demonstrate its trust in him the Constituent Assembly, made up largely of Gómez appointees, within forty-eight hours voted Rojas constitutional president with a mandate to fill the balance of Gómez' term, expiring in 1954. For the law-conscious Colombians this act legalized the June 13 coup and removed whatever objections may have lingered after the ouster of the old president.

Rojas named a cabinet of ten civilians and three officers, thus allaying fears of a possible military junta. But Colombians who applauded the composition of the new government may have overlooked the appointment of Lucio Pabón Nuñez as war minister. Switching a few weeks later to the Ministry of Interior, this pudgy little man of fascist inclinations was to exercise a sinister influence on Rojas. In time he became the chief political theoretician of the regime, and it is believed that he pushed Rojas, a man without clear ideas of his own, into the morass of the new dictatorship. It was Pabón Nuñez who thought up the offensive against the free press, sold Rojas on attempts to form a political party, and masterminded the disastrous re-election scheme of 1957. Intellectually and politically Pabón Nuñez was no different from Gómez. His presence in the Rojas cabinet thus provided a line of continuity between the two regimes. In the end, Rojas fell because, under Pabón Nuñez' aegis, he was trying to do exactly what Gómez had tried so unsuccessfully.

But, in the meantime, all, or almost all, was sweetness and light in Colombia. Rojas released political prisoners, immediately abolished censorship on foreign correspondents, and soon proclaimed a general amnesty. Thousands of guerrillas, particularly Liberals, came down from their mountain hideouts and from the vastness of the llanos to turn in their weapons. Although the Rojas government had a Conservative tinge—all the civilian ministers were moderate, or Ospinista, Conservatives—the long persecuted Liberal party was given all the guarantees and busied itself with the reorganization of its shattered cadres.

Rojas, however, had not opened the floodgates of freedom in the country. He refused to lift the state of siege already four years in force, because violence in the provinces had not yet completely abated. Similarly, he declined to abolish internal press censorship once and for all, though he held enforcement in abeyance. Instead, he worked out a voluntary agreement with the publishers to refrain from printing material likely to revive political passions, particularly references to incidents of violence. This seemed reasonable enough.

For a year Colombians had little to complain about in Rojas. Seen as a whole, his leadership was uninspired, but the rhythm of the civil war had diminished considerably—and peace was still what counted most in Colombia. There remained a good deal of fighting in the hilly countryside—some of the fighters were simply bandits, others unreconstructed partisans of either party—but violence was far from the paroxysm of Gómez' days. A bizarre Communist "state" had established itself along the banks of Sumapaz River around the municipality of Viotá, and the authorities somehow could not dislodge it. Rojas himself often ran personal risks flying to guerrilla areas to talk to guerrilla leaders and persuade them to lay down arms. And frequently he was successful. While many restrictions were in force public liberties were not yet suffering too much interference.

Around that time, as he celebrated the first anniversary of his coup, Rojas had convinced himself that, indeed, he was Colombia's savior. The corollary was that he should go on being a savior. Although he had always been identified with Conservatives and his first cabinet was exclusively made up of Conservatives, he now concluded that all the ills of Colombia stemmed from the existence of political parties. He proclaimed that his Government of the Armed Forces was above parties and expressed the belief that it should stay that way for a long time to come. It must be said in all justice that both the Liberals and the Conservatives were providing justification for his position. Their own honeymoon was coming to an end, their rivalries were re-emerging, politicians and newspapers were spewing forth bitter accusations and recriminations. This was quickly reflected in the provinces, where men once again were reaching for guns and torches.

A propitious climate existed, therefore, for Rojas to take the first step to perpetuate himself in power. About July, 1954, the General declared that the situation had not improved sufficiently to warrant the holding of popular elections, as provided in the 1886 constitution, and he prevailed upon the Constituent Assembly to suspend a series of pertinent constitutional articles. Like all Latin-American dictators, Rojas wanted to disguise his arbitrarities in legal clothing.

The Assembly was that same body that Gómez had put to-

gether to revise the constitution, and it had been virtually inactive since Rojas took power. Now, however, he increased its
membership from sixty-one to ninety-nine, giving it just
enough lease on life to arrange for his re-election. Obediently,
the Assembly put aside the provisions calling for only one
consecutive presidential term and for universal suffrage in
presidential elections. With these obstacles out of the way, it
voted on August 3, 1954, to elect Rojas for the 1954-1958
period.

All this was clearly illegal and in violation of the constitution. But, concerned as they were about the maintenance of
peace, Colombians let Rojas get away with the infractions
they had denied to Gómez. In rationalizing this "election"
they stretched the interpretation of the electoral farce to the
point of asserting that the Assembly had the right to suspend
as many articles of the constitution as was required by the
situation. And, after all, the Assembly was technically a legal
body; it was its business if it did not mind being raped. And
until the end of the Rojas dictatorship even his most outspoken
enemies never challenged the legality of his government. The
method of packing the legislature in order to bend it to his
wishes and thus be free to alter the laws of the republic had
worked for Rojas this first time. He was to remember it on
future occasions.

Four days later, on August 7, 1954, Rojas was sworn in for
the new term and the scene was ready for the launching of a
full-bodied dictatorship.

6

The new authoritarian rule over Colombia materialized slowly,
gradually, even imperceptibly at times. Rojas was too uncertain of himself to implant his dictatorship in broad swift
strokes as a Perón might have done. Public opinion, pre-

occupied with the continuing Liberal-Conservative feud, the fighting in the backlands, and worsening inflation in the country, overlooked many of Rojas' measures that tended to cement his hold on power for an indefinite period. And there was always the excuse of keeping peace in the blood-covered nation. By the end of 1954 Colombians counted more than 100,000 dead in six years of civil war, thousands of burned homes, destroyed villages, and millions of pesos worth of ruined crops.

What Rojas was doing, however, was picking up where Laureano Gómez had left off in 1953—with certain personal variations. In his austere office in the Ministry of Interior, decorated with a crucifix and a portrait of Rojas, Lucio Pabón Nuñez was preparing for a Falangist system with overtones of Jesuit severity, also very much what Gómez had in mind. It sought to capitalize on Colombia's social problem and, in the best Mussolini or Franco tradition, it aimed at bringing labor unions under government control. The National Confederation of Workers, affiliated with Perón's ATLAS, was to be Rojas' instrument for capturing union allegiance. But where Gómez had fully identified himself with the class of owners and managers, Rojas brought a touch of Peronista demagoguery. He was to stand between the people and the oligarchs, furthering the cause of social justice.

As early as September, 1954, Rojas created the National Secretariat of Social Assistance, known by its Spanish initials of SENDAS, and named his young daughter, Maria Eugenia, to run this new enterprise that became part of his dictatorial trappings. SENDAS was evidently patterned after Fundación Eva Perón, although Maria Eugenia had neither the unlimited funds nor the showmanship talents of her Argentine mentor in order to construct a good imitation of Eva's Foundation. While SENDAS undoubtedly helped thousands of refugees, workers, and farmers—its stated objective—it was primarily conceived as a political tool for the Rojas dictatorship. The regime was thus developing along classical lines.

At the same time Rojas took several steps intended to alleviate the very real situation of social injustice in Colombia. He raised taxes—a move on behalf of the government's shaky finances as well as a social gesture—and issued some legislation protecting rural laborers. Maximum and minimum wages were decreed. The labor ministry engaged in programs of workers' training and betterment. But, seen as a whole, these policies had limited impact and scarcely touched on the fundamentals of the social problem. Therein lies one of the basic failures of Rojas' regime: coming into power with the unanimous support of the entire nation he had a chance of introducing a true, peaceful social revolution in Colombia. But he missed it. This revolution, if there was going to be one, became lost amidst his fumbling politickeering and fuzzy thinking.

The Supreme Chief did not even await his formal "re-election" to embark upon a series of arbitrary acts. Late in 1953 he ordered the release from prison of a number of Conservative bandit chiefs who were serving court-imposed sentences passed after the fall of Gómez. This was not comparable to the liberation of political prisoners held without trial and it could not be part of an amnesty. It was riding roughshod over established legal procedure and using troops to release prisoners over the protests of judges and wardens. The most notable case involved Leon Maria Lozano, the Condor, who was the most feared and bloodthirsty of Conservative guerrilla leaders. Rojas had befriended him while commanding the brigade in Cali, and until his death in 1957 Lozano led bands of Pájaros Azules in pro-Rojas raids of extermination of the regime's foes. The Condor incident became the basis for a charge of abuse of power against Rojas during his trial by the Senate in 1958 and 1959.

On June 10, 1954, or almost two months before his "re-election," Rojas' police shot and killed twelve Bogotá students demonstrating against the government's highhanded methods. First to sense the dictatorial dangers of the Rojas regime in 1954, the students later spearheaded the 1957 revolution against him.

His administration called itself the Government of Armed Forces, and Rojas saw to it that the armed forces lacked nothing while he was the boss. Thus, in 1955, the national budget assigned twenty per cent of all appropriations to them. It was only second to public works and exceeded manyfold the appropriations for agriculture, health, or education—all of them in dire need of funds. In 1956 $25,000,000 were spent on the military. Although coffee prices began to fall alarmingly early in 1955, dealing a painful blow to Colombia's foreign exchange resources, Rojas thought nothing of ordering in Sweden a flotilla of destroyers for his navy and in the United States and Canada a wing of F-86 Sabre-Jets for his air force. Special commissaries were established for the armed forces where officers and men could purchase imported goods at a fraction of the market price. In time, this system of privilege, which included permits for officers to import cars, became a severe drain on Colombia's dollar reserves.

In the field of economic development Rojas was not opposed to grand gestures. In 1954 he inaugurated the Paz del Rio steel mills, begun under the Gómez government and financed mostly by French capitalists. There was talk of building a jeep plant near Paz del Rio and Henry J. Kaiser came down to Bogotá to talk it over with Rojas. But throughout the Rojas regime the steel mill was an inefficient, money-losing enterprise, desperately seeking additional foreign financing to make it function better. Rojas also signed a law creating the Autonomous Regional Corporation of Cauca, an ambitious project designed to use the waters of Cauca River to irrigate the huge valley and generate power for Cali's industries. David E. Lilienthal was invited to co-ordinate the plans of this Colombian version of the Tennessee Valley Authority. But Rojas made no funds available for the Cauca project, and when he left the government three years later virtually nothing had been accomplished.

The World Bank was presented by Rojas in 1955 with a vast plan for economic development and asked to lend money for it. After detailed studies a bank mission cut Rojas' requests to the bone because it felt that most of the dictator's projects were either unworkable or completely out of tune with Colombia's economic realities.

As a president Rojas ran the country casually, often leaving major decisions to his ministers. His personal interest was in road building—he had been a highway engineer himself—and under his government Colombia did gain some vitally needed roads. He took the word of other people for most other things, and the results were often disastrous.

Cabinet meetings were often held at Rojas' country home in Melgar under conditions that at times reminded one of a Marx Brothers comedy. A foreign official who visited Melgar to address the cabinet on an economic subject related that in the middle of his explanation he became aware that a cabinet minister was lying on the floor shooting photographs of him. Orderlies walked in and out looking for army officers who were being called to the telephone. At one point, the official said, a bowl of fruit was thrust before his face while he was deep in his speech.

7

On August 3, 1955, Rojas Pinilla ordered the closing of Bogotá's Liberal newspaper *El Tiempo,* and this act marked the imposition of open dictatorship in Colombia. Until then only an erratic censorship had operated, but now Rojas was determined to prevent free newspapers from speaking freely.

The excuse for closing *El Tiempo* (it was owned by the former Liberal president of Colombia, Eduardo Santos) was its refusal to print daily for thirty days the retraction of a charge of lying made against Rojas by the paper's editor, Roberto Garcia Peña. While on a state visit to Ecuador, Rojas had said that the Liberal newspapers had exploited for political reasons the death of three men in an automobile accident. Cabling a Quito newspaper Garcia Peña asserted that the men were assassinated and added that "it is not possible that truth be deformed with the aid of your generous Ecuadorean hospitality."

If Rojas could perhaps justify his stand on *El Tiempo* on grounds that he had been insulted, the persecution of other independent newspapers that ensued was entirely gratuitous— except for the fact that the dictator could not stand criticism. Using Perón's techniques in dealing with the opposition press, Rojas began heavily fining newspapers for disrespect (the local version of the Peronista desacato law). Bogotá's *El Espectador*, another traditional Liberal daily, was the first target of this attack. Later, government accountants discovered that the newspaper and the Cano family who owned it were guilty of tax evasion. This was another favorite Perón trick, as was the denial of newsprint to opposition papers at a special low exchange that had always been available to the Colombian press. Declining the offer of civic groups to pay the fines through public subscription, *El Espectador* finally suspended publication. On August 10 police and troops dispersed violently a protest manifestation of Bogotá women.

The campaign against the press coincided with a series of steps Rojas was taking to assure his indefinite enjoyment of supreme power in Colombia. Already on December 31, 1954, he had announced in his New Year's message that he would not end the state of siege so long as he remained in office. He did not elaborate on how long this would be. The explanation was that violence in the provinces was worsening instead of improving. One-half of the Colombian army, including crack battalions of Korean veterans, was permanently tied down in fighting the hopeless guerrilla war. Air force planes bombed guerrilla strongholds, fighter aircraft sprayed the villages and jungles with flaming napalm, but the guerrillas were as elusive as ever. After eighteen months in power Rojas had thus failed to achieve his primary goal: to re-establish peace in the country. He blamed the two parties and their newspapers for inciting violence, and it soon became apparent that he had to distract the attention of the nation from the bloody happenings in the interior of Colombia.

Censorship took care of keeping from the people the truth about the fighting. But something else was needed to capture their interest. What Rojas produced was a plan to build political support for his regime. Early in 1955 the Perón-controlled National Confederation of Workers and a group calling itself Movement of National Action (MAN) began agitating, clearly with Rojas' encouragement, for the formation of a Third Force to replace the Liberal and Conservative parties and help the Supreme Chief battle the oligarchs in defense of the workers. Curiously, the co-ordinator of this movement was General Rafel Calderón Reyes, the army's chief of staff. The Government of the Armed Forces, which proclaimed in neon signs atop Bogotá's public buildings that Motherland Is Above Parties, was thus busying itself with its own party. It must be recorded at this point that a large number of Colombian officers took a dim view of this excursion by Rojas in the realm of Peronista politics.

The quiet opposition of these officers combined with the outspoken displeasure of the Roman Catholic Church over Rojas' efforts to break up Catholic unions temporarily took the wind out of the Third Force scheme. A mass rally scheduled for February 26 was canceled by Rojas. But in November the dictator was ready for another try along these lines. Liberal newspapers were no longer able to criticize him— Bogotá now lacked what could be called an opposition press, except for one or two Ospinista Conservative publications— and Rojas' propaganda office worked overtime to glorify the Third Force. This propaganda bureau was named DINAPE and it was a faithful copy of Vargas' DIP and Perón's Subsec.

Rojas felt powerful and sure of himself. Before going to Ecuador in July he had reorganized his government and he felt the climate was now ripe for making his big political bid. If it worked, Rojas could depend on the Third Force to propel him into still another presidential term in 1958, in a Perón-style Justicialista election. And the technique was identical: Perón had the General Confederation of Labor to backstop the Peronista Party; and Rojas presently unveiled his plan for creating a Gran Central Obrera, a regime-controlled, catchall union federation. In a speech Rojas primly denied that his government was promoting state syndicalism, but admitted that it "would favorably regard syndical organization in accordance with conditions which would permit labor to achieve a program of Peace, Justice, and Liberty." It was just a play on words.

By the end of 1955 it was already obvious to most Colombians that Rojas had every intention of remaining in power forever. The Liberals and the Conservatives reacted by taking their first step toward unity and launched a Civic Front. It was largely inspired by a letter written late in 1954 by former President Alfonso López proposing a coalition government of the two parties. Rojas countered in his New Year's message on December 31, 1955, charging the opposition with "abusing the full liberty of the press."

But he was in a definite minority in claiming that the press was free in Colombia. Early in January, 1956, Henry Holland, United States Assistant Secretary of State for Inter-American Affairs, visited Bogotá and told Rojas that American public opinion would not tolerate further economic assistance to Colombia if the government persisted in its violations of freedom of the press. The overthrow of Perón four months earlier was still fresh in all memories. The dictator promised Holland that a solution would be found for the problem of "reconciling the freedom of the press with a need for press responsibility" and a few days later named a five-man commission of lawyers to draft a Statute of the Press. Eduardo Zuleta Angel, a respected moderate Conservative who had just resigned as ambassador to the United States, accepted the chairmanship of the group with the explicit understanding that Rojas would honor its recommendations.

On February 21, 1956, the Zuleta commission presented Rojas with a 105-article draft of the statute, based largely on provisions of the laws of the state of New York on libel and slander. Rojas not only broke his promise to Zuleta about enforcing the statute, but chances are that he never read it.

Meanwhile, opposition to Rojas was growing by leaps and bounds even as he kept bandying about his latest slogan, that of an "Armed Forces-People's Government." This was the latest disguise for his Third Force movement. The Civic Front of the Liberals and Conservatives was picking up momentum, although its leaders still insisted that no attempt would be made to prevent Rojas from serving out his current term.

On February 5 came the Bogotá Bull Ring Massacre by Rojas' police agents and the Roman Catholic Church jumped into the situation. A pastoral letter by Crisanto Cardinal Luque of Colombia denounced the killings. It was published in the Church weekly *El Catolicismo*, but other newspapers were not permitted to run it. The aftermath of the Bull Ring affair may have scared Rojas, for he made some conciliatory moves. *El Tiempo* and *El Espectador* were permitted to resume publication under the names, respectively, of *Independiente* and *Intransigente*, although they were subject to severe censorship. Alberto Lleras Camargo, chief of the Liberal Party, became editor and columnist of *Intransigente*, and his office in the newspaper's building became the center of anti-Rojas opposition. From there it radiated to the private dining rooms of the Bogotá Jockey Club, where Colombia's influential men gathered for lunch, to offices of banks and big corporations, to universities and schools, and even to labor unions. The final battle was approaching, but another year was to elapse before Rojas brought about his own fall.

8

It was the Supreme Chief himself who hastened to fire the first salvo of that battle. On June 13, 1956, celebrating the third anniversary of his power grab, Rojas officially unveiled the Third Force in ceremonies that combined religious mysticism, mob rabble-rousing, and extreme poor taste. Standing in front of a huge cross erected alongside Bolívar's statue on Bogotá's Plaza Bolívar, the dictator received the oath in the Name of God from the officers of the armed forces that they would stand by him and the Third Force. The new party was to be operated openly by the government. Atop the national Congress palace in the background an immense neon sign proclaimed Motherland Above the Parties. A Christian-Bolívarian State had thus been launched. The following day Rojas moved his circus to the city's big, new Campin Stadium to receive the oath from civilian throngs, particularly labor leaders and rank-and-file workers brought there by government trucks. It was a slightly pathetic imitation of Perón's Plaza de Mayo rallies, since Rojas somehow could not whip

Colombians into the screaming frenzy that characterized Peronista meetings.

Within a few weeks the General took additional steps to set the stage for perpetuating his dictatorship. He established the Gran Central Obrera, the pro-regime labor confederation, and arranged for the Administrative Council of the department of Caldas to nominate him for re-election for the term starting two years hence.

But Rojas was not to ride very long the crest of this wave he had created. The Roman Catholic Church, long resentful of his activities, struck out against the Third Force and condemned Rojas for presuming to extract oaths of loyalty to himself in the name of God. And the Liberals and Conservatives signed what turned out to be the basic pact of their anti-Rojas unity. Representing the Liberals Alberto Lleras Camargo traveled to Spain to meet with old Laureano Gómez at the resort of Benidorm to discuss collaboration. Gómez was anathema to the Liberals and their archfoe, but he also was the top Conservative chief, and now the need for a joint opposition front against the dictator, overshadowing all other considerations, plunged old hatreds into oblivion. On his return to Bogotá, Lleras, a former president of Colombia, suffered the humiliation of being detained and searched at the airport.

About the same time Rojas delivered an hysterical, rambling radio and television speech defending himself against charges of graft and corruption and enrichment in office. He was replying to an article in a United States magazine that had made a profound impression in Colombia. It was translated, mimeographed, and widely circulated among the military. However, Rojas' speech backfired. Instead of convincing the military of his probity it led them to think that the charges may have been true. A small group of important army officers, already unhappy over Rojas' demagoguery and his bid for re-election, began to think in terms of getting rid of the dictator. The leader of this secret group was, strangely enough, no lesser a personality than Brigadier General Luis Ordoñez, chief of SIC, the Colombian intelligence service, which was Rojas' secret police. And anti-Rojas sentiment was spreading among other officers as well. Visiting the guerrilla regions of Tolima Department this writer was surprised at the willingness of colonels and majors, all of them combat commanders, to discuss with him the need for ousting Rojas. The officers were sick of the interminable war in Colombia's interior, of the nauseating cycle of reprisals and counter-reprisals. They had become convinced that there could be no victory in this civil war. And they had completely lost faith in Rojas' leadership. These officers took the view that the dictator was dishonoring the armed forces by his immorality and dishonesty and that he was breaking the tradition of the army's neutrality in politics. They were opposed to the Third Force and to Rojas' arbitrary methods. In their criticism they singled out the closing of *El Tiempo*.

In August, 1956, this military criticism of Rojas brought about the greatest crisis in his three-year dictatorial career. Actually the crisis was triggered by an accident unrelated to the political situation. On August 7 six army trucks, loaded with dynamite, exploded in Cali, leveling thirty city blocks and killing over one thousand persons. It appeared to have been a case of pure negligence, but arriving in Cali the next day Rojas made the mistake of accusing his Liberal-Conservative opposition of sabotage. The reaction against his unjustified charge was instantaneous. The sense of justice of Colombians, military and civilian alike, was outraged, and on returning to Bogotá on August 9 Rojas was faced with military demands to resign. Coming in the wake of his other political excesses the sabotage charge seemed to have broken the camel's back of the nation's patience with him.

In the capital generals and politicians freely discussed the creation of a junta to replace Rojas. But this time the dictator succeeded in saving his skin. Appealing to the sense of discipline of the military and invoking his status as commander in chief Rojas managed to retain their support. But he had to offer concessions and he outlined them in a closed conference on August 15 with hundreds of top officers at Patria theater, a soldiers' cinema at the suburban Usaquen military reservation. He thus promised to drop the Third Force; not to seek re-election; to call the Constituent Assembly, inactive since 1954, back into session; and to put an end to graft practices. He also warned the officers that their privileges, ranging from the sumptuous Military Club to the army commissaries, would likely be taken away from them should a civilian government be allowed to replace him.

Having thus weathered the storm Rojas proceeded to relax his controls and to give the impression that he was backtracking on his plans for forcing an immediate re-election. The moribund Third Force was allowed to die and nothing further was heard about it. Press censorship was not lifted but opposition newspapers suddenly began to enjoy unaccustomed freedom. In September the cabinet was reorganized, and on October 11 the National Constituent Assembly held its first meeting. Tensions diminished and it appeared for a while as though Rojas would have no difficulty serving out his term —if he only watched his step.

But Rojas' vanity was too great for him to exercise even the most elementary caution. And he rushed to demonstrate that the last vestiges of political sense had left him. When the Assembly convened the dictator sprang on it his proposals for a revision of the 1886 constitution along corporativist lines—exactly what Gómez had tried to do in 1953—and for the enlargement of the Assembly's membership by twenty-five deputies. This was a barefaced scheme to assure himself of re-election in 1957—a year ahead of time—and Rojas made no secret of it. The new majority would be enough to vote again the suspension of the constitutional ban against re-election as was done in 1954 and to keep him in power at least until 1962.

Having lost the Third Force Rojas now declared himself a Conservative, forgetting that his regime was to be "above parties." Lucio Pabón Nuñez, Minister of Interior and author of this whole scheme, became head of the progovernment faction of the Conservative Party. It was backed by a group of dissident Liberals. Ranged against the government bloc were Gómez and moderate Conservatives. Former President Ospina Pérez accepted the chairmanship of the Assembly in the vain hope of defeating the Rojas-engineered maneuver. When this writer asked Rojas in an interview in November what he would do if the Assembly refused to enlarge its membership, the dictator replied with disarming frankness: "Why, I'll just dissolve it."

But this was not necessary. After weeks of bedlam in the Assembly—Rojas had filled the public galleries with hoodlums who drowned the speeches of opposition deputies in a cacophony of shouts and catcalls—the legislature voted by a slight margin on November 3, 1956, to add the twenty-five members. Then, as Ospina Pérez resigned in protest, the Assembly proceeded to dissolve itself and order the creation of a new body for early next year. The first act of the great electoral farce was over.

9

The year 1957 began inauspiciously for Colombia. The economic situation was deteriorating rapidly and it developed that the mismanagement by the Rojas government had run the nation into a $450,000,000 short-term foreign debt. The cost of living was soaring on the wings of new inflationary pressures. In the interior guerrilla violence—motivated in equal parts by political hatreds, economic difficulties, and pure banditry—was still on the upswing, and estimates for the death toll in the nine years of civil war now mounted to 200,000.

Political unrest in the nation loomed high, with the promise of troubles ahead. And again Rojas' boundless vanity had stampeded him into recklessness. An article in a New York magazine had described him as nothing more than the "chairman of the board" of a ruling military group, with his own powers curtailed and his future in doubt. The magazine writer had been wrong—Rojas remained the undisputed ruler of the country—but the dictator was not going to let such wrong impressions prevail abroad. Besides, it could give ideas to restless officers at home. As the article also happened to coincide with the publication in Bogotá newspapers of letters by Alberto Lleras Camargo and Mariano Ospina Pérez declaring that any Rojas bid for re-election would be unconstitutional, the Supreme Chief resolved to settle matters once and for all.

Calling General Gabriel Paris, the war minister, to Melgar Rojas ordered him to make a public statement of the armed forces' support. Obediently, Paris dictated an interview for *Diario Oficial*, the new paper the government had just launched as part of a projected chain of proregime press, announcing that the military stood united in demanding that Rojas continue as president until 1962. Simultaneously the President opened his own campaign for "nomination." In a January speech before an army regiment at Pasto he declared that the "armed forces will rule Colombia for the rest of the century." On February 4 he went to the town of Arbelaez, near Bogotá, to speak of plans for "a new republican order against the old democratic disorder." And three days later Rojas formally accepted the military's "demand" that he run for re-election, stating that "the people must be protected from political oligarchs who wish only to hurt and to hurl them into barbarism."

Desperately casting about for scapegoats for his difficulties the dictator turned on Protestant missionaries in Colombia. Having sanctioned for three years persecutions against them now he accused the missionaries and Protestants in Colombia in general, of Communist associations and plots to enlarge the civil war.

On March 23 Rojas was ready to raise the curtain on his re-election show. The new Constituent Assembly met that evening under the chairmanship of Pabón Nuñez, who had resigned as Minister of the Interior to devote himself full-time to stage-managing the affair. Of the ninety members, thirty had been directly appointed by Rojas while the others were "elected" by government-controlled departmental assemblies. At the opening session Pábon Nuñez ruled out of order Ospina Pérez—all the ex-presidents of Colombia held seats in the Assembly and were the only opposition voices in that rubber-stamp body—as he tried to read a manifesto of the Civic Front against Rojas' re-election. Simultaneously, severe press censorship was reimposed and a wave of harassment arrests got under way. One evening twenty-one guests at a graduation ceremony at a convent school were arrested. Another day Señora Berta de Lleras, wife of Colombia's former president and Liberal chief, was detained.

But in many instances the Colombian intelligence service of General Ordoñez was merely going through the motions. His sympathies were now completely with the opposition and he did only the minimum required to preserve appearances. The nascent anti-Rojas conspiracy had better chances of success as long as Ordoñez remained the secret-police boss. Distinguished political prisoners were usually held briefly in his private office, and often he made a point of driving them home in his own car. His agents looked the other way as society

ladies mimeographed clandestine manifestoes and their hus-
bands held political meetings at the Jockey Club and elsewhere.

The result of all these activities was the nomination on
April 8 of Guillermo Léon Valencia, a moderate Conservative, as the joint presidential candidate of the Liberal and
Conservative parties in opposition to Rojas. The Liberals are
a majority in Colombia, but for the sake of unity Lleras was
willing to defer to the Conservatives. It was a protest gesture
because nobody expected Valencia to be allowed to run, let
alone to be elected. A colorful, mustachioed politician who
helped Laureano Gómez form the pro-Nazi National Action
group during the war, Valencia had broken with the old man
and joined the ranks of progressive Conservatives. Now he
loomed as the symbol of freedom and democracy in Colombia
on the eve of what was to be Rojas' final assault on the nation's liberties. Instantly, Valencia received the backing of all
of Colombia's political leaders. Associations of industrialists
and bankers issued public declarations of support with thousands of signatures. National revulsion against Rojas was
mounting.

On April 23 Valencia's candidacy was proclaimed at a private house in his home town of Popayán because the government refused permission for a public ceremony. That same
day Valencia was received by the Archbishop of Popayán in
what constituted the Church's first official endorsement of the
opposition's fight against Rojas.

Two days later, on April 25, Rojas touched off what was
to be the two-week crisis that ended in his downfall. He sent
bills to the Assembly calling for the suspension of constitutional provisions which banned a president's re-election and
established universal suffrage in a presidential election. Other
bills were for general constitutional reform. The Assembly
was to meet on May 1; the traditional Labor Day was to

mark the re-election. On April 30 Colombia's Crisanto Cardinal Luque refused a conference with Rojas and wrote him that the re-election would be illegal.

Because of the opposition of the Church and internal difficulties—Rojas refused to meet Pabón Nuñez' demand for the election of a civilian vice-president—the Assembly's meeting was delayed. Instead, Rojas made the stupendous error of trying to arrest Valencia, who had gone to Cali to campaign as best he could for his candidacy. This was the dictator's political suicide, as the move against Valencia was fated to set off the final explosion.

Barricaded in a friend's house Valencia announced that he would not let himself be taken alive. As army troops maintained a desultory siege of the two-story house, students in Cali went on strike and began rioting throughout the city. Their leaders established headquarters at the archbishop's palace, with the blessings of the Church's hierarchy. The next day, on May 2, students at Bogotá's Jesuit university occupied the building and launched anti-Rojas demonstrations, demanding freedom for Valencia. All day long the students, encouraged by their Jesuit teachers, withstood the police and their attacks with tear gas and jets of red-dyed water. A memorable news photograph taken that afternoon showed three youths clutching a Colombian flag bending under twin jets of red water shot point-blank from a police tank truck. Late in the evening the government announced that Valencia was free to go where he pleased. Instantly, the candidate returned to Bogotá to join with Lleras in directing what was suddenly developing into open revolution.

On Friday, May 3, student riots spread to all the Bogotá universities. Valencia was no longer an issue; now the students clamored for Rojas' resignation. They smashed the dictator's portraits on the campus of the National University, and in the afternoon staged a march in downtown Bogotá.

Police fired on them with tear gas, bullets, and streams of colored water. Revolutionary councils were organized in the schools, and rioting spread to other Colombian cities. Student squads sprinkled the streets with broken glass and nails to stop police cars, others launched a fund-raising campaign to finance the people's revolution. Stickers reading "Death to Rojas" were slapped on backs of passers-by. It was a spontaneous explosion, not really planned by any of the political leaders but spreading like wildfire across the nation, picking up momentum and support among people in all walks of life. It was being improvised from moment to moment, from hour to hour. Anti-Rojas military chiefs, such as General Ordoñez, watched the situation, waiting for the right moment to move. Because of the army's tradition of discipline, most generals were still reluctant to turn on their commander in chief. But it was becoming increasingly clear that a further deterioration in the situation might leave them no other choice.

On Sunday, May 5, Rojas committed another of his unbelievable errors: he let his police attack a church. The occasion was high Mass at La Porciuncula church in the fashionable Chapinero district of Bogotá. The parish priest there was Father Severo Velasquez, famous for his antidictatorial attitude. Expecting fireworks, worshipers and students filled the church to capacity, spilling out into wide Avenida Chile. In a sermon Father Velasquez roundly condemned Rojas, and the congregation broke out in unprecedented applause and began to sing the national anthem. At the end of Mass worshipers streamed out of the church chanting the slogan of "Cristo, Sí—Rojas, No," as student leaders climbed on garden walls around the church to deliver speeches. Then the police struck. Jeeploads of troopers hurled themselves into the crowd in clouds of exploding tear gas. Tank trucks spraying red-colored water followed. The façade of the church was desecrated by streams of red dye while maddened policemen hurled tear-gas grenades inside the church.

In the evening another riot broke out around the church and two students were killed by tear-gas grenades fired at them point-blank from riot guns. Cardinal Luque publicly charged Rojas with murder. But the dictator was not to be stopped any more; he was fighting for his life and he knew it. On Monday, May 6, the army occupied Bogotá, and Rojas in an hysterical speech insisted that the armed forces stood squarely behind him. He was doubtless convinced of it, vainly unaware that his commanders were wavering and preparing to abandon him.

On Tuesday, May 7, employers and workers joined in paralyzing most of the industry and commerce in a general strike against the Rojas regime. The dictator went back on the air to accuse the oligarchs of turning their workers into cannon fodder, but his ranting charges only had the effect of strengthening the unions in their determination to oppose him. Banks were closed, factories and stores stood silent, and most of the economic activity in Colombia came to a standstill as the nation united in its effort to overthrow the dictatorial yoke.

On Wednesday, May 8, with troops and tanks surrounding the National Congress building, Rojas had his hour of triumph —or what he took to be triumph. His Constituent Assembly re-elected him president for the 1958-1962 term. Pabón Nuñez had fled the country several days earlier and now Rojas was left alone to reap the harvest of his ex-minister's scheming. He did not savor his bitter victory very long. Colombians greeted his re-election with derision and a new wave of rioting. On Thursday, May 9, army troops in Cali fought rebel crowds, killing at least fifteen persons. Several children were bayoneted to death. Returning to Bogotá for a quick inspection trip, General Deogracias Fonseca, chief of national police, reported to his colleagues gathered at army command headquarters that the situation in Cali was hopeless. The generals in the capital agreed that the picture everywhere was hopeless, too.

In midevening General Ordoñez drove to Colombian air

force headquarters and obtained the agreement of the air force for an immediate move against Rojas. Simultaneously, General Rafael Navas Pardo, army commander, contacted Conservative political leaders. Shortly before midnight he called on Rojas to tell him that the Civic Front demanded the President's immediate resignation and that they had the means to force him out of office. Rojas countered with the proposal that he would forget his re-election if he were allowed to serve out his present term. The answer was an emphatic no.

The generals held another conference, and in the small hours of Friday, May 10, went to the palace to inform Rojas that they no longer could stand by him and that to save the nation from chaos and revolution he must step down. A military junta was formed at once. It was exit for Rojas as president, dictator, and Supreme Chief of Colombia.

With incredible speed the word of Rojas' fall spread across Bogotá. By five o'clock in the morning tens of thousands of Bogotános, many in night clothes, filled the streets and avenues, deliriously cheering the return of freedom. *"Se cayó, Se cayó"* ("He fell, He fell") was the chant that echoed among the hills of the mountain city. Colombian flags were broken out by the thousands over buildings and private homes. Strangers kissed strangers in the streets. It was an explosion of joy surpassing anything ever seen in Colombia. In mid-morning, in a moment of unexplained confusion, troops fired at the celebrating crowds in Plaza Bolívar, killing ten persons. But not even this tragedy took the edge off the intoxicating happiness of the people as they danced and sang late into the night.

Unnoticed by the merrymakers, a small motorcade sped to Techo airport under the mantle of darkness. There, Gustavo Rojas Pinilla was whisked aboard a waiting aircraft. An era ended in Colombia when the plane roared off the runway, taking a course toward the north and eventual foreign exile in Spain for the deposed dictator.

Chapter Seven

MARCOS PÉREZ JIMÉNEZ
OF VENEZUELA

1

In the small hours of January 23, 1958, a date that will long be remembered in the history of Venezuela, a vicious and ruthless dictatorship met its death in the conquering surge of a bloody revolution.

In toppling from power General Marcos Pérez Jiménez, Venezuelans ended nearly a decade of military rule that in its second half had become a nightmare of oppression, imprisonments, assassinations, corruption, graft, and immorality. This five-year period began late in December, 1952, when Pérez Jiménez, the moonfaced artillery officer with a psychopathic craving for power, established a regime that functioned under the disguise of a false and inhuman political philosophy that took the name of New National Ideal. It undertook to mold Venezuela into a technocracy, a nation in which the economic motive overrode all other normal aspirations of the people for the sake of antiseptic material progress. In the New Venezuela of Pérez Jiménez and his theoreticians, there was no room for any form of political life—not even that pathetic little dose that Perón tolerated in Argentina—or any vestige of independent thought. One of the regime's slogans was the "Transformation of the Physical Environment," and commendable as it was in some of its aspects the human element of this environment was forgotten. The dictator had imposed a system of spiritual and mental regimentation, and his lethally efficient secret police stood poised to enforce it with methods unrivaled by any modern organization of repression outside of Hitler's Germany or Stalin's Russia.

With its emphasis on the supremacy of the economic motive in human life and the eradication of political intercourse, the regime of Pérez Jiménez came incredibly close to re-creating certain fundamental Marxist doctrines in the easygoing tropical setting of Latin America. Much as he thundered against communism, this intense little general was in truth generously borrowing from Marxist economic-political thinking. He stopped short, however, of such ideas as state ownership or dictatorship of the proletariat. He preferred to do as much owning as possible himself and to clasp the dictatorial rule in his own pudgy hands and those of his henchmen.

If Pérez Jiménez thus succeeded in strangling Venezuela's spiritual life and distorting her moral values, he similarly distorted her economy, thereby removing any valid excuse there might have been for his presence in government. True, Caracas, and one or two other Venezuelan cities, gained a spectacular face-lift, and showy public projects were superimposed on the Venezuelan landscape. Costly new industries were launched, often with dubious justification in terms of the national economy. A certain degree of prosperity in the cities favored the nascent middle class and the nouveau riche of the artificial boom. But this outward prosperity, born from

Venezuela's great oil wealth, existed in spite rather than because of the dictator's policies.

When Pérez Jiménez finally left power and the curtain of propaganda and deceit was lifted from Venezuela, the nation realized that the sacrifice of liberty—the price it had paid for the mirage of the New National Ideal—had been in vain. Behind the façade of brave accomplishments, a Potemkin Village type of thing, there loomed chaos, confusion, and inadequacy. Having spent billions of dollars of Venezuela's vast petroleum revenues—the kind of money that could have made her a model of healthy development for the world—Pérez Jiménez left behind him a short-term debt that exceeded a half-billion dollars.

Once the fabulous program of public works was slowed down by the new government that could not afford them severe unemployment set in. And one wonders how much longer Pérez Jiménez himself could have managed to go on with his eye-catching projects, financing them as he did with secret indebtedness and covering them up in budget ledgers with symbolic entries of one Bolivar each.

When the bubble burst Venezuelans who had not wished to see the truth before discovered the terrible misery that prevailed in the backlands of their country. Now they believed the words of their archbishop, uttered in warning nine months before the dictator's demise, that the majority of the population lived in "subhuman conditions." With his immense resources, the envy of the rest of Latin America, Pérez Jiménez hardly made a dent in the awesome social problem of Venezuela. If a social explosion should occur in Venezuela someday, as it well may, his dictatorship will have helped to set it in motion.

Whereas all the Latin-American countries gradually lower their index of illiteracy, Venezuela, unbelievably, saw her index rise between 1950 and 1958. Although a fairyland hotel had risen atop Mount Avila overlooking Caracas, with an aerial train connecting it with the city below, one-half of Venezuela's children had no schools to go to. A steel mill designed to produce three times as much steel as Venezuela was likely to consume in the next generation was ordered by Pérez Jiménez, but hundreds of thousands of Venezuelans lived in hovels. Other thousands went hungry because not enough money went into irrigation and other agricultural schemes which would make the land produce more and better food.

At the same time, uncounted hundreds of millions of dollars streamed into the bulging pockets of the dictator, his family, friends, and associates in the most grandiose example of public graft known in the annals of Latin America. As a cynical observer of the Venezuelan scene once remarked, the graft in Venezuela was greater than elsewhere because there was so much more money there. With their income from graft the dictator and his fun-loving acolytes financed lives of luxury and dissipation that would have been notable even in the days of Bacchus. And as a collective playground for sex, pleasure, and gay imbibing, Pérez Jiménez and his friends set aside a lovely island off the Venezuelan coast.

The extraordinary fact about the regime of Pérez Jiménez was that this travesty of government was so readily accepted by so many people in Venezuela, citizens and foreigners alike, and by so much of the outside world. United States ambassadors and United States businessmen in Venezuela—the latter taking vastly profitable advantage of the country's phony prosperity—assiduously praised Pérez Jiménez for his accomplishments, oddly ignorant of the true economic and social picture of the nation and strangely unaware of the existence of the torture chambers of the regime's secret police. In fact, the American business and industrial community in Venezuela constituted one of the most enthusiastic cheering sections

Pérez Jiménez ever had. He kept order, they said, he favored investments and business, and this made him a regular guy in the eyes of the majority of the forty thousand Americans in the country.

In sum, Pérez Jiménez' regime, perhaps even more drastically than Perón's government, negated the comfortable theory, current for so long among many North and South Americans, that a nation lacking in democratic experience cannot develop properly unless it is guided by a strong man whose wisdom curtails and regulates the excesses of irresponsible politicians. None of the fumbling and quarreling politicians who preceded him during the brief interlude between the two successive nightmares of Venezuelan dictatorships acted with more irresponsibility than Pérez Jiménez.

For Venezuela, a nation rich in dictatorial tradition, the rule of Pérez Jiménez was in a sense worse than the now legendary twenty-seven years in power of Juan Vicente Gómez, the Tyrant of the Andes. While in effect Pérez Jiménez took up where Gómez left off at his death in 1935, his dictatorship had a special touch of the ludicrous, particularly in the formulation of his technocratic political philosophy. And he did not have Gómez' merit of leaving Venezuela in a state of fiscal solvency.

Actually the parallels between Gómez and Pérez Jiménez are many, and they are revealing. Both came from the same mountain Indian stock of the Andes, both were cunning and coldly calculating, both had an all-consuming passion for power and wealth. In fact, it is impossible to think of Pérez Jiménez without thinking of Gómez, and in both instances the thought occurs of what a happy and truly prosperous nation Venezuela could have been—with her tremendous natural resources—had she been blessed with wise, honest, and democratic-minded rulers instead of these two hard-eyed dictators and the inept men who bridged the gap between them.

The parallel between Gómez and Pérez Jiménez ends in the manner in which their respective dictatorships terminated. For Gómez, it was by death at the age of seventy-eight, after twenty-seven years of personal rule and fifteen earlier years as gray eminence under President-Dictator Cipriano Castro. When Gómez passed away the long pent-up hate against him exploded in the bloodshed of vengeance. But such was the hold of Gómez on Venezuela—called by the people El Brujo (the Sorcerer)—that he probably would have succeeded in remaining in power no matter how many more years he had lived. Gómez often and confidently predicted that he would live to be a hundred years old. Interestingly enough, Pérez Jiménez, imitator and spiritual heir of Gómez, was ousted by revolution on almost exactly the one hundredth anniversary of the birth of El Brujo.

2

Marcos Pérez Jiménez was a man thoroughly obsessed with the idea of power. The craving for power has been a characteristic shared by dictators throughout the ages, but in Pérez Jiménez, combined as it was with a crushing inferiority complex, it soared to dizzying heights.

A short, stocky, and rather ugly human specimen, Pérez Jiménez was an introverted and repressed individual. When his hunger for power was finally satisfied, his repressions bloomed forth into a love of showy uniforms and a penchant for orgiastic pleasures. When fulfillment of his cravings was denied Pérez Jiménez—as was the case in 1948 when a fellow officer assumed the presidency of the victorious revolutionary junta and he was relegated to a secondary spot—he reacted with an emotional glandular disturbance taking the form of sudden obesity. Explosions of hysterical behavior also punctuated his career.

Venezuelan psychiatrists, who studied Pérez Jiménez' record as a clinical case after the revolution that ousted him in 1958, found him to be a "paranoiac, megalomaniac, neurotic." Dr. José Luis Vethencourt, a Caracas specialist, described the ex-dictator as an "abnormal character . . . characterized by rapidity of thought," in an explanation of Pérez Jiménez' ability to act with disconcerting speed under pressure. Dr. Abel Sánchez Pelaez wrote that Pérez Jiménez "is the type of man who can live only . . . in absolute power. . . . Psychologically, he is unable to live in an atmosphere of liberty."

To win power—and, later, to keep it—Pérez Jiménez stopped at nothing. After living for two years in the shadow, or on the brink, of total power, the path to the presidency was opened to him by the assassination in mysterious circumstances in 1950 of Lieutenant Colonel Carlos Delgado Chalbaud, the junta chief. Much evidence was uncovered after Pérez Jiménez' fall to suggest that if he had not ordered it personally, he had known ahead of time of the plot to murder the popular, well-liked Delgado Chalbaud. In 1958 the Colonel's widow actually filed murder charges against Pérez Jiménez in a Caracas court, but no immediate action was taken. And the death of Delgado Chalbaud is strangely reminiscent of the equally mysterious killing, in 1923, of Juancho Gómez, then vice-president of Venezuela and brother of the Tyrant of the Andes. Nothing has been definitely proved in either case, but old Gómez and Pérez Jiménez did have in common an intense dislike of rivals.

Pérez Jiménez did not reach for the top job immediately after Delgado Chalbaud's assassination; it would have been too obvious and he was too cunning for that. Instead, he let a civilian figurehead take the presidency while he remained a member of the junta, pulling the strings from behind the throne. After two full years of thus functioning in the background Pérez Jiménez risked a free election. As soon as the

first returns indicated that he was being defeated, he stopped
the counting and in a few days issued a new set of figures proclaiming his victory. The military named him provisional
president, and his chief opponent was lured to the Ministry
of Interior to be arrested and deported. A few months later
arrangements were made for the legislature to "elect" him
for a five-year term and reform the constitution in a way that
would give him unchecked control over the fate of Venezuela.
The old dictatorial preoccupation with apparent legality of
arbitrary acts was not absent from Pérez Jiménez' thoughts.

Upon reaching the presidency Pérez Jiménez was thirty-
eight years old, the youngest chief of state in the history of
his country. He then proceeded to use the energy of youth
not only to implant a terrible dictatorship, but, the craving
for power satisfied, to give vent to his other repressed desires.
Sex was the foremost of them, and in practicing it he put to
shame Perón and even possibly old Gómez, the man who is
credited with illegitimate progeny in the range of four score
and ten.

Married and the father of four small girls, Pérez Jiménez
was conspicuous for the sex orgies at his many "retreats,"
especially his playground on the island of Orchilla off the
coast of Venezuela. A mansion, said to cost over $2,000,000,
and an airfield with a runway long enough to serve four-en-
gined aircraft were built in 1956 for the sole purpose of providing pleasure for the dictator and his friends. At the inaugural party eyewitnesses have said, two hundred beautiful
women were flown from the mainland to participate in the
three-day revelry. Many of them were invited by a business
partner of Pérez Jiménez who was known in those days as the
"Sexual Minister." On other occasions airplanes were chartered to bring women from Havana, and once from as far
away as Santiago in Chile. One of the stories told about Orchilla has to do with Pérez Jiménez' predilection for chasing

girls along the beach on a motor scooter. Skin-diving was another of the dictator's favorite sports.

In addition to power and sex, Pérez Jiménez had a vast craving for wealth. Actually, financial and sexual pursuits are often sublimations of a basic power drive. Such was the case with Gómez and Perón. Through practices of graft, extortion, and kickbacks, Pérez Jiménez is believed to have built a fortune in excess of $250,000,000 in cash, not counting the property and corporate shares he left behind when he fled Venezuela. There were hefty bank accounts in the name of his wife, his octogenarian mother, and even his four little daughters. Pérez Jiménez' friends also did extremely well during the years of the New National Ideal. In some instances, cabinet ministers charged industrialists as much as thirty per cent of the total cost of a project in exchange for a government contract. It was a bonanza of corruption on a scale unmatched even by old Gómez, who concentrated on acquiring land and cattle.

As he continued to get away with everything he did—politically and personally—Pérez Jiménez allowed himself to be lulled into a false sense of security. Remembering the 1952 experience he did not want to risk an open election in 1958, and in its place staged a "Yes" or "No" plebiscite on his continuation in the presidency. He and his advisers were convinced that Venezuelans had been beaten into such a state of submission that the farce of a plebiscite would be accepted by the nation. But two weeks after the plebiscite, the air force rose in rebellion against Pérez Jiménez, triggering the national revolution that in twenty-two days deposed him.

The dictator fought with all the means at his command to save himself, and for days it was touch and go whether he would succeed. He sacrificed his two closest friends, his interior minister and the chief of his secret police, to placate rebel officers, and the next day, in a masterful coup, he arrested and exiled the general who had come to demand his resignation. But it was too late; all Venezuela was aroused against him and all his cunning and talent for intrigue were not enough to contain the explosion.

As a personality Pérez Jiménez was plain dull. Unlike Perón and Vargas, he was never able to extract even a scintilla of excitement from his people, to say nothing of popular support. His speeches were rare, colorless, monotonous, and uninspiring. Except for the 1952 elections when the junta slapped together an Independent Electoral Front to sponsor Pérez Jiménez, he never bothered to form a political party of his own. But, then, his theory was that Venezuela did not need political parties of any kind. Oddly enough, Pérez Jiménez was not interested in self-glorification. Practically nothing was named after him in Venezuela, and the nation was spared the sight of his portrait on every wall.

His personal vanity took a special form: that of emphasizing his military profession. He insisted on wearing uniforms at all times—at the conference of American presidents in Panama in 1956 Pérez Jiménez was the only one to appear in uniform, although seven other participants also held the rank of general —and he often looked grotesque in an oversized peaked cap that seemed to fall over his ears.

He was an excellent rifleman and pistol shot and official photographs often showed him lying on the ground at a firing range, a rifle at the ready. A professional soldier with a distinguished background of military schools, he did much to reorganize and modernize Venezuela's armed forces. He gave the army an impressive military academy and the officers a multimillion-dollar Military Circle, probably the world's most luxurious officers' club. He also sought to instill into Venezuelans a sense of tradition and pride in their history.

Pérez Jiménez' dictatorship may have outdone Gómez' rule in ruthlessness and refined cruelty, but fundamentally the two men had very much in common. Both of them were Andeans and both had in their veins the blood of the mountain Indians. In Venezuela this is a fact of immense human, historical, and political importance, for the *Andinos* are the dominant and toughest strain in the country's population. Coming down from their cool, high peaks and valleys into the languid coastal lowlands and the vast, hot llanos they have time and again forced themselves upon the rest of Venezuela, sometimes as small, private armies snowballing in size as they rolled toward Caracas, the seat of national power; other times as just ambitious, well-equipped individuals. Gómez reached Caracas helping to lead a revolutionary army; Pérez Jiménez was the individual whose combined gifts of highland hardness and Indian cunning overcame in the end all opposition in the capital. The Andes, then, had a tradition of leadership in Venezuela; the dark-skinned *Andinos* were both the nation's curse and her glory. Much of the country's history can be told in terms of a contest between Caracas and the Andes. Yet Venezuela's greatest and most famous son, Simón Bolívar, was born in Caracas.

3

Marcos Pérez Jiménez was born in the remote town of Michelena in the state of Táchira, deep in the mountains of the west, on April 25, 1914. His father, a farmer and tradesman, was seventy years old when Marcos, the third of four children, came along. Thirty years younger, Pérez Jiménez' mother had been a schoolteacher.

The family belonged to one of the scores of Andean clans but, unlike the militaristic Gómez clan, it lived peacefully, devoting itself to the quiet pursuits of tilling land and practicing commerce. Marcos' father, Juan Severo Pérez, had provided modestly but comfortably for his family. Their home was a one-story whitewashed structure, and, many years later, as Pérez Jiménez graduated to dictatorial luxury and his many mansions, the regime's propaganda attempted to make something out of these unspectacular beginnings.

When Marcos was twelve years old his father died, and the family was broken up. Señora de Pérez went back to school-teaching in her home town of San Antonio, keeping two of the children with her. Juan Pérez Jiménez, the oldest son, was dispatched to Gómez' military school at Maracay, some forty miles from Caracas, while Marquitos, as his mother called him, was sent to live with an aunt in Cúcuta, across the border in Colombia.

By all accounts, young Marcos was a quiet, withdrawn, precocious, and sanctimonious child. He retained in manhood these traits of character. Pérez Jiménez' official biographer wrote that Marcos never looked for fights but knew how to defend himself with his fists when provoked. His latter-day career bears this statement out; the dictator was always happier when he could get what he wanted without a fight, but he was a slugger when someone or something stood in his way.

Shortly before his seventeenth birthday Pérez Jiménez was enrolled as an Alferez (a cadet) at the Maracay military school, following in his brother's footsteps. Under Gómez' army-oriented regime, this was the most promising career in Venezuela for an ambitious young man of limited resources —as was also the case in most of Latin America in those days. Thus, unwittingly, Pérez Jiménez was following the careers of Perón, Odría, and Rojas Pinilla.

The old dictator had transformed the once ragged and amateurish Venezuelan military establishment into a fairly modern force, notable for the favored treatment granted officers. This mother-hen approach to high-ranking officers was one of the many lessons of the Gómez period that Pérez Jiménez remembered and applied in his own heyday.

Gómez had won his generalcy, and subsequently ultimate power, as a result of his revolutionary campaigns with Cipriano Castro, the bearded lawyer-warlord, and of ensuing wars against their common enemies. Gómez never had any formal military training, was just a notch above illiteracy, but possessed that rare natural military genius that makes true leaders of men at arms. He also had been exposed for years to Castro's masterful guerrilla techniques—probably the most important military factor in the civil wars that raged throughout Venezuela from the peaks of the Andes to the lowlands of the Caribbean coast for decades on end.

But in the 1930's the days of the warlords were very much over in Venezuela, and the boy who aspired to be a general had to work for it by the dull way of a military academy. Pérez Jiménez was a brilliant student—he graduated first in his class and received a wrist watch as a prize—specializing in artillery, ballistics, and ordnance. But even as Gómez learned the military arts without schooling and through sheer experience, so Pérez Jiménez emerged as the theoretician who never saw combat duty.

The Maracay military school where the short, slim Marcos became a student in 1931 was a brand-new establishment. It was founded by Gómez to replace the Caracas military school that the dictator closed in 1928, following an antiregime revolt that came within minutes of success. Gómez then resolved to have the academy where he and his powerful and loyal garrison could keep an eye on the cadets and their teachers. The late 1920's and the early 1930's, during which many Latin-American dictators around Gómez were falling out of power, were dangerous years for the aging El Brujo. But because he took no chances with anybody or anything, he managed to weather this period of conspiracies and crises.

Thirty years later, Pérez Jiménez, in his turn watching the collapse of dictatorships everywhere, also used utter distrust and suspicion as the cornerstone of his strategy and tactics. But times had changed and Venezuela's public opinion, now ever so much more enlightened than three decades earlier, had united against him as it never could have against Gómez.

There is no recorded indication that as a young cadet Pérez Jiménez was disturbed in any tangible way by Gómez, his dictatorship, or the excesses of the corrupt regime that had turned Venezuela into the nearest thing to a prison-dotted personal estate of the old man and his innumerable relatives and friends. Gómez owned directly or indirectly millions of acres of land, thousands and thousands of heads of cattle; he held controlling interest in a vast number of industrial and commercial enterprises; and he was cut in personally on the immense oil taxes and royalties paid by foreign companies, as well as on practically everything else that constituted a profitable economic activity in Venezuela. Officers and soldiers were frequently used to harvest crops on the dictator's haciendas or to supervise road gangs of political prisoners for whom there was no room in the country's overflowing penitentiaries.

All this did not seem to bother Marcos Pérez Jiménez, the studious cadet at the Maracay military academy, although it did disturb in an increasing degree quite a few of his fellow students. His own brother, Francisco, the youngest of four, was arrested briefly in 1931 when he was fourteen years old for participating in anti-Gómez student demonstrations.

Curiously enough, as Marcos Pérez Jiménez was learning the military arts in Maracay under the watchful eye of Gómez' henchmen, the young leaders of the continuous conspiracies against El Brujo were the very men whom Pérez Jiménez was to strike down years later in his own march to power. Among them was Rómulo Betancourt, the future president of the Acción Democrática Party whom Pérez Jiménez and his Military Junta colleagues exiled in 1948 after

overthrowing the constitutional government of President Rómulo Gallegos. Betancourt was one of the most active student
leaders in Caracas. Another student leader busy working
against Gómez in those days was Jovito Villalba, the man who
defeated Pérez Jiménez in the 1952 elections and was immediately exiled as the regime went to work on falsifying the
returns.

Then there was Carlos Delgado Chalbaud, the young engineering graduate from the Sorbonne in Paris, who helped
his father, General Ramón Delgado Chalbaud, stage an unsuccessful guerrilla landing on the Venezuelan coast. And in
1950, Delgado Chalbaud, then junta president, lay dead in a
Caracas villa.

Thus Pérez Jiménez, symbolically and probably unwittingly, paid a debt of gratitude to his dictatorial mentor, Juan
Vicente Gómez, the Sorcerer of Maracay, whom he never
met, by eliminating one by one all of his surviving enemies.
But it may be poetic justice that the 1958 revolt which ousted
him began in Maracay, and that in 1959 Betancourt again became president. History had gone full circle.

In his military school days Pérez Jiménez was a quiet young
man who minded his own business, stayed away from the
cadets' bull sessions and group associations, and was slow and
reluctant in making friends. It was his admiring biographer
who described him in this fashion. But, he also added self-
consciously, Pérez Jiménez "is sensitive and conscious of his
own value, but always modest."

On December 5, 1934, Pérez Jiménez graduated with honors from military school, received his wrist watch, and as a
brand-new twenty-year-old second lieutenant stood on the
threshold of the spectacular career that was to culminate in
a relatively short time in his ascension to the exalted position
of military dictator of his country.

4

Second Lieutenant Marcos Pérez Jiménez, boyish-looking and moonfaced, was in command of a section of the second battery of the Ayacucho artillery regiment in Maracay as Juan Vicente Gómez lay dying on December 17, 1935, in his bedroom at Las Delicias hacienda, a few miles from the town's garrison barracks.

Imperturbably, Pérez Jiménez watched the overnight collapse of the entire Gómez dictatorial edifice. And the crash came as soon as the word spread that El Brujo was dead. After twenty-seven years of the peace and tranquillity that Gómez had enforced by police terror and corrupt rule, the lid blew off the nation, and vengeance against the henchmen of the dictatorship mixed with the joy of liberty regained.

Until General Eleázar López Contreras, war and marine minister of the old regime, succeeded in re-establishing a semblance of order several weeks later, Venezuela lived in bloody chaos. Eustoquio Gómez, the old dictator's brother, who had attempted to wrest power away from provisional President López Contreras, was shot and killed. Dozens of minor tyrants of the Gómez heyday were massacred by bloodthirsty crowds.

Finally, López Contreras, who amazed Venezuelans by restoring all civil freedoms to the nation, put an end to the killings and lootings. Then political agitation burst forth as ideas of every degree, ranging from extreme left to extreme right, clamored for their share of public attention after decades of suppression. Elected to the presidency by Congress in April, 1936, López Contreras represented the transition from severe dictatorship to burgeoning democracy. His last contribution to the cause of democracy in Venezuela came twenty-two years later: long retired from public life and a tired octogenarian, he broke his silence in January, 1958, to encourage the military and civilian leaders in their revolt against the dictatorship of Pérez Jiménez.

Pérez Jiménez observed this birth of democracy in his country with disapproval and disgust. He had no direct participation in the events of 1935 and 1936 by virtue of his youth and low rank, but his biographer makes a point of reporting that "Second Lieutenant Pérez Jiménez, along with other officers, formed part of the national army that re-established public order saving the Nation from the catastrophic consequences of a social anarchy."

For Gómez' young disciple, wrote the biographer, the revolt of the people against oppression, their freedom of speech, and "audacious criticism . . . of the leaders" were, purely and simply, "constitutional anarchy." Pérez Jiménez concluded that this would not do, because "true freedoms" can be guaranteed only by the military and, therefore, the military establishment must be perfected so that peace, social order, and "a high sense of responsibility" may be secured. His reasoning was simple: if political liberties interfere with material progress—and they undoubtedly did in the confused initial years of democracy in Venezuela—then they must be abolished.

These, then, were the first recorded and coherent political thoughts of Pérez Jiménez. His lifelong obsession with public order—later the excuse for his own ruthless dictatorship—had taken roots as he watched the debacle of the Gómez empire. He dedicated his ensuing years of military obscurity to preparing for the self-appointed mission of saving Venezuela from herself. For the sanctimonious young Lieutenant it was a comfortable rationalization of his ambition for power. It had all the proper overtones of patriotism and righteousness.

But this cool, orderly, and calculating officer who had learned so many lessons so well failed to absorb the most crucial lesson of the post-Gómez period. He did not understand then, or twenty-odd years later, that no matter how long the night of oppression and how tough and exacting the dictatorship, a nation never forgets its craving for freedom. What Gómez could not accomplish in twenty-seven years in a much more primitive society, Pérez Jiménez could not have hoped to do in less than a third of the time and in a changed world.

5

As total war raged throughout the world—and his own country, influenced by the liberalizing currents of the day, fumbled through its democratic infancy under the government of President Isaías Medina Angarista—Pérez Jiménez studied and worked in Peru.

A first lieutenant since 1936, he was sent in March, 1939, to Lima's artillery school to perfect his military knowledge. He remained in Peru for nearly five years, graduating from the Chorillos military academy and from Peru's Superior War College. In 1941, already a captain, he served for ten months with a Peruvian mounted artillery group. This was the time of Peru's war with Ecuador, and although Captain Pérez Jiménez saw no action he had at least the experience of being part of an army at war. It was also at the Superior War College that he met another officer destined to become a dictator: Manuel A. Odría, Peru's future strong man. Curiously, one month after the 1948 Peruvian events, Pérez Jiménez emerged as the key member of the military junta that overthrew the constitutional government in Venezuela.

There was no direct relation between the 1948 military revolutions in Peru and Venezuela—except that these were the good days of the postwar dictatorial season—but it is interesting to note that their respective leaders were the product of the same army environment and that they shared the same political philosophical ideas hatched in the intense atmosphere of the Lima War College.

It is probable that his five years in Peru were crucial in crystallizing Pérez Jiménez' political concepts. He was twenty-five years old when he went there and twenty-nine when he returned to Venezuela. His views as well as his personal ambitions evidently matured during his Peruvian stay, and, significantly, a high Peruvian official had warned President Medina in Caracas to keep a careful eye on young Captain Pérez Jiménez. While in Lima, Pérez Jiménez befriended a number of fellow Venezuelan officers studying there. Later they became his associates and faithful supporters in the campaign for power. This group included Luiz Felipe Llovera Paez, subsequently a general and a member of the 1948 Military Junta, and Colonel Pulido Barreto, one of the few officers who remained faithful to Pérez Jiménez until the last hour in 1958. These men constituted the first nucleus of the future dictator's military clique.

Pérez Jiménez' friends say that he was fascinated by the Inca empire of four centuries ago. The patriarchal system under which the Inca emperor and the caciques (the regional chiefs) reigned wisely but with absolute power and considerable cruelty for the greater good of their peoples appealed to him. Coming from the Andes, Pérez Jiménez may have felt closer to the Indians of the Peruvian cordillera than to his fellow citizens in Venezuela. At any rate he seemed more receptive to these Andean ideas than to the realities of Venezuela, with which he appeared to be completely out of touch.

The brain trusters of the Pérez Jiménez regime put great stock in catchwords about "social and economic democracy" as the truly American solution to American problems. Chances are that some of those ideas were brought to Venezuela by Pérez Jiménez, student of the Inca empire and of the Indo-American "social democracy" of the Andes.

His biographer, seeing an almost metphysical experience in Pérez Jiménez' visit to Peru, wrote that the Captain returned to his country with this "national mission": "to preserve the values of the past and never to destroy them as a sacrifice to the false idols raised by demagoguery." This assessment is probably correct if it is remembered that to Pérez Jiménez freedom and political democracy were equated with "demagoguery" and that he developed in time a Bolívarian complex, presenting the Liberator as the forerunner of his dictatorial ways. Under Pérez Jiménez, Venezuela was to build a tremendous cult of Bolívar, and his cynical regime constantly invoked Bolívarian traditions to justify its actions. Juan Vicente Gómez had the same attachment to Bolívar, and in this, too, Pérez Jiménez imitated the old man of Maracay.

In the meantime, Pérez Jiménez was returning from Peru with observations on a more immediate political level. What he had seen in his five years there was a weak constitutional government in the crossfire between the traditional moneyed aristocracy and the surge forward of leftist parties demanding leadership in the political and social transition to a new age.

This phenomenon was part of the over-all Latin-American revolution in eruption since the end of World War II. When this revolution became distorted and the truly democratic elements failed to set it back on the right tracks, the stage in Peru was ready for Odría's dictatorship. The same thing was happening in Argentina with Juan Perón. And in Venezuela, to which Pérez Jiménez was returning in December of 1943, events were also marching toward the protracted convulsions that were to lead to a new military dictatorship.

6

Coming home, Captain Pérez Jiménez found a nation that was prosperous economically but politically unstable. President Medina, an easygoing man of liberal tendencies and a weakness for comfort, was in his third year in office. He had been overwhelmingly elected by a Congress controlled by his predecessor, General López Contreras. Backed by big business and farm interests he defeated Rómulo Gallegos, a famous writer and the leftist candidate.

Medina's idea of government was, essentially, to get along with everybody. Thus, he granted amnesty to leftist exiles, among whom the most outstanding was Rómulo Betancourt, the defiant student of Gómez' days and now a hardened politician. Medina, who allowed political parties of all shades to organize, said in his inaugural address that he believed that there were useful men in all factions, regardless of their ideology. To him, perhaps in innocence, this was democracy. To Pérez Jiménez, then taking stock of the situation in Venezuela, it was "social utopia."

Enjoying the political freedom, Betancourt and Gallegos soon organized their own party: the leftist Acción Democrática. It immediately became the center of opposition against Medina.

The new petroleum law and the advanced social legislation promulgated during Medina's term under Acción Democrática prodding propelled Venezuela fully into her period of transition from the feudalism of the Gómez era to the social, economic, and political modernism of the twentieth century. Yet the country still could not find stability, what with the agitations of Acción Democrática and the fundamental political weakness of Medina.

In the local elections of 1944 the power alignments became astonishingly weird. Medina's party, the Venezuelan Democratic Party, originally a right-of-center group, allied itself with the Communists. Acción Democrática, pronouncedly leftist and not itself lacking in strong Communist influences, picked up the support of other right-wing elements. In the end Medina triumphed, and Acción Democrática turned to conspiracies and revolutionary thoughts.

To carry out a successful revolt it needed military support. To win it, Betancourt and his friends set out to attract young officers who had their own axes to grind against Medina. Their principal complaint was that the President had kept the old system of army patronage that worked in favor of senior commanders, leaving the younger men in uniform without much hope of profitable advancement.

Like everything else, this approach had to be backed up by rationalization. Acción Democrática and the Military Patriotic Union, a secret organization of young officers, promptly took care of this problem. And emerging as one of the top rationalizers in the military group was Marcos Pérez Jiménez, chief of the first section (G-1) of the general staff since January, 1944, or a month or so after his return from Peru, and a major since July, 1945.

Only thirty-one years old, Pérez Jiménez had quickly become influential among his fellow officers, and when the conspiracy got solidly under way he emerged as one of the chief plotters. Serious and intense, he still looked young despite his moonface and spectacles. His official wedding picture—in February, 1945, he had married Señorita Flor Maria Chalbaud Cardona, a slim, rather pretty brunette, an inch or two taller than her husband—suggests a cadet rather than a ranking officer of the general staff.

Although the fundamental dissatisfaction among the young officers was directly caused by Medina's neglect of them, their individual motivations for wanting a change of government varied widely. For Pérez Jiménez it was a chance to identify himself with a victorious movement and to advance a step nearer limelight and ultimate power. His rationalization of the conspiracy was that Medina, though a general himself, was minimizing the military establishment and that he had abandoned "national ideals" for "international ideas."

Several of the other plotting officers, notably Major Carlos

Delgado Chalbaud, the Sorbonne graduate turned anti-Gómez rebel, and Captain Mario Vargas were sincerely worried by the growing corruption under Medina. Acción Democrática's propaganda astutely fed this spreading sentiment against Medina and corruption. Only a plausible excuse was now needed for springing the coup. This was provided by reports that former President López Contreras was seeking re-election in 1946, and that he was planning a revolution if Congress did not comply.

The alliance between the young officers and the Acción Democrática was a strange one—virtually none of the military subscribed to the party's leftist policies—but it appeared to be serving the immediate goals of each group. The officers promised to keep the armed forces out of direct policy making, while Acción Democrática committed itself to look after the officers' interests. Betancourt's idea was that he would use the politically naïve captains and majors for his own purposes—and he did, up to a point.

So tenuous was this coalition that Pérez Jiménez had no difficulty in saying later that Acción Democrática had betrayed the military and thus made a new revolution necessary. But for the sake of expediency Pérez Jiménez was willing to forget momentarily his theories on military governments and go along with the Acción Democrática idea of a civilian government of the left backed by the army. Aside from expediency his readiness to work with Betancourt made no sense, unless one is prepared to accept the explanation of a latter-day Pérez Jiménez admirer, one Ramón David León, that the young officers wanted "to change an intolerable social situation, without knowing exactly in what form they would attempt to solve the problems of the country." The suggestion that, in effect, he did not know what he was doing is little flattering to Pérez Jiménez. Finally, the conspirers announced that their movement was designed to "condemn to death the ideology of the past century," that it was a social revolution against the "feudal oligarchy," and that it stood for a rebirth of the nationalistic spirit. After removing the sugar-coating, it does remain true that the 1945 revolt did pave the way for profound social changes in Venezuela.

The coup d'état was to take place in November, but on October 18 Major Pérez Jiménez was arrested by Medina's agents. The plotters then decided to launch the rebellion at once. By evening General López Contreras was detained, President Medina had fled the capital, and the rebels occupied Miraflores Palace. But fierce fighting between the rebels and pro-Medina forces, including the Communists, went on for three days in Caracas and in many other points of Venezuela. Armed crowds—weapons had been stolen from the arsenals— were in control of the streets of the capital, and there was looting and arson.

On October 21, 1945, the revolution had triumphed at the cost of more than five hundred lives and uncounted hundreds of wounded and injured. Immediately, a seven-man Junta of Government, presided over by Betancourt, was formed. It had as its members Major Carlos Delgado Chalbaud, Captain Mario Vargas, Dr. Raul Leoni, Dr. Edmundo Fernández, Dr. Luis Beltrán Prieto, and Dr. Gonzalo Barios.

Major Pérez Jiménez was liberated from prison on the second day of the revolt—years later he was credited with great bravery during the fighting in and around the Ministry of Defense—but he did not make the junta this time. Instead, he was named to the key post of chief of general staff. Betancourt and his civilians were in control of the government, but Pérez Jiménez as boss of the army was in an excellent position to go on planning his own future. His friend Delgado Chalbaud held the defense ministry concurrently with his junta seat.

Not yet thirty-two years of age, Pérez Jiménez thus stood within reach of complete power over Latin America's wealthiest nation. But seven more years of patient intrigue were needed before he formally attained his objective.

7

The so-called Acción Democrática period—the only time during this century prior to 1959 that Venezuela lived under civilian chiefs of state—lasted for three years and twenty-seven days. At the end of this interlude the military struck again, returning the nation to rule by soldiers. The bloodless coup d'état of November 24, 1948, was faultlessly planned and executed by Pérez Jiménez, who thereby took the penultimate step toward the fulfillment of his obsession for absolute power.

It would be vast exaggeration, however, to say that the 1948 revolution was the direct consequence of Pérez Jiménez's activities. It was Acción Democrática—and more specifically Betancourt and Gallegos—that brought it about through their reckless policies and behavior. But Lieutenant Colonel Pérez Jiménez (he rose in rank on July 5, 1946) knew how to take advantage of a ready-made situation by keeping his cards close to the chest and playing them correctly at the right moment. He quietly consolidated his personal strength within the armed forces in preparation for the next jump ahead.

While Betancourt and his junta colleagues launched their breathless program of reform government from the yellow-walled Miraflores Palace, Pérez Jiménez and his small clique of army friends established themselves at the defense ministry building at Planicie, not quite a mile from the palace. Although Delgado Chalbaud was nominally defense minister, it was Pérez Jiménez who actually controlled the armed forces with the assistance of his old Peru schoolmate, Lieutenant Colonel Luiz Felipe Llovera Paez, now assistant chief of the general staff.

Soon after the junta grabbed power, a split began to develop between Acción Democrática and the military. It was hardly noticeable at first, but positions were taken immediately by all those concerned and there they remained until the revolutionary denouement three years later. While Captain Vargas, a member of the junta, maintained his active loyalty to the civilian regime until fatal illness overtook him within a few years, Colonel Delgado Chalbaud desperately sought to conciliate the civilians and the military up to the very last moment. Only then did he side with the rebelling officers. Pérez Jiménez had waited from the outset for the disintegration of the Acción Democrática government and all his bets went that way.

His work was carried out in his customary unobtrusive, unostentatious, and pedantic fashion. Miraflores officials hardly remember him at all. His appearances at the palace were rare and caused no impression. Despite his high position, Pérez Jiménez hardly mixed socially—in contrast with Delgado Chalbaud—preferring stag military gatherings to the glittering functions of Caracas society. This self-effacing pattern of behavior, a combination of conscious tactics and his deep-seated inferiority complex, stood him in good stead: few people thought of suspecting him of anything more sinister than keeping papers flowing regularly to and from his desk at Planicie.

Late in 1945 he made a brief visit to the United States in his capacity of Venezuelan chief of staff. United States officers remember him vaguely as a competent and quietly pleasant officer. Visiting military centers, he showed interest in technical matters, asked all the right questions, and seemed to absorb easily the explanations. He had not yet fallen victim to the obesity that was to come soon, and his photographs in the United States showed a smiling, young man in spectacles, and wearing an overseas cap.

Meanwhile it was becoming apparent in Venezuela that the growing difficulties between Acción Democrática and the military were stemming essentially from Betancourt's determination to nullify as completely as possible the influence of the army. Even though the armed forces had agreed in 1945 to stay out of politics officers began to think that Betancourt was overdoing his policies. Simultaneously the military were taking an increasingly dim view of the administrative and political practices of the Acción Democrática-dominated junta. Betancourt had gradually assumed near-dictatorial powers; vast sums were being expended on such things as the organization of labor and on party propaganda; new laws that the military thought to be too far to the left were being promulgated; and something of a social and economic chaos started to develop in Venezuela. To officers like Pérez Jiménez, who had no use whatsoever for civilian governments, this was proof that they had been right all along. But the majority still hoped that this state of affairs would improve after the elections, when Betancourt and the junta would be replaced by a freely chosen president.

On December 14, 1947, Rómulo Gallegos, the sixty-three-year-old novelist, was elected to the presidency on the Acción Democrática ticket, carrying seventy per cent of the popular vote. It was Venezuela's first direct choice of a president in this century. The new president retained Colonel Delgado Chalbaud as defense minister and Colonel Pérez Jiménez as chief of staff. Betancourt withdrew to the post of secretary-general of Acción Democrática, but his power was undiminished. He was the gray eminence of the Gallegos government, and upon him ultimately hinged the collapse of Venezuela's civilian administration.

Inaugurated in February, 1948, the Gallegos regime turned out to be unexpectedly authoritarian and it lost no opportunity to antagonize the military. Criticism of the government or Acción Democrática was not tolerated. Those who insisted on criticizing them anyway often found themselves under arrest. Seguridad Nacional, the secret police, turned to beatings and tortures, though it took the Pérez Jiménez era to elevate these practices to the status of art.

At the same time the regime sponsored the expansion of the old Mobile Guard of the junta days into a civilian militia of Acción Democrática. There were reports that weapons purchased abroad for the regular army were finding their way to Acción Democrática arsenals throughout Venezuela. As a clash with the armed forces loomed inevitable sooner or later Acción Democrática concluded that to retain power it must build its own fighting arm.

To the military this was a slap in the face and the final act of betrayal. Unrest spread in the officers' corps and talk of conspiracies blossomed forth once more. The regime reacted through the time-honored expedient of shifting officers suspected of plotting from one command to another. Some of them were sent on "official missions" abroad, a Venezuelan euphemism for exile with pay. In this group was Lieutenant Colonel Julio Vargas, inspector general of the army. He was the brother of Colonel Mario Vargas, member of the original 1945 Junta and later Minister of Interior. On his return from a trip to Europe he issued a public letter denouncing the Acción Democrática government for betraying the ideals of the 1945 coup. To escape an arrest warrant he finally sought refuge in a foreign embassy in Caracas.

The Vargas incident set off a flurry of excitement in the army. Officers held meetings to discuss the situation and pressures began to develop in favor of a drastic solution. About February, 1948, shortly after Gallegos' inauguration, Pérez Jiménez attempted to force the situation at a gathering of high-ranking officers at the Caracas military school. But the climate was not yet ripe for rebellion, and in the end he was shipped out on an "official mission."

The plan was for Pérez Jiménez to make a tour of South

American capitals and then join the Venezuelan delegation at the Conference of American Foreign Ministers that was to meet in Bogotá, Colombia, in April. Although this voyage was clearly intended to remove him from the Caracas scene for a number of weeks Pérez Jiménez did not appear too unhappy over it. He called at the Miraflores Palace to present his respects to President Gallegos and to arrange for the usual dollars expense fund.

Pérez Jiménez got only as far as Buenos Aires. Summoned home by Delgado Chalbaud he interrupted the trip and flew back to Caracas. He did have time, however, to meet Perón. It is not known what they said to each other, but evidently the Pérez Jiménez visit was the beginning of their strange friendship that culminated in the Venezuelan's stubborn defiance of hemisphere public opinion in offering asylum to Perón in 1956.

Back in Caracas Pérez Jiménez encountered a growing sentiment for a change. Throughout summer and early autumn anti-Acción Democrática feeling coalesced and the crisis finally began to take shape in the first days of November. From conspiratorial and military viewpoints, Colonel Pérez Jiménez had everything ready and now it was just a question of the right moment and the right excuse.

The crisis was triggered by the death of a Copei (Catholic Party) leader in Los Teques, near Caracas. He was said to have been shot by a high Acción Democrática official. The incident had the effect of greatly exciting political tensions in the country, and at this juncture of events the military prepared to step in. Delgado Chalbaud, still Minister of Defense, conveyed the demands of the armed forces to Gallegos: the formation of a military-civilian cabinet under the President, the end of Acción Democrática influence in the government, and the exiling of Betancourt. Gallegos refused. Simultaneous reports circulated that the government planned to fire Delgado

Chalbaud from the defense ministry and replace him with an Acción Democrática civilian.

While on November 19 Gallegos still insisted in press interviews that everything was normal, the military renewed their pressure. Troops and officers were kept in barracks while Delgado Chalbaud continued his efforts to mediate between Gallegos and the military group now openly led by Pérez Jiménez. On November 22, after the Gallegos government suspended constitutional guarantees and imposed strict press censorship, the military presented him with a forty-eight-hour ultimatum. It was signed by Delgado Chalbaud, Pérez Jiménez, and the commanders of the ground forces, the air force, the navy, and the National Guard. Signing for the navy was its commander in chief, Captain Wolfgang Larrazábal, who exactly nine years and two months later was to present a similar ultimatum to Pérez Jiménez and then replace him as chief of state in the wake of the 1958 revolution.

The ultimatum stated that the "extremist wing of the Democratic Action Party has launched a series of maneuvers designed to dominate the National Armed Forces, seeking to sow discord and divisions among them." Gallegos was thus requested to act against his own party or be ousted. He refused, and on Thursday, November 24, his government was overthrown without the spilling of a drop of blood as the military smoothly occupied all the vital spots in Caracas.

The plan for seizing all the strategic centers in the country, surrounding Miraflores with tanks and troops, and taking over Caracas had been worked out in detail by Pérez Jiménez. He had been ready to strike for several days, but his colleagues, notably Delgado Chalbaud, preferred to wait to give Gallegos a final chance to come to terms with them.

While the wait went on Pérez Jiménez was exposed to tremendous pressures from younger officers to move at once. A master of timing, he resisted the pressures only to discover that he was being called "traitor to the army." At this point Pérez Jiménez had his first recorded case of public tantrums. According to his secretary, Juvenal Vivas Jahn, he smashed china against the walls of his office and broke down weeping. Vivas described the incident as "the grief of a military wounded in his honor and high sense of responsibility."

But in the end the deed was done and the armed forces assumed the government. President Gallegos was arrested while Betancourt sought asylum in the Colombian embassy. That same night the victorious officers met at Miraflores Palace behind a shield of tanks and helmeted infantrymen to organize the new regime. Pérez Jiménez, the man who had directed the military operations against the Gallegos government and still held the nation's military power in his hand, became a member of the new three-man junta, but not its chairman. This post went to Lieutenant Colonel Delgado Chalbaud while Lieutenant Colonel Llovera Paez, the stone-faced Pérez Jiménez hatchetman, was named the junta's third member.

Pérez Jiménez missed the chairmanship because Delgado Chalbaud outranked him in seniority and because, at least as a front man, he was more palatable to the nation and the armed forces. There was no question, however, that it was Pérez Jiménez, assisted by his faithful friend Llovera Paez, who exercised the real power. He took over the duties of defense minister while Llovera Paez was appointed Minister of Interior, with control of the police and secret service. Between them they had Delgado Chalbaud at their mercy and they used him for their own purposes as long as it was necessary.

To secure United States recognition and to convince Venezuelans that the new regime was not to be just another military dictatorship, the junta took several steps to emphasize its respectability. With the exception of defense, interior, and communications, all cabinet posts went to civilians. No immediate steps were taken to curtail important national liberties—this was to come later. In a press statement two days after taking office Delgado Chalbaud announced that "the military movement does not constitute in any way a step directed toward the establishment of a dictatorship." Well meaning as he was, he probably believed it, but he did not reckon with the private plans of Pérez Jiménez and Llovera Paez.

While Pérez Jiménez remained convinced that rough military rule was the only answer to Venezuela's problems, he had enough political sense to realize that the social improvements brought about by the Acción Democrática government could not be taken away from the people without setting off a serious reaction. In a proclamation issued on the day of the revolt he promised that the armed forces would maintain "all the measures of progressive order" and that new ones "necessary for the betterment and welfare of the people" would be effectively applied. This was Pérez Jiménez' first major step toward his policy of giant-scale social demagoguery that, backed by the bayonets of his soldiers and the torture chambers of his secret police, was to be the cornerstone of his dictatorship.

A few years later Pérez Jiménez saw to it that the record would explain plausibly his participation in the 1945 and 1948 coups—first to bring to power, then to oust the Acción Democrática government. In a 1950 speech he said that in 1945 the army had liquidated the "feudal oligarchy," and that in 1948 it intervened to prevent the creation of a "new oligarchy . . . a sectarian minority with a foreign ideology."

In a passage of splendid rhetorical double talk Pérez Jiménez went on to clarify that "the depuration and rehabilitation of the fundamental institutions of [our] nationality, constitutes for us a mission that is imperative in its fulfillment." This mission, made to fit his own interests, was to become the guiding light of Marcos Pérez Jiménez in the coming years which would witness his final assault on power, in name as well as fact.

8

For nearly two years Marcos Pérez Jiménez lay low. As a member of the Military Junta he deferred publicly to Delgado Chalbaud, its chairman. As defense minister he quietly went about his job of streamlining the armed forces—and building up his own strength among the officers. Although he was considered the strong man of the regime, he avoided ostentatious attitudes.

For Venezuela these two years brought relative peace, political calm, and economic prosperity. The junta did not look kindly upon criticism, and the press and other organs of public opinion knew better than to antagonize the government, although there was no out-and-out persecution of those who dared to question the status quo. But, after all, elections had been promised, and Venezuelans, with their gift for rationalization, were willing to think of the junta rule as a period of transition. That certain constitutional guarantees had been suspended and that some persons were jailed or exiled did not disturb the people too much. It was not being done on a wholesale basis and, anyway, such practices were part of Venezuelan political tradition.

Tired of the continuous upheavals and troubles that had beset the country in its democratic apprenticeship since the death of Gómez, most Venezuelans were content to accept the tutelage of the junta. Business was good, oil production was booming, foreign investors—no longer harried by the unpredictable policies of Acción Democrática politicians—were pouring new money into the country. The government, surrounding itself with technicians, launched new public works projects—some of grandiose scope—and as far as such things went in Venezuela life ran smoothly.

By mid-1950, while the press remained barred from political discussions, it became known that Colonel Delgado Chalbaud was seriously thinking of calling national elections and returning Venezuela to some form of constitutional system. His candidate was believed to be Dr. Arnoldo Gabaldón, a noted malaria specialist. It appeared that the Colonel's idea was to move from the junta's unobtrusive dictatorship to a civilian regime in which a nonpolitical figure like Dr. Gabaldón would be allowed to govern under a discreet surveillance of the military. This would be something of a compromise, and under the circumstances it sounded reasonable to most Venezuelans.

But there were silent dissenters, and Marcos Pérez Jiménez was the most noteworthy among them. He never came out openly against Delgado Chalbaud's plan, but, clearly, the election of a civilian president would put an end, possibly forever, to his ambitions for absolute power. Were Delgado Chalbaud allowed to carry out his plan of gradual democratization Pérez Jiménez would be relegated to the pathetic role of a frustrated strong man. Having gone this far in his march to power Pérez Jiménez, the man with an obsession, could not be thwarted in his ambitions. He suffered acutely during that period, fearing that his hunger for power would not be satisfied. And Delgado Chalbaud became the great obstacle.

This, then, was the man—obsessed and neurotic but quick-thinking and cunning—who rose to challenge the plans for a democratic restoration to Venezuela. But his challenge was not a frontal one; it was surreptitious and underhanded, and it was aided by what may have been—but not necessarily—luck.

The extraordinarily lucky event, if it is to be called that, in Pérez Jiménez's life came at 8:30 A.M. on November 13, 1950. At that precise moment the limousine taking Lieutenant Colonel Delgado Chalbaud to Miraflores Palace from his home was stopped by a group of twenty-six men led by an old conspirer, General Rafael Simón Urbina, at the entrance to the country-club residential district of Caracas. He was seized by the assailants, forcibly taken to an empty villa in the near-by suburb of Las Mercedes, and there he was shot to death.

Pérez Jiménez went immediately on a nationwide radio hookup to announce in a funereal voice that Delgado Chalbaud was the victim of a "criminal act." The murder of the President, he said, was "an attempt without precedent in the history of the country and alien to the proverbial nobility of our people" and it left Venezuela in "deep mourning." Later in the day an official communiqué declared that Urbina was "the head of the assassins" and that he and several of his ac-complices were captured. Subsequently, the government an-nounced that Urbina was shot by policemen when he attacked them in an attempt to flee from custody.

To Pérez Jiménez the case seemed at first to be as simple as that: just a quickly solved whodunit. But the immediate and widespread reaction to Delgado Chalbaud's death was that "the *Andino* will now jump to Miraflores," and Pérez Jiménez and Llovera Paez were forced to take stern measures to fore-stall any rebellious movement. Delgado Chalbaud had been well liked, many hopes were placed in him, and his murder shook the nation out of its passivity. In short Venezuelans were not as gullible as Pérez Jiménez had expected, and the official version of the November 13 events found little accept-ance.

Starting out by declaring a state of siege and imposing an early curfew for several days Pérez Jiménez succeeded in con-trolling the situation. But it had become politically impossible for him to rise to the presidency at once. The majority of the officers' corps had been loyal to the assassinated President and feelings in the country ran high. Pérez Jiménez realized that to play it safe he had to be patient for a while longer.

While going through all the required motions of pious regrets over Delgado Chalbaud's murder—he promoted him posthumously to full colonel, awarded him the Liberator's Cross, placed the body in state at the Capitol, organized a funeral with a twenty-one-gun salute, and delivered himself of a number of tearful speeches—Pérez Jiménez began searching for a political solution that would safeguard the appearances without ruining his own future chances.

Thus, his first move was to offer the presidency of the junta to Dr. Gabaldón. But it failed when Gabaldón refused to act as a figurehead and demanded effective power as a condition for acceptance. Pérez Jiménez was more fortunate, however, in his approach to Dr. Germán Suárez Flámerich, a lawyer and diplomat, who was perfectly willing to become a puppet president as the price for his emergence from obscurity into national limelight. With Flámerich's connivance, the military junta was reorganized into a Junta of Government, and Pérez Jiménez became the undisputed strong man of Venezuela.

Years later the regime's official propaganda claimed that Urbina killed Delgado Chalbaud to settle old scores and in reprisal for the President's refusal to give him money. It also took the opportunity to praise Pérez Jiménez for his patriotism in *not* grabbing power for himself after Delgado Chalbaud's death. Pérez Jiménez' biographer offers the following deadpan explanation for his subject's strategy:

> Pérez Jiménez, the supreme chief of the Armed Forces, did not have to conquer power that he already held, but simply to declare himself the Chief of State; and precisely in not having done so, he gave the irrefutable proof of being a statesman who looks toward a distant future, subjecting

himself faithfully to his avowed ideas. . . . The *Andino*
did not assault Miraflores. . . . Not because he felt too
weak to do it, but because he felt so strong in serving his
motherland as the Minister of Defense that he did not have
the personal ambition to dominate her and, to make the
nation's surprise even greater, the two high military elected
as president of the new Junta a lawyer, Dr. Germán Suárez
Flámerich. . . .

To this extravagant outpouring of praise Pérez Jiménez
added his own touch: in his study at Miraflores Palace he
always kept by his desk a life-size color portrait of Delgado
Chalbaud. He may have regarded it as a trophy.

9

With Pérez Jiménez and Llovera Paez running the country—
the fiction of Dr. Suárez Flámerich being the junta's chairman
was so transparent that nobody took it seriously—Venezuela
began to enter the phase of total dictatorship, in contrast with
the relative freedom enjoyed while Delgado Chalbaud was
still alive.

Acción Democrática was the chief target of the regime's
hatred, but Pérez Jiménez' dislike of all forms of organized
political life also kept all other parties from functioning.
Effective press censorship prevented the newspapers from
debating political issues, and gradually Venezuela was sliding
into the antiseptic, apolitical condition that its strong man was
recommending as the ideal state of affairs.

This was strange, to say the least, because the government
had proclaimed its intention of holding elections soon had
gone to work on a new electoral law. But Pérez Jiménez' idea
was that there should be no electioneering or politickeering
before the elections. Presenting himself as a candidate in a

political vacuum he had fully expected to be elected without difficulty by a lethargic nation. The plan was for the voters to choose a Constituent Assembly that, in turn, would select a president for the 1953-1958 term. It was simplicity itself, but as usual Pérez Jiménez was underestimating his fellow citizens.

In the meantime the regime busied itself eliminating all opposition. When students rioted at the Caracas university Pérez Jiménez suspended its autonomy in a classical dictatorial act reminiscent of Perón. From the early days of his rule Venezuelan students had formed the hard core of opposition to him, and in 1958 helped to lead the revolution that toppled Pérez Jiménez from office.

Constantly charging Acción Democrática with plots and acts of sabotage Pérez Jiménez kept up a campaign of hate and denunciation against the party of Betancourt and Gallegos. Hundreds of A. D. leaders were exiled, others were imprisoned, often tortured. His feeling about A. D. was so strong that Pérez Jiménez went to the childish extreme of banning automobile license plates in Caracas that bore the letters AD. The serial letters thus jumped from AC to AE and on down the alphabet.

Shortly after it took office the new junta launched an expanded program of public works, a foretaste of the extravaganza of spending that was to come later. Some of the projects were useful and necessary, but many others just smacked of the demagogic techniques of the regime. Whereas Perón based his demagoguery on "social justice" through legislation and favoritism of the descamisados, and using showy construction projects as a secondary appeal, Pérez Jiménez, wallowing in oil revenues, took the opposite tack.

"The regime," he said in a speech, "wishes to be judged on its achievements and not on its words, and I have more trust in the evidence of deeds than in statements oriented toward exclusively political aims."

While this may have sounded very commendable, what Pérez Jiménez was trying to do was to tell Venezuela that nothing else mattered except what he could build. When he "accepted" the demands of the military that he run for president in the 1952 elections he explained that he was willing to take on "this great responsibility" to demonstrate that a country can be governed without political parties.

His "nomination" as presidential candidate was the logical outcome of his preparations since the death of Delgado Chalbaud two years earlier. Nobody except the students would have protested if, after waiting for a decent interval and mending his political fences, he had simply sent Suárez Flámerich home and taken over the presidency himself. But in traditional dictatorial fashion Pérez Jiménez preferred to keep the mantle of legality about his shoulders. Convinced that he could win the elections he found it more convenient to try for the respectability of being a constitutional president than to settle for the uncomfortable status of a usurper of power. Since he thought he could have it either way he naturally chose the more pleasant way of doing business. Besides, an election would make him look good in the United States and elsewhere abroad.

The elections took place on November 30, 1952, and Pérez Jiménez made what was a grievous error for a dictator: he allowed free and clean balloting. Acción Democrática was barred from the polls as an independent political party, and the five other parties opposing Pérez Jiménez' Independent Electoral Front had been prevented from campaigning and were thought to have made no impact on public opinion. Newspapers and radio stations carried only Pérez Jiménez propaganda and rarely could opposition candidates hold public meetings. Indeed, there was nothing to indicate that the voters were aware of opposition parties, let alone that they would vote for them. Pérez Jiménez was assured by his advisers, particularly Llovera Paez, who as Minister of Interior was responsible for organizing the elections, that he did not have a thing to worry about.

But when the returns began rolling in during election night, the regime realized with a horrible shock that it had completely misjudged the situation and miscalculated in its strategy. Instead of voting for Pérez Jiménez and his project-building achievements, the majority of Venezuelans, exhibiting deplorable ingratitude, threw their ballots in favor of the Republican Democratic Union, a leftist party led by Jovito Villalba, the opposition's candidate for president. Tens of thousands of Acción Democrática sympathizers, unable to vote for their own candidates, cast ballots for the Union's men.

Acting swiftly the regime stopped counting the returns and imposed a news blackout over Venezuela. At the rate the opposition pluralities were growing it would have soon become evident that the government had lost the elections and that the Constituent Assembly, if left to its own devices, would elect Villalba as president of Venezuela. This had to be avoided, and at the same time the nation had to be kept from knowing the truth about the scope of Pérez Jiménez' defeat.

For two days and two nights the regime toiled to revise the returns more to its liking. When the curtain of censorship was lifted on December 2 official tabulations showed that out of a total of 1,800,000 votes the government's ticket had received almost 150,000 more than Villalba's Union. For what it was, the new returns were presented fairly skillfully: it would have been too obvious to claim too great a margin of victory. But, projecting the results, Pérez Jiménez wound up with fifty-nine representatives in the Constituent Assembly and the combined opposition with only forty-five. This was enough to elect him to the presidency.

Yet, skillful or not, the electoral maneuver had generated so much resentment in the country that Pérez Jiménez did not want to take any more chances with the continuation of the Junta of Government. His formal election was not scheduled until April of the next year, and it may have been dangerous for him to stand much longer in the wings. Consequently, the disbanding of the junta was announced together with the publication of the returns. Dr. Suárez Flámerich vanished from the scene as suddenly as he had appeared, and Pérez Jiménez was named at once provisional president.

Llovera Paez, the man who fumbled the ball on the elections, was at once dropped from the Ministry of Interior, but for the sake of his earlier services was given another top job. The new minister was Dr. Laureano Vallenilla Lanz, a brilliant lawyer and a Sorbonne graduate, who had helped Pérez Jiménez formulate his political thinking in past years. Venezuela's foremost advocate of eradication of politics from the national life, Vallenilla Lanz, a psychologically unstable man, was to become the top brain truster of the regime and one of its most evil influences.

His first task in those December days was to invite Jovito Villalba for a conference at the ministry. Leaving Vallenilla Lanz's office, Villalba was arrested, taken to the airport, and put on a plane to Panama without so much as a by your leave.

10

On January 10, 1953, the docile Constituent Assembly held its first session and by April 15 it had written a new constitution for Venezuela and elected Pérez Jiménez to the presidency. Now everything was moving as smoothly as clockwork, and on April 19 Pérez Jiménez was sworn in.

The sanctimonious little colonel with the will power of iron thus finally reached the ultimate goal of his life. He was thirty-eight years old.

Installed at Miraflores Palace, Pérez Jiménez set in motion what was to be one of the hemisphere's most ruthless and efficient dictatorships under the guise of a legal government. The New National Ideal was proclaimed, and it immediately took the shape of a frenzy of public works coupled with unforgiving repression of any form of opposition to the regime.

Llovera Paez, heading a new Office of Special Projects, took over the task of reshaping the appearance of Venezuela. Working on the principle of the iceberg, the regime concentrated on the one-tenth of the country that was visible on the surface, particularly in Caracas. The remaining nine-tenths, including the backward rural areas, were simply forgotten.

Over the years Pérez Jiménez' government indeed changed the face of the capital. A multilane modern highway connected Caracas with the airport of Maiquetia and the port of La Guaira. Two long tunnels were cut through the mountains in order to build the road. Along the narrow valley of Caracas an impressive freeway now runs from east to west. Glancing up and to the north, the *Caraqueno* could see atop Mount Avila the silolike structure of the striking Humboldt Hotel. An aerial train carried tourists and occasional guests up and down the mountain. Plans were drawn to burrow through Mount Avila for a tunnel linking Caracas with La Guaira, but, mercifully for Venezuela's exchequer, the revolution put a stop to that. On the slopes of the hills dotting the city the government erected huge boxlike, low-cost housing developments for the workers of Caracas. Painted in a nightmarish combination of screaming and gaudy colors these Super Blocs were said to have Venezuela's highest suicide rate per one thousand of population. It was never determined whether the color schemes of the buildings had anything to do with it. The Super Blocs were doubtless needed to improve the living standards of the tens of thousands of miserable dwellers of Caracas' hillside ranchos or squatter huts. But what Pérez Jiménez accomplished in this field in five years hardly made a dent in the housing problem of Caracas.

The money the government poured into Caracas and La Guaira projects could not fail to produce a special kind of prosperity in the capital. Spectacular homes of wealthy men rose throughout the city, the middle class built their own comfortable modern houses. Office buildings mushroomed. Rapidly, Caracas became filled with chic stores and night clubs, and acquired the garish appearance of a neon-lit southern California town. Thousands of Spanish, Italian, and Portuguese immigrants poured into Caracas attracted by Pérez Jiménez' immigration schemes which, as it developed later, had more than one purpose.

Soon the city gained the spectacular, multimillion-dollar Centro Bolívar, a complex of ministry buildings and shopping areas. A vehicular tunnel carried traffic under the Centro. A vast modern campus was built for Central University, but it did not bribe the students into supporting Pérez Jiménez any more than the Super Blocs made its inhabitants into followers of the regime. Two big sports stadiums rose along the University campus.

Outside the city, the four-lane Pan-American highway followed the coast of Venezuela, east and west. Blueprints were ready for a bridge across the wide mouth of Lake Maracaibo, but again the revolution intervened to halt this giant undertaking.

In the field of industrial and related projects, the Pérez Jiménez regime liberally blended the foolish with the useful. A harbor for ore ships was built at Ciudad Bolívar to bring iron ore from near-by mines operated by a United States company. But, on the other hand, the government invested un-counted millions of dollars in ill-conceived, uneconomical, and probably unnecessary steel and petrochemical industries. They were never completed, but their planned capacity ex-ceeded by far the consumption possibilities of Venezuela. And they cost millions in graft and kickbacks. A $50,000,000 physics and medical research center, complete with an atomic reactor, was being erected atop a mountain near Caracas when the revolution came. It was an important contribution to science and education in Latin America, but like everything built by Pérez Jiménez it was designed to be the biggest and most spectacular of all establishments of its kind.

With record budgets, some public and some hidden, the economy appeared to be booming. Foreign investments in many fields outside of oil were pouring into Venezuela. From the outside the picture seemed rosy. But the truth was that this rich nation was going quickly broke in magnificent, unpro-ductive undertakings. And the insatiable thirst for money of the dictator and his friends helped to empty the treasury. In 1956 Pérez Jiménez raised $500,000,000 from new oil con-cessions. But even this was not enough; when he left and the books were examined, Venezuela owed hundreds of millions of dollars to creditors at home and abroad.

If the living standards of the majority of the fast-growing population, already well in excess of 6,000,000, were not go-ing up as fast as they should with Venezuela's income, the ruling group was doing magnificently. Pérez Jiménez main-tained several homes in Caracas and in the country, in addi-tion to his pleasure island. He also liked privacy: when he visited his house at Macuto, near the Caribbean beach, army tanks stood guard over him. Vallenilla Lanz lived in a splendid villa surrounded by a high wall, collected French modern paintings, and cruised aboard a yacht named after his wife. Colonel Pulido Barreto, an army friend of the dictator, filled

his home with medieval armor suits. General Romúlo Fernandes, army chief of staff, lived in a modernistic mansion of
vast luxury perched on the edge of a cliff overlooking the
Caracas valley. And so it went, a monotony of opulence and
ostentation.

11

The man in charge of keeping the regime secure was a professional policeman named Pedro Estrada. He was the director
of Seguridad Nacional, the secret police, and theoretically sub-
ordinate to his archenemy, Vallenilla Lanz. But Estrada, a
tireless investigator of conspiracies and a great inquisitor hark-
ing back to the days of Castille, worked directly with Pérez
Jiménez.

Every morning Estrada briefed the dictator on intelligence
matters, then returned to his gray, five-story headquarters
building on Avenida Mexico, from where he directed the most
efficient and far-reaching police network of South America.
His agents were everywhere in Venezuela and could be found
throughout the Caribbean, in Central America, in New York,
and Washington. Because of his avowed anticommunism
Estrada was a favorite of United States investigative agencies,
which did not perhaps know that Estrada protected known
Communists at home in exchange for their labors as informers.

A charming, extroversive man who invariably impressed
United States visitors with his colloquial knowledge of English and his cordiality, Estrada headed a huge contingent of
degenerates, psychotics, and plain criminals who made up his
secret police. The basement of Seguridad Nacional was a
honeycomb of cells where actual or suspected enemies of the
regime underwent the most refined tortures. Nobody knows
how many men died in Seguridad cells in Caracas and elsewhere but it must have been thousands. When army troops

and civilians stormed its building in Caracas after the fall of
Pérez Jiménez, four hundred emaciated, beaten, tortured men,
many walking like zombies in a dreamlike world, emerged
from the cells in the burning structure.

Estrada also maintained Venezuela's most complete filing
system, an extraordinary dossier on tens of thousands of persons, Venezuelans and foreigners. The data kept in Estrada's
files often came in handy for the regime's blackmail purposes.
Actually, few things escaped Estrada's attention in Venezuela. Citizens were required to have visas to leave and enter
their own country so that the government could keep tabs on
them—and prevent its foes from returning.

This system of spying and torture was backed up in Caracas
by the district police who handled the rare student riots and
other disturbances with machetes and tear gas. Despite police
brutality the students never quite gave up. There were ugly
riots in the spring of 1956, again in 1957, and finally in January of 1958, as the revolution against the dictatorship picked
up momentum.

It was not surprising that Pérez Jiménez and his collaborators lived in constant fear of their lives. Thousands of Venezuelans hated them for the deaths or tortures of their kin and
friends. When Pérez Jiménez drove between Miraflores Palace
and his home in a Caracas residential area all traffic was halted
along the capital's main avenue to let his motorcade rush
through. In 1957 Pérez Jiménez ordered in New York a bul-
let-proof limousine equipped with submachine guns, a television set, a record-player, and a bar.

Both Vallenilla Lanz and Estrada rode with Tommy guns
fitted into the footrests in the backs of their limousines. Secret
police agents sat in front, tear-gas grenades within their reach.
In Vallenilla's car, books by French philosophers often rested
on the submachine guns. Plain-clothesmen armed with rifles
and Tommy guns stood around-the-clock watches inside the

high walls enclosing Vallenilla's villa, patrolling the grounds and the cages containing his rare tropical parrots.

Vallenilla was by far the most interesting personality in the Pérez Jiménez regime. An excellent conversationalist, he made himself into the apostle of the New National Ideal and its political aberrations. He could talk for hours to foreign visitors about the superiority of the Pérez Jiménez system, which freed the country from the scourge of politics and replaced it with "peace and social security." He had only scorn and contempt for the Western concept of democracy; considered Thomas Jefferson and Abraham Lincoln passé figures. He argued that democracy was not applicable to the tropical temperament of Latin Americans and he ominously predicted that in time the Pérez Jiménez type of regime would spread to all Latin America.

With the press gagged by incredibly stern censorship, Vallenilla Lanz was the only writer on the subject of politics who could be read in Venezuela. A few times a month he wrote for his newspaper *El Heraldo* an anonymous column of musings about the inadequacies of democracy. It was his task to keep democracy from ever returning to Venezuela; but it was his carefully prepared plan to keep Pérez Jiménez in power indefinitely that accomplished precisely that which he sought to avoid.

12

The dictator's "constitutional" term in office was to expire in April, 1958, but when summer of 1957 came along the regime began to make plans to extend it for another five years.

There was no question that Pérez Jiménez had every intention of staying in power, but the problem was how to stage his "re-election" in the least objectionable fashion. Regardless of what he may have thought about it, his advisers, particu-

larly Vallenilla Lanz and Estrada, had no illusions that Pérez
Jiménez would not be defeated in a free election. His personal
popularity was almost nonexistent, the country was kept in
line only through the efforts of the secret police, and, in effect,
the regime was admitting its failure to sell Venezuela on the
apolitical New National Ideal. Whether this showed the ingratitude of the nation or was the result of sinister opposition
scheming, the fact remained that Pérez Jiménez could not face
again the embarrassment of a 1952-type election.

The regime was aware of rumblings of restlessness in the
country in the last year or two and knew that it had to proceed carefully not to upset unnecessarily the political apple-
cart. There had been student riots early in 1956, and after
giving it a quick try the government promptly abandoned
announced plans for an amnesty. Too many "undesirables"
could have taken advantage of it. Late in 1956 Pérez Jiménez
played host to Perón, and for a variety of reasons this caused
unhappiness among many officers. The fall of Rojas Pinilla
in Colombia in May, 1957, had a deep impact upon Venezuelan public opinion, and people were beginning to ask
themselves why they, too, could not oust their dictator. When
the rebellion broke out in Bogotá, Venezuelan newspapers
rushed correspondents to Colombia and, inexplicably, the
Pérez Jiménez censorship allowed publication of full accounts
of the victorious revolution next door.

The Colombian revolution coincided with the pastoral letter issued by Monsignor Rafael Arias Blanco, Archbishop of
Caracas, analyzing the social and economic situation of Venezuela and concluding that the majority of its population lived
in "subhuman conditions." It was an indirect but unmistakable
way of declaring publicly that the New National Ideal was a
failure. Monsignor Arias also condemned the absence of
spiritual life in Venezuela and deplored the corruption.

The letter, read from all church pulpits in Venezuela and

circulated throughout the country in pamphlet form, had the effect of a bomb on the nation as well as on the regime. It was an open attack on the dictatorship, striking at the very heart of its system, and it came from a source that could not be silenced by the usual methods. Vallenilla Lanz asked the Archbishop to withdraw his charges but was ignored. Then he published a deprecating article in his newspaper denying all of the statements made by Monsignor Arias. It was laughed off by independent readers. The first chink had appeared in the armor of the dictatorship.

Undismayed by the Church's attitude Pérez Jiménez announced in July that elections would be held before the end of the year; but he set no date, gave no details, and failed to say whether opposition candidates would be allowed to run. A few weeks earlier he had become embroiled in the dispute with Argentina over his refusal to expel Perón, who was abusing his right of asylum by directing a campaign of sabotage in his country by remote control, and the Buenos Aires government broke relations with Venezuela. About that time reports circulated that Perón was advising Pérez Jiménez on how to stay in power and that he had suggested holding an election.

By October, however, Vallenilla Lanz came up with a better idea. Instead of elections he proposed a plebiscite in which voters would be simply asked to say whether they wanted Pérez Jiménez to stay in the presidency. There would be no other candidates in the race and, besides, the only man in Venezuela who could have been a real opposition candidate was in the Seguridad Nacional prison. He was Rafael Caldera, head of the Christian Democratic Copei party, and he had been arrested in August on a charge of inciting the Roman Catholic Church against the regime.

Several key military leaders and Estrada took a dim view of the plebiscite plan. They felt that it was too transparent a bid for retaining power and suggested that either Congress simply extend Pérez Jiménez' term or that an election be held in which he would be opposed by a safe, figurehead candidate with no conceivable chance of winning. Estrada also warned Pérez Jiménez that the plebiscite could lead to trouble, but the dictator was finally swayed by Vallenilla Lanz. In November Congress obediently approved a new electoral law providing for the plebiscite, and Pérez Jiménez delivered a speech declaring that Venezuela's national interest required him to stay in office to finish his work.

To simplify matters the government then announced that there would be no electoral campaign. Vallenilla said it would be a waste of time, interfering with the nation's normal labors. Next it was decided that all foreigners who had lived two years in Venezuela would be eligible to vote in the plebiscite. Without precedent anywhere in the world, this step aimed at throwing to Pérez Jiménez the ballots of the tens of thousands of new immigrants who presumably felt gratitude to the regime. Taking the cue from the government the Italian community took an unprecedented step of its own in buying newspaper space to pledge its support of Pérez Jiménez. Because of his involvement in this affair the Italian ambassador had to leave Venezuela after the revolution.

Difficult as it is to trace back the precise moment when a nation's cup of bitterness overflows, it is likely that it happened in Venezuela when foreigners were given the vote. Even those people who were not actively opposed to Pérez Jiménez—and, by and large, Venezuelans had accepted the dictatorship with immense patience and a great deal of passivity—resented the implication that foreign votes were needed to elect a Venezuelan president.

It is possible that Pérez Jiménez was so worried by the plebiscite that he wanted to garner every available vote. But it is more likely that Vallenilla had simply been excessively zealous.

As the dictator thus prepared his re-election, an underground movement was being organized in Venezuela. Formed by four political parties—Acción Democrática, the Republican Democratic Union, Copei, and the Communists—it received basic instructions from exiled leaders abroad but had tactical independence at home. It called itself the Patriotic Junta and it developed into the most successful conspiratorial enterprise in Latin America, one that even Pedro Estrada could not discover or break. Its president was Fabricio Ojeda, a young Caracas newspaper reporter, and the organization was so carefully built that none of the four top leaders knew the true identity of the others.

When the plebiscite was held on December 15, the junta, in existence since July, did not have sufficient strength to oppose it effectively. All it could do was to circulate leaflets denouncing the re-election farce and calling for a general strike. But the revolutionary spirit had not yet swept Venezuela and the junta's appeals had no effect. Yet its quiet efforts did help to lay the groundwork for the approaching revolution.

In the plebiscite, voters wishing Pérez Jiménez' re-election were asked to deposit a "yes" card in the ballot boxes. But to insure that they voted right, government employees were requested to produce the unused "no" card when they reported to work the next day. An inkstain on the finger indicated that a person had gone to the polls. And it was dangerous for a man or a woman hoping to keep a job to come to the office or workshop with the "yes" card, the admission of having voted against Pérez Jiménez. The government claimed that nearly eighty per cent of the voters cast affirmative ballots, but obviously it was a foregone conclusion. Thirty minutes after the polls closed, Vallenilla Lanz called in foreign correspondents to give them the percentages. The dictatorship was eager to claim its victory.

Pérez Jiménez had a busy fortnight: on December 2, the

anniversary of his assumption of power in 1952, he inaugurated many of the new public projects that were rushed for
completion on that date; then he sailed smoothly through the
plebiscite. All he had to do was to await his swearing-in for the
new term in a ceremony scheduled for April of the next year.
Satisfied with himself, he now settled to enjoy the Christmas
holidays.

13

Pérez Jiménez did not have much time or opportunity to enjoy his latest success. The plebiscite had sparked the spirit of
revolt in Venezuela—it was the final insult that the docile
nation had received from its dictator—and now events began
to move rapidly.

A few days after the "election" hundreds of students
staged a manifestation in Caracas. As usual, it was dispersed
by the police, but this time the student protest against Pérez
Jiménez had a special significance. It was no longer one of
those periodic riots, that led to the closing of the Caracas Central University in the middle of 1957, but the awakening of
a desperate reaction against the degradations to which Venezuela had been subjected for so many years.

On New Year's Eve Estrada received word that a military
group was plotting an uprising. Acting rapidly he arrested
General Hugo Fuentes, commander of the ground forces, and
Colonel Jesus Maria Castro Léon, assistant chief of air staff,
the leaders of the conspiracy. But the government did not
take the incident seriously, and Pérez Jiménez was convinced
that he had nipped the revolt in the bud with the two arrests.
Refusing to read obvious signs he felt certain of his strength,
and after the plebiscite even began to release certain political
prisoners, including Copei's chief, Rafael Caldera.

The dictator slept restfully after his New Year's Eve party. He was awakened early the next day by the sound of bomb explosions, the noise of jet fighters swooping low over Caracas, and the thud of antiaircraft artillery. A revolt had broken out, precipitated by the night's arrests. But the planning was faulty and the execution unlucky. Only a few ground units moved to support the rebel aviators, and by nightfall their base at Maracay had been taken by government forces and the leaders had to flee to Colombia. At noon the next day the army units that had joined the abortive revolution surrendered.

Pérez Jiménez was certain he had quelled the movement for good. To make a show of force and to eliminate possible centers of conspiracy he ordered hundreds of arrests of officers and civilians. The editor of the Church newspaper, *La Religión,* outspokenly against the regime, was among those detained. It was the first time the dictator had arrested a Catholic priest. Caldera hid at the Papal Nuncio's residence.

While Pérez Jiménez bragged about his victory in the January 1 revolt, the nation was talking of an inevitable second round against him. Now Venezuela was aroused; the myth that the military stood squarely behind the dictator had been destroyed, and it was only a question of time before the next showdown came.

Before a week had elapsed following the air force rebellion, Pérez Jiménez was faced with new military problems. Top commanders of the armed forces were demanding that he relax his oppressive dictatorial controls, and as a sign of good faith dismiss Vallenilla and Estrada, the two men hated by all Venezuela. Pérez Jiménez temporized for days, showed extreme nervousness, and began making bad mistakes. His police detained four more priests, causing an open clash with the Church as the Vatican threatened to excommunicate all those responsible for the arrests. Having minimized the importance of the Church in Venezuela, a rather anticlerical country, Pérez Jiménez repeated the classical error of dictators in tangling with it.

On the evening of January 9 Pérez Jiménez ran into a major crisis. General Fernandes, chief of staff, apparently speaking for most of the military, warned him that the armed forces would not support him unless he dropped Vallenilla Lanz and Estrada immediately. The dictator fought the pressure most of the night but finally gave in. The day before, in one of his explosions of uncontrolled rage, he had slapped Vallenilla Lanz and heaped invective on him for having planned the plebiscite that was now producing such disastrous results. In the courtyard of Miraflores Palace Pérez Jiménez tore off rank insignia from the uniforms of officers he had court-martialed for participation in the New Year's Day revolt.

As Vallenilla and Estrada fled the country the dictator grimly swore in a new cabinet on January 10. General Fernandes was the defense minister and he was believed to be the new strong man of the regime. For three days Pérez Jiménez remained on the defensive, allowing General Fernandes to make his moves at will. Then, on the morning of January 13, when Fernandes drove to Miraflores Palace to demand his resignation, Pérez Jiménez arrested him and threw him out of Venezuela. The armed forces were split and disorganized, and Pérez Jiménez succeeded in marshaling enough support to win the round with Fernandes.

But is was a Pyrrhic victory. The Patriotic Junta had established contact with anti-Pérez Jiménez officers and had expanded its revolutionary organization into most segments of the population. Students were rioting and battling the police day and night. One evening hundreds of women staged a demonstration demanding the release of political prisoners. Professional men were signing manifestoes urging the return of freedom to Venezuela. The nation was in a state of ebullition and Pérez Jiménez was now fighting for his life. His palace was surrounded by tanks and armored cars; troops patrolled the city.

There was drama in the air and the final explosion was near. On Monday, January 20, a school strike was declared, and on the 21st the Underground Command staged a general strike. Cars full of people careened across the city, horns blaring. Soon, crowds gathered in downtown Caracas, smashing store windows, setting buses and cars on fire. The police countered by firing into the throngs of demonstrators. Dispersed in one spot the rioters reorganized elsewhere and all day long there was fighting in the capital. On January 22 the battle was resumed with greater intensity. Now the rebels had acquired arms and were facing the police. By the end of the day, as the revolution raged openly, at least one hundred persons, including children, had been killed by police bullets. But the rioters fought back with such arms as they could procure, with Molotov cocktails and rocks and stones.

Early in the evening of January 22 the navy served notice that it would bombard Caracas from the sea and land marines ashore for an attack on the capital if Pérez Jiménez did not resign at once. Shortly before midnight navy chiefs met with army commanders still loyal to the dictator. At a dramatic conference at the Military School, agreement was reached that Pérez Jiménez must go if a full-fledged civil war were to be avoided.

At one o'clock in the morning of Thursday, January 23, 1958, Pérez Jiménez was informed of the decision. He was given just enough time to gather together his family and closest friends before an army-led motorcade took them to La Carlota airport and a waiting airplane. At three o'clock in the morning, as the sound of rifle fire echoed over the city, the aircraft took off. It flew low over Caracas and disappeared over the mountains in the direction of the Dominican Republic, the last refuge of dictators. Three days later Juan Perón, who had been hiding at the Dominican embassy in Caracas, joined Pérez Jiménez in exile in Ciudad Trujillo.

The long night of oppression and dictatorship had finally ended in Venezuela.

Bibliography

Araujo Lima, Claúdio. "Mito e Realidade de Vargas." Rio de Janeiro. Editora Civilização Brasileira S.A., 1955.

Delgado, Luis Humberto. "Las Guerras del Peru: Batalla del Zarumilla." Lima. Latino America, Editores, 1949.

Dirección General de Informaciones del Peru. "Educación Rural"
—— "Guano"
—— "Fondo Nacional de Salud y Bionestar Social"
—— "La Corporación Peruana del Santa"
—— "Voto Feminino" Lima. 1955.

Fluharty, Vernon Lee. *Dance of the Millions*. Pittsburgh. University of Pittsburgh Press, 1957.

Frischauer, Paul. "Presidente Vargas—Biografia." Rio de Janeiro. Companhia Editora Nacional, 1944.

Marquet, Paul. "Manuel A. Odría: Breve Ensayo Biografico." Lima. Ediciones Peruanas S.A., 1953.

Ministerio de Gobierno y Policia. "La Verdad Sobre el Apra," Lima.

Ministerio de Gobierno y Policia "Los Crimenes del Apra," Lima.

Ministerio de Relaciones Exteriores. "Venezuela 1956." Caracas. 1956.

Ministerio de Trabajo. "Obra del Movimiento Restaurador en el Campo de la Justicia Social." Lima. 1955.

Odría, Manuel A. "Message to the Nation," 7/27/1949
—— "Message on Economic Policy," 11/17/1949
—— "Message to National Congress," 7/28/1951
—— "Economic and Financial Policy of Peru," 10/24/1953
—— "Message to National Congress," 7/28/1954
—— "Message to National Congress," 7/28/1955
—— "Political Situation and Electoral Process of 1956," 9/9/1955

Owen, Frank. *Perón: His Rise and Fall*. London. The Cresset Press, 1957.

Perón, Eva. *My Mission in Life*. New York: Vantage Press, 1953.

305

Pessôa C. de Albuquerque, Epitacio. "Getúlio Vargas." Rio de Janeiro. Imprensa Nacional, 1938.

Pimpão, Hirose. "Getúlio Vargas e o Direito Social Trabalhista." Rio de Janeiro. 1942

Portal, Magda. "Quienes Traicionaron al Pueblo?" Lima. Empresa Editora Salas e Hijos, 1950.

Tarnói, Ladislao T. "El Nuevo Ideal Nacional de Venezuela—Vida y Obra de Marcos Pérez Jiménez." Madrid. Ediciones Verdad, 1954.

Zalamea, A. "Las Jornadas de Mayo" (Collection of Documents). Bogotá. Ediciones Documentos Colombianos, 1957.

Zenha Machado, F. "Os Últimos Dias do Govêrno de Vargas." Rio de Janeiro. Editora Lux Ltda, 1955.

"1950," Semanario Peruano, January 9, 1950 issue.

"Elite," La Revista Venezolana, Article on Pérez Jiménez, March 15, 1958 issue.

Index

Acción Democrática Party (Venezuela), 262, 269-72, 273-75, 276, 277, 280, 281, 285, 286, 287, 299
Acción Nacional (Colombia), 218
Alberto Lins de Barros, João, 82
Aloé, Carlos, 149
Alzamorra, José R., 176
Américo de Almeida, José, 80, 86, 92
Andinos (Venezuela), 259
Antonio, Jorge, 149
APRA (Peru), 30, 31, 160-61, 162, 168, 170, 171, 173, 174-76, 177, 178, 179, 183, 184, 185, 186, 187, 193, 203, 218
Aprismo, in Peru, 175
Apristas, in Peru, 161, 164, 171, 174, 176, 177, 180, 183, 188, 193, 203
Aramburu, Pedro E., President of Argentina, 101, 157
Aranha, Oswaldo, 49, 65, 67-68, 69, 79, 83, 92
Argentine Institute of Trade and Promotion (IAPI), 131-32
Armed Forces Government (Colombia), 205-6, 227, 231, 234
"Armed Forces-People's Government" (Rojas' slogan), 236
ATLAS, labor confederation in Argentina, 138
Avalos, Gen. Eduardo, 120, 121, 122

Balbin, Ricardo, 146
Barios, Dr. Gonzalo, 272
Barreto, Col. Pulido, 267, 292
Batista, Fulgencio, 4, 7, 28, 39, 158
Belaunde Terry, Fernando, 203
Belmont, Francisco Tovar, 177
Beltrán, Pedro, 186, 192, 202
Benavides, Oscar, President of Peru, 170

Berle, Adolph, 87
Bernardes, Arthur, 60, 62
Betancourt, Rómulo, 5, 262, 269, 270, 271, 272, 273, 275, 277, 279, 286
Blanco, Msgr. Rafael Arias, 296-97
Bogotá: Bull Ring Massacre, 211, 236, 237; student uprisings, 245-46
Bogotá, Act of, 184
Bolívar, Simón, 17, 259; cult of in Venezuela, 268
Bonsal, Philip, US Ambassador to Colombia, 11, 212
Borges de Madeiros, Antonio Augusto, 55-56, 57, 60, 61, 62, 65, 68, 74, 75
Braden, Spruille, US Ambassador to Argentina, 126
Bramuglia, Juan Atilio, 139
Brasil, Dr. Assis, 61
Brazilian Integralist Action, 78-79
Brazilian Labor Party, organized by Vargas, 90
Bull Ring Massacre (Bogotá), 211, 236; aftermath, 237
Bustamante Rivero, José Luis, President of Peru, 160-61, 166, 168, 173, 174, 175, 176, 177, 178, 179, 180, 181, 187, 193

Café Filho, João, 91, 95
Caldera, Rafael, 297, 300
Calderón Reyes, Gen. Rafel, 234
Campo, Carlos Ibañez del, 137
Campos, Francisco, 66, 81
Capanema, Gustavo, 92
Caracas, Venezuela, antiregime riots in, 301, 303
Castilhos, Júlio, 52, 54, 55, 56, 58, 60, 83
Castilhos Academicians' Bloc, 56

Castillo, Luciano, 187
Castillo, Ramón S., 102-3, 110, 111
Castro, Cipriano, President of Vene-
zuela, 16, 254, 261
Castro, Fidel, 4
Castro Léon, Col. Jesus Maria, 300
Cerro, Col. Sanchez, President of
Peru, 170
Chalbaud Cardona, Flor Maria, 270
Christian Democratic Copei Party
(Venezuela), 297, 299, 300
Christian Democratic Party (Argen-
tina), 152
Civic Front (Colombia), 235, 236,
243; demands Rojas' resignation,
248
Civilian Revolutionary Government
(Peru), 188
Collor, Lindolfo, 71
Communist Party: in Peru, 183, 195;
in Venezuela, 20
Communists: in Brazil, 78, 90, 92; in
Colombia, 209, 227; in Peru, 188;
in Venezuela, 20, 269, 272, 299;
thrived under dictatorships, 19-20
Conservative Party (Colombia),
205-7, 209, 216-17, 221, 223, 225,
227, 229, 234; united with Liberals,
208
Conservatives (Colombia), 235, 236,
238, 241, 244. *See also* Conserva-
tive Party
Copei. *See* Christian Democratic
Copei Party
Copello, Cardinal, 152
Costa, Zenobio da, 95
CTAL (Argentinian labor confed-
eration), 138
Cunha, Flores da, 75, 76, 80

Death Brigades (Colombia), 209
"Declaration of Economic Independence" (Perón), 131
Delgado Chalbaud, Carlos, junta
president (Venezuela), 255, 263,
270-75, 277, 278-82, 285; assassinated, 283-84
Delgado Chalbaud, Gen. Ramón,
263

Democracy, trend toward in Latin
America, 4-8, 15, 17-18
Democratic Action Party (Vene-
zuela), 20, 218, 278
Democratic Front (Peru), 173
Democratic National League (Peru),
186
Democratic National Union (Bra-
zil), 91
Democratic Party (Venezuela), al-
lies with Communists, 269
Desacato, law of in Argentina, 134
Descamisados (Shirtless Ones), 116-
117, 140
Descartes (pseudonym of Perón),
134
Diario Oficial (government news-
paper, Colombia), 242
Diaz, Porfirio, 15, 21, 102
DINAPE (propaganda bureau, Co-
lombia), 235
DIP (propaganda department, Bra-
zil), 82, 86
Dornelles, Dinarte, 55
Dutra, Gen. Eurico Gaspar, 80, 83,
87, 88, 90; elected president of
Brazil, 89

Echandía, Darío, 222
Eisenhower, Dwight D., 196, 197
Eisenhower, Dr. Milton, 9, 149, 197
El Brujo. *See* Gómez, Juan Vicente
El Catolicismo (Colombia), 236
El Comércio (Lima), 170, 193
El Espectador (Bogotá), 233; re-
sumes publication as *Intransigente*,
237
El Heraldo (Venezuela), 295
El Siglo (Colombia), 220
El Tiempo (Bogotá), 211; sus-
pended, 232, 233, 239; resumes
publication as *Independente*, 237
Ernesto, Dr. Pedro, 76
Esparza, Alejandro, 196, 202
Espejo, José, 149
Estado Novo (New State), Vargas
proclaims, 26, 81, 82
Estrada, Pedro, 11, 293-94, 296, 297,
298, 299, 300, 301, 302

Farrell, Gen. Edelmiro, President of Argentina, 114-15, 119, 120, 121, 122, 123, 124, 126, 127, 128
Fascists, influence of in Argentina, 108-9
Fernandes, Gen. Romúlo, 292, 302
Fernández, Dr. Edmundo, 272
Figueres, José, 10
Fiuza, Yedo, 90
Five-Year Plans: Argentina, 129, 131, 149; Peru, 194
Fletcher, Warren, US Ambassador to Venezuela, 11
Fonseca, Deodoro da, 53
Fonseca, Gen. Deogracias, 247
Fontes, Lourival, 92
Ford, Henry, 74
Fortunato, Gregório, 94
Francia, Dr. José Gaspar Rodriguez (El Supremo), 14-15
Franco, Francisco, 142
Frondizi, Arturo, President of Argentina, 4, 8, 29, 101, 137, 146, 158
Fuentes, Gen. Hugo, 300
Fundación Eva Maria Duarte de Perón, 104, 139-40, 141, 147

Gabaldón, Dr. Arnoldo, 282, 284
Gaitán, Jorge Eliecer, 209, 218, 219, 220, 221
Galland, Adolph, 136
Gallegos, Rómulo, President of Argentina, 262, 269, 273, 275, 276, 277, 278, 279, 286
Garcia Peña, Roberto, 233
Garland, Francisco Grana, 175
Gaúchos, 51, 52-53, 59
General Confederation of Labor (CGT), in Argentina, 115, 148, 154
"Glorious Revolution" (Argentina), 103, 110-11
Goes Monteiro, Col. Pedro Aurelio, 68, 75, 76, 80, 88
Gomes, Eduardo, 91
Gómez, Eustoquio, 264
Gómez, Juan Vicente (Tyrant of the Andes), 15, 21, 24, 37, 38, 39, 253, 254, 256, 257, 258-59, 260, 261, 262, 263, 264, 266, 268, 281
Gómez, Juancho, 255
Gómez, Laureano, President of Colombia, 33, 204-5, 206, 208, 218, 219, 220, 222, 223, 224, 225, 226, 227, 229, 238, 244
Goulart, João, 45-46, 49, 92
"Government of the Armed Forces" (Colombia), 205-6, 227, 231, 234
Graf von Spee, 84
Gran Central Obrera (Colombia), 235, 238
Grandi, Dino, 136
Grupo de Oficiales Unidos (GOU), 110, 111

Haya de la Torre, Victor Raúl, 183, 185, 193, 195
Holland, Henry, 236

IAPI. *See* Argentine Institute of Trade Promotion
Independente. See El Tiempo
Independent Electoral Front (Venezuela), 258
Integralista Party (Brazil), dissolved, 83
Integralistas (Brazil), 79, 83
Intransigente. See El Espectador
Irigoyen, Hipólito, 108

Jockey Club: in Bogotá, 237, 244; in Buenos Aires, 151
Junta of Goverment (Brazil), 69, 75
Junta of Government (Venezuela), headed by Betancourt, 272, 273, 274-75, 278; by Delgado Chalbaud, 279-81; by Suárez Flamerich, 284; disbanded, 289
Justicialismo, doctrine of in Argentina, 136-37, 138, 139, 141, 142, 149-50

Kaiser, Henry J., 231
Kelly, Guillermo Patrick, 149, 157
Klinger, Bertoldo, 69, 75
Kubitschek, Dr. Juscelino, President of Brazil, 6, 20, 46

La Nacion (Argentina), 34
Labor Party (Argentina), 125-26
Lacerda, Carlos, 93, 94
La Prensa (Argentina), 134, 147-48; (Lima), 175, 186, 192, 202
La Religión (Venezuela), 301
Larrazábal, Capt. Wolfgang, 278
Lavalle, Hernándo de, 164, 203
Leguía, Augusto, 21
León, Ramón David, 271
Leoni, Dr. Raul, 272
Liberal Alliance (Brazil), 42, 66
Liberal Party (Colombia), 205, 206, 209, 217, 218, 219, 221, 223, 225, 226, 229, 234, 244; united with Conservatives, 208
Liberals (Colombia), 235, 236, 238. *See also* Liberal Party
Lilienthal, David E., 232
Linhares, José, 89
Lleras Camargo, Alberto, President of Colombia, 5, 36, 209-10, 211, 219, 237, 238, 242, 243, 244, 245
Llosa, Lt. Col. Alfonso, 178, 181, 185
Llovera Paez, Luis Felipe, 267, 273, 279, 285, 288, 289, 290
Lonardi, Gen. Eduardo, 155
López, Alfonso, President of Colombia, 235
López Contreras, Gen. Eleázar, President of Venezuela, 264-65, 269, 271, 272
Lozano, Leon Maria (the Condor), 230
Lucero, Gen. Franklin, 155
Luque, Crisanto Cardinal, 236, 245, 247

Machado, Pinheiro, 57
McIntosh, Dempster, US Ambassador to Venezuela, 11
Marshall, Gen. George C., 220
Medina Angarista, Isaias, President of Venezuela, 266, 267, 268-69, 270, 271, 272
Mendoza, Gen. Juan, 203
Menendez, Gen. Benjamin, 145
Mercante, Col. Domingo, 125
Merinos, Gen. Marcial, 202

Military Juntas: in Brazil, 69, 75; in Colombia, 206; in Peru, 183, 185, 190, 192; in Venezuela, 262-263, 266, 267. *See also* Junta of Government; Patriotic Junta
Military Patriotic Union (Venezuela), 270
Miñano, Col. Carlos, 172
Miranda, Miguel, 129
Miró Quesada, Antonio, 170, 193
Mittelbach, Col. Aristóbulo, 121
Montagne, Ernesto A., 187, 188, 192
Moreno Diaz, Samuel, 215
Mosca, Dr. Enrique M., 125, 127, 128
Mostajo, Dr. Juan Francisco, 187, 188
Motherhood Above the Parties (Rojas' slogan), 34, 234, 237
Movement of National Action (MAN), in Colombia, 234
Muller, Col. Flinto, 84
Mussolini, Benito, influence of on Perón, 109, 111

National Alliance (Argentina), 149
National Coffee Council (Brazil), 73
National Confederation of Workers (Colombia), 229, 234, 235
National Democratic Union (Brazil), 87, 92, 93
National Liberating Alliance (Brazil), 78
Nazis: in Argentina, 103, 136; in Brazil, 79
Neves da Fontoura, João, 66
New National Ideal (Venezuela), 36, 39, 249, 250, 257, 290, 295, 296
Newspapers, censorship of: in Argentina, 134, 148; in Colombia, 232-34, 237, 240, 243; in Venezuela, 295
Nixon, Richard, South American visit, 12
Noriega, Gen. Zenón, President and Premier of Peru, 181, 187, 189, 195, 196

Odría, Col. Manuel, 169
Odría, Maria Delgado de, 167
Ojeda, Fabricio, 299
Ordoñez, Brig. Gen. Luis, 239, 243, 246, 247-48
Ospina Pérez, Dr. Mariano, President of Colombia, 217, 219, 221, 222, 223, 224, 241, 242, 243

Pabón Nuñez, Lucio, 16, 225-26, 229, 241, 243, 245, 247
Pájaros Azules (Blue Birds), pro-Rojas guerrillas, 219-20, 230
Pardo, Gen. Rafael, 248
Paris, Gen. Gabriel, 242
Patriotic Junta (Venezuela), 200, 302
Pavelich, Ante, 136
Paz, Dr. Alberto Gainza, 148
Pedro the Second, 42
Peixoto, Ernani de Amraral, 92
Peixoto, Floriano, 53
Penna, Affonso, 57
Pérez, Juan Severo, 259
Pérez Jiménez, Juan, 260
Peronismo, 101, 105, 119, 138, 152
Peronista Party (Argentina), 104, 109, 135, 153, 154, 235
Peronistas, 29, 122, 125, 131, 133, 134, 144-46, 151, 153, 154, 157
Pessôa, João, 66, 68, 93
Pius XII, 142
Popular American Revolutionary Association. *See* APRA
Prado y Ugarteche, Manuel, President of Peru, 4, 31, 168, 203
Prestes, Júlio, 42, 66, 67, 69, 75
Prestes, Luiz Carlos, 42, 64, 78, 87
Prialé, Ramón, 183, 203
Prieto, Dr. Beltrán, 272
Protestant missionaries, Rojas' criticism of, 243
Pumarejo, Alfonso López, President of Colombia, 218

"Queremismo" (Vargas slogan), 91
Quijano, Juan Hortensio, 125

Radical Party (Argentina), 125, 128, 133, 146, 148
Ramírez, Gen. Pedro, 111, 113
Ramos, Nereu, 92
Rawson, Gen. Arturo, 111, 145
Republican Democratic Union (Venezuela), 288, 299
Revolution of Restoration (Peru), 180-81, 183
Revolutionary Union Party (Peru), 188
Ribeiro de Andrada, Antonio, 66
Richter, Ronald, 130-31
Rivas, Nelida, 150, 151, 156
Rojas, Adm. Isaac F., 155
Rojas, Julio, 215
Rojas, Maria Eugenia, 34, 211, 215, 229
Roman Catholic Church, 8, 101; attacked by Perón, 152-53; attacks dictatorship in Venezuela, 296-97, 301-2; opposes Rojas, 35, 207, 212, 234, 236, 238, 245-46
Rosas, Juan Manuel de, 135
Rudel, Hans, 136
Rural Societies (Argentina), 141

Saldia, Adm. Roque, 176, 177, 181, 189, 195
Sales de Oliveira, Armando, 80
Salgado, Plinio, Integralista leader, 79, 80; exiled, 83
Sánchez Pelaez, Dr. Abel, 255
Santos, Eduardo, President of Colombia, 218, 233
Sarmanho, Darci, 59
SENDAS (National Secretariat of Social Assistance), in Colombia, 211, 229-30
SIC (Rojas' secret police), 239
Sisters of Evita, 148
Skorzeny, Otto, 136
Social Democratic Party (Brazil), 87
Socialist Party (Peru), 187
Somoza, Anastasio, President of Nicaragua, 4, 24, 157
Souza, Washington Luiz Pereira de, 39, 42, 64, 66, 69, 71, 75, 93

Stroessner, Gen. Alfredo, 15, 24, 25, 136, 137, 156
Suárez Flamerich, Dr. German, 284, 285, 287, 289

Tamborini, Dr. José P., 125, 127, 128
Tank, Dr. Kurt, 136
Tessaire, Adm. Alberto, 146
Third Force (Colombia), 207, 234-235, 236, 239, 240, 241
Tittman, Harold, US Ambassador to Peru, 197
"Transformation of Physical Environment" (Perez Jiménez slogan), 250
Tribuna da Imprensa (Brazil), 93
Trujillo Molina, Rafael Leonidas, Dominican President, 4, 16, 19, 24, 38, 133, 158
Turbay, Gabriel, 219

Unión de Trabajardores Colombianos, 222
Urbina, Gen. Rafael Simón, 283, 284
Urdaneta Arbeláez, Roberto, 222, 223, 224
Ureta, Brig. Gen. Eloy G., 171, 172, 173, 174, 181
Uriburu, Gen. José, 108

Valencia, Guillermo Léon, 218, 244, 245
Vallenilla Lanz, Dr. Laureano, 16, 289, 292, 293, 294, 295, 296, 297, 298, 299, 301, 302
Vargas, Alzira, 83, 96
Vargas, Benjamin ("Beijo"), 80, 83, 88, 92, 96
Vargas, Darcy, 48
Vargas, Lt. Col. Julio, 276
Vargas, Lutero, 94, 96
Vargas, Gen. Manoel do Nascimento, 52
Vargas, Capt. Mario, 271, 272, 274, 276
Vargas, Viriato, 59
Vaz, Rubens Florentino, 93
Velasquez, Fr. Severo, 246
Velazco, Col. Filomeno, 121, 127, 134, 136
Vethencourt, Dr. José Luis, 255
Villalba, Jovito, 263, 288
Vinatea, Col. Luis, 172
Vivas Jahn, Juvenal, 279

Women's Peronista Party, 134

Zuleta Angel, Eduardo, 236